1984

Michael A. Faletti
117 Seeser Street
Joliet, Illinois 60436

Books by Arthur Krock

The Editorials of Henry Watterson

In the Nation

Memoirs

The Consent of the Governed
and Other Deceits

The Consent
of the Governed

The Consent
of the Governed
and Other Deceits

Arthur Krock

Little, Brown and Company — Boston–Toronto

LIBRARY OF CONGRESS CATALOG CARD NO. 77-149466

T 06/71

FIRST EDITION

*Published simultaneously in Canada
by Little, Brown & Company (Canada) Limited*

PRINTED IN THE UNITED STATES OF AMERICA

Contents

1

The Second Oldest
Profession

H ENCE, loathèd Melancholy," said Milton, inviting us instead to "come, and trip it . . . on the light, fantastic toe." This book is an attempt to obey that summons in part: it deals with the ways and works of American politicians and the government that is largely composed of them.

For while the favorite mouthings imposed on schoolchildren by politicians are that this is "a government of laws, not men," and is a government with "the consent of the governed," these are the falsest of the shibboleths which extol a democratic system that, as I shall attempt to demonstrate, has proved inadequate to deal with the problems confronting the United States.

Insofar as "the consent of the governed" is concerned, that is acquired nearly always by the campaign promises of politicians, to be forgotten as soon as they have accomplished their purpose — getting elected. Meanwhile, until or unless government and the victimized American mass combine to require an evenhanded code of laws, and their enforcement, and of judicial interpretation that places foremost the general interest, the United States governing system will dissolve into the dust heap of history.

However, in a lifetime spent in the company of politicians, observing their personal traits and official behavior, I have developed a fondness for the professionals and found them vastly entertaining on and off the rostrum. They are the cast of an American classic comedy, and in the following pages I have set down the lines of certain of the performers in a script I began to record in Kentucky, in the first decade of this century.

Classic comedy embodies serious and dramatic elements as well as the witty, the humorous and the farcical. Certainly it was wit, though tipped with a searing point, in Clay's reputed response to John Randolph of Roanoke when they approached each other on a plank sidewalk over the quagmire that was nascent Washington, D.C. "I never step aside for scoundrels," said Randolph. Said Clay, "I always do," suiting the act to the word. Or so goes the story, and I want to believe it.

The ways of the professional American politician in office, in the back room of the party committee and on the stump, have not materially altered since the Age of Reason passed into history in the Eighteen Twenties. Between the Northern and Southern species, each encompassing adjacent regions such as the Border, the Middle West, the Southwest and the Pacific littoral, there were and remain certain superficial differences — of accent, local interest, dress and bearing. The Southerners and the Yankees are the better raconteurs, the former given to broad sweeps of humor and invective, the latter to arid wit. But, to use the inspired descriptive with which the late John Nance Garner expanded the vocabulary of politics, they all "bloviate."

In the Wilson era all the characteristics of the Southern section of this ruling congressional group were to be found in the Kentucky delegation, and as the Washington correspondent of the *Courier-Journal* of Louisville, I was in a privileged position to observe them. Among their most representative exemplars were three who sat for Kentucky in the United States Senate or House, or both: William O'Connell Bradley, Ollie M. James, and Augustus Owsley Stanley.

Bradley was a Republican, the first of that party to be elected Governor. This was in 1895, and it forecast the deep and bitter Democratic party split on the issue of free silver that for years rent the Democrats asunder nationally. Bradley went on to become Kentucky's second Republican Senator, again as the beneficiary of the abiding Democratic division. He was a native of Lancaster, the seat of the rural county of Garrard, the son of a Union soldier whose regiment had been among the troops that scaled Missionary Ridge. Bradley could at will turn from educated speech to earthy diction according to the etymology common to the audience he was addressing. In Louisville, Lexington and Frankfort, a polished orator; in the countryside a liberal user of the raw vernacular.

One illustration of the latter that evoked guffaws all over the state was Bradley's inquiry of a young mountain man named Wash who had greeted him with that most embarrassing of all approaches, particularly to a politician: "I'll bet you don't remember who I am." On Bradley's confession that he did not recall at the moment, but was sure he would if given a clue, the youth suggested that the Governor think of "the first thing you do ever' mornin'." With pretended concern Bradley asked, "Your name isn't 'piss,' is it?"

The Democrats concentrated on the Governor's calculated coarseness, urging churchgoing citizens and particularly their womenfolk, to repudiate Bradley as a "vulgarian." "If the ladies will pardon me," Stanley piously would say, "I will now quote from Billy Bradley's latest speech." But Bradley, who was a worthy political descendant of Lincoln in that sort of exchange, always had a withering anecdote or witticism for riposte. One example of this talent was the following:

When Bradley was elected Governor, he was the lone Republican to be chosen for state office. One of the successful Democrats was John K. Hendrick, of Paducah, the Attorney General. Hendrick somewhat resembled the Governor in that he was short, stocky, and bearded. Entering Bradley's office in the Capitol, Hendrick explained his errand by saying he "wanted a pardon." (Then and perhaps still the Governor of Kentucky had unlimited pardoning powers in offenses against the Commonwealth from the moment a suspect was convicted.)

Instantly Bradley reached for the form on which pardons were officially issued, remarking only, "Of course, John." And not until he had filled out the form and was signing it "William O'Connell Bradley," did he inquire, "What did you do?" "Well," Hendrick replied, "as I was walking across the Capitol square just now a man called out, 'Good morning, Governor,' and naturally I killed him." "Naturally," said Bradley, finishing his signature with a flourish. "If you hadn't killed the son-of-a-bitch I would have done it myself."

Bradley died while serving in the Senate, but not before he had become one of the members of the Republican power structure and gained great personal popularity in intimate bipartisan Senate social circles — singing old frontier songs such as "Camptown Races," accompanying himself on the piano while Democratic Senator Robert Taylor ("Fiddlin' Bob") of Tennessee exercised the talent from which his sobriquet derived. But old and moribund though Bradley was when attacked by his young Democratic colleague Ollie James on the Senate floor over a partisan issue, he was still able to have the last word in an exchange, couched as this was in the Southern rural idiom.

James (six feet six, circa three hundred pounds in weight, twenty years younger and the most effective crowd-spellbinder then in the Democratic party) had borrowed from the idiom by pretending deep sorrow that Bradley, a short, stumpy man, had "lost his ironwood and oak." "But," responded Bradley, "true as this may be, the junior Senator from Kentucky will never lose his dogwood and brass."

The laugh at James's expense was heard from the Senate chamber to the remotest Kentucky hamlet, for Bradley had employed the common descriptive of callowness that prevailed in that time before American native speech and wit became a casualty of the vast urbanization of the United States, and the English language was debased into a dialect in which the constant repetition of barren lines, "man," "you know," and "like what" comprised the entire vocabulary of words more or less than four letters long.

Ollie M. James first attracted national attention as an orator during his terms as a member of the House of Representatives from the Paducah district. His early political hero was William Jennings Bryan for whom he thundered on stumps all over the country in Bryan's presidential campaigns of 1896, 1900, and 1908, in a voice proportionate to his gigantic stature. This physical bulk and the roar it emitted led the *Baltimore Sun's* famous political commentator, Frank R. Kent, to refer to James jovially as "the Caveman."

Among the most celebrated examples of an oratorical style which entranced his hearers were his anti-Republican philippic at the Democratic national convention at St. Louis in 1916 that renominated Wilson; and a plea to the Senate, during the debate on Wilson's proposal in 1917 to arm American merchant ships bearing cargoes to the Allies. "The President," James admonished the opposing Senators, "is like Blondin crossing the rim of the Niagara Falls on a tightrope. [The only person to accomplish this feat.] Do . . . not . . . shake . . . the . . . rope!" The appeal to these Senators failed and they were denounced by Wilson as "a little group of wilful men." But James's graphic simile thrilled the Senate and the galleries.

So massive a man was this Kentuckian that when, after he had displaced the incumbent Senator, Thomas Paynter, in a Democratic state primary and won the subsequent election, it was necessary to explore the basement storeroom of the Capitol to find a chair large enough to accommodate him. Its last occupant had been Senator David Davis of Illinois, who later became a Supreme Court Justice and was strongly backed for the Democratic presidential nomination in 1880.* From this oversize seat, reclining comfortably, with his legs — which resembled California redwoods — on a giant hassock, James received his visitors, among whom, as correspondent of Kentucky's most important newspaper, I regularly was one.

The telephone rang constantly, often but not always on matters of politics or legislation. Once, when I had just received James's usual reply to my queries whether there was any news he might have created or heard ("Don't know a thing, ole feller; haven't been nowhere and ain't seen nobody"), the phone rang. It was soon evident that the caller was the Representative from the Second Kentucky (Owensboro-Henderson) District, Augustus Owsley Stanley. It was equally evident that the subject was a notification by James to Postmaster General Albert Burleson that he opposed Stanley's nominee for postmaster of Owensboro — "personally obnoxious" was and remains the standard and sufficient explanation of a Senator in such cases.

---

* One of Davis's Illinois supporters for the presidential nomination was Adlai E. Stevenson the First. In scouting the prospects he made a visit to the county in Kentucky where he was born and summoned a citizen widely reputed to be an expert in assaying political trends. "Who are they talking about, Adlai?" asked the rural seer. "There's a good deal being said about Davis," Stevenson replied. The local authority scratched his head a moment and made this comment: "That's all right with me, Adlai. But don't you think it's a little arly [early] to bring old Jeff back?"

"Yes, Stanley," said James after what obviously was a long and passionate plea at the other end of the phone for reconsideration, "I know; you've made it clear; this feller is your devoted friend and supporter — as you say, he is your dog. . . . But he was for Paynter in the primary. Why should your dog bite *me?*" The ensuing explanation was patently unsatisfactory. Stanley was obliged to choose a postmaster acceptable to James.

Another time when the telephone sounded the caller was Representative Arthur B. Rouse of the Sixth Kentucky District, an area which included the racetrack at Latonia. It chanced that on the day previous, James had been at the Laurel racetrack in Maryland and lost every bet — some of which, most significantly, Rouse had recommended.

"No, Arthur," said the Senator in a doomsday voice. "Don't give me any excuses. Horse racing is corrupt, rotten all the way through. And I'm introducing that bill and no one can stop me this time. [The bill was James's oft-threatened legislative proposal to ban betting on horse races and the sport as well throughout the United States.] No, I won't change my mind, like you got me to do before." After a long and plainly intense last effort at conciliation by Rouse he continued: "No, sir, the bill goes in the hopper today. . . . What did you say his name is? What race? Where? . . . I'm warning you, Arthur. . . . But put $100 for me on his nose."

The legislation was never introduced. But the threat was repeated every time the Senator felt himself betrayed by surething tipsters — the jockeys that rode the horses recommended to him, the trainers and owners whose optimism James again had relied on.*

* I was with the Senator one day at Laurel when a young man entered the box, identified himself as a member of a Kentucky family known to James, and offered a tip on the first race. James followed the counsel, remarking "That's a fine family, knows all about horses, and that's a fine young man."

Stanley was elected Governor in 1915 by less than five hundred votes amid suspiciously one-sided returns from certain Democratic counties; and went to the Senate in 1919. In a previous book I have related how, if Majority Leader Oscar W. Underwood of Alabama had agreed to go along in accepting the mildest of the proposed reservations, the votes of Stanley and Underwood would have made possible the approval of the Covenant of the League of Nations in 1919, with an effect that might have averted World War II.

Underwood, in his role as Wilson's spokesman in the Senate, felt that not only would his support of any reservation to the Covenant be a direct repudiation of the President; it would induce the strongly pro-Wilson votes in Alabama to defeat Underwood for reelection, even though the beneficiary would be Thomas J. Heflin — or, in the Shakespearean trope, replace "Hyperion" with "a satyr." For Underwood was one of the ablest and most statesmanlike men who ever sat in Congress.

Stanley, like James, was a powerful political orator of the same school as James. But he was possessed of a subtle wit, a gift for satire and an intellect not matched by Frank Kent's "Caveman." These talents he had brilliantly disclosed in Kentucky and also in the larger and more critical congressional theater.

On one occasion, Representative Clark of Florida, a dependable low-tariff Democrat except when citrus fruit was involved, was opposing a related section in the classically Democratic "tariff-for-revenue only" Underwood bill in 1913. In a colloquy with Stanley the Floridian compared his colleague to "that great product of his state, the Kentucky mule," and unfavorably at that. Stanley, an excellent actor, pre-

---

The horse lost. Whereupon James observed that he should have remembered the young man was the black sheep of his flock.

tended to be stricken by the asserted resemblance and began his retort in mournful, penitent tones that left the House totally unprepared for, and Clark open to, this peroration:

"I would rather be a doorkeeper in the House of the Lord than dwell on a dais in the tents of iniquity. And I would rather be an honest ass than the gentleman from Florida."

During the House debate, in the first decade of the century, on what was styled the Pure Food and Drug Act, Stanley was championing the section which required the manufacturers of blended whiskey to specify on the label and in advertising that such a concoction was not the noble "straight" (undiluted) bourbon of Kentucky. In a low and caressing voice he described the physical and mental sensations that followed a drink of true Kentucky bourbon — a mood of peace toward men, a sense of listening to a great symphony played by a perfect orchestra, a desire to go about the world doing good. "But, Mr. Speaker," said Stanley to a House he had lulled into tranquillity, "what follows taking a drink of this Peoria [blended, rectified] whiskey? Why gentlemen, this unspeakable mixture turns an anchorite into a howling dervish and makes a rabbit spit in a bulldog's eye!"

The House exploded with delight, was convinced, and the consumer was thereafter protected from having bourbon debased with neutral spirits foisted on him as the pure Kentucky article.

When I first came to Washington, the late South Trimble, who had been the member of Congress from the Ashland (Bluegrass) District of Kentucky, was Clerk of the House. Somebody said of him and another Kentuckian, Representative Swagar Sherley of Louisville, that their names sounded like English country estates.

Trimble was a remarkable person, an antebellum type with

the kind of cold courage that is associated with the Kentuckians of his breed. He was Speaker of the Kentucky House at the time of the contest for the Governorship initiated by William Goebel, the unsuccessful Democratic candidate against William S. Taylor in 1900. On the face of the returns at the polls Taylor, a Republican, was declared Governor, and the Democrats filed a contest petition in the legislature.

A corollary matter of great moment was who should serve on the investigating committee. It was decided to leave the selections to a lottery. Slips bearing the names of the members of the legislature were put into a box and the Speaker was authorized to draw them out. The first eleven slips drawn would constitute the Senate (4) and House (7) members of the contest committee. At that time the Senate had a fragile Democratic majority and the House was tied.

During the drawings at the Speaker's desk in the House it was estimated that there were nearly one thousand mountaineer Republicans in the gallery, many with their rifles resting on the rail of the balcony, to make sure there was no cheating. And, also observing Trimble's every move, were official Republican watchers standing beside him. Trimble — as always, cool and calm — reached his hand into the box eleven times and read out the name on each slip he withdrew. When the proceeding ended it miraculously developed that all eleven chosen in the lottery were Democrats. But, though fraud was charged, no solid evidence of it was produced.

This miracle of the fortuitous was accounted for at the time as follows: Of the slips in the box, listing all the members of the legislature, those with the names of the Republicans and all but eleven of the Democrats were tightly rolled so that, when the box was shaken preparatory to drawing, as the Republican watchers insisted, these slips would rest atop the others.

Years later I asked Trimble about the drawing, and he gave me a different and much more dramatic explanation. "Well," he said, "I had a hollow ring on a finger of my right hand and in it were duplicated slips on which were written the names of the eleven Democrats. They were also in the box, of course. As I reached into the box I used my left hand to shake up the slips and with my right hand I extracted from the ring one at a time." I asked, "Were you scared?" "No," he said; "nothing to be scared about."

He probably was spoofing me with a tall tale, for I was young and presumably gullible. But whichever is the true explanation, the result was that the committee found for Goebel and he was declared Governor.

The oath was administered on his deathbed because in the meantime he had been mortally wounded by an assassin stationed in a window of the Capitol as he walked toward the building. There followed a "confession" by a mountaineer, one Youtsey, that he had fired the fatal shot, and long trials of Secretary of State Caleb Powers, "Babe" Jett, and other mountain characters. Powers went to prison, but since it was never satisfactorily established who killed Goebel, Powers's exculpation (pardon) by a subsequent Republican Governor, Augustus E. Willson, put a quietus on the bloody history, and Powers was elected to Congress from his mountain Republican district.

This kind of contested election, while still known today, was more common then and certainly more colorful. The anthologies of courtroom wit and satire that are known to me omit one of the most brilliant examples of this color. It was an observation addressed to the Kentucky Court of Appeals, the Commonwealth's highest tribunal, by James P. Helm, Sr., a leader of the American bar.

The issue was the validity of a contest over the outcome of

the election for mayor of Louisville in 1905. The contestants made a strong point of a voting phenomenon in the Twelfth Ward. There the returns recorded that, not only had every eligible voter gone to the polls, but that they had voted in strict alphabetical order, from names beginning with Aa to those begining with Za.

Said Helm to the judges in Frankfort: "To accept returns of this character is equivalent to accept as a fact that, if the letters of the Greek alphabet were tossed into the air they would, when they came down, spell out the *Iliad* of Homer!"

The Democratic mayor elected on the face of the returns was deposed by the Court on the ground of palpable fraud.

South Trimble was a gray-eyed, level-browed man, the type one also associated with gunslingers of the old West who, however quick on the draw, had a keen sense of humor. Once he was accused by his opponent in a campaign for Congress of being in the pay and under the influence of the Louisville & Nashville Railroad. An item of supporting evidence was the specific charge that he carried a pass on the L & N.

This was a usual and accepted gratuity in the politics and by the press of the time, but the charge provided Trimble with a riposte which turned it into effective ridicule. Addressing a group at the Forks of the Elkhorn, one of the loveliest spots in the Bluegrass country, he said, 'Boys, they say I sold you out to the L & N, and that one of the things I got for selling you out was this pass. Let me read you this pass. . . . It reads 'good only within the State of Kentucky and excluding the following trains . . .' And all of them are the only good trains on the L & N! Boys, I might sell you out some day to the L & N or somebody else, but I'm never going to sell you out for a stingy pass like this."

Swagar Sherley was the most intellectual of the Kentucky delegation in the House in this century and he eventually became chairman of the Appropriations Committee during World War I. Previously he was chairman of the subcommittee that built the Panama Canal and fortified Guam, a controversial issue the nation has come to honor Sherley for resolving affirmatively before Pearl Harbor was even conceived of as a possibility.

He was afflicted from childhood with polio, wore leg braces which gave him a rolling walk, and moved about with a cane. But, like Franklin Roosevelt, from the waist up he was muscular and finely built. After Sherley was defeated for reelection in the Republican sweep of 1918, he practiced law in Washington with great distinction and applied the most rigid ethical code in the choice of clients he felt it proper for an ex-chairman of Appropriations to represent.

Later this delegation was joined by Fred M. Vinson who became Secretary of the Treasury, Justice of the Court of Appeals, and Chief Justice of the United States.

The Kentucky delegation I first encountered as a Washington correspondent from 1910 to 1915 included the celebrated Ben Johnson. He represented the Fourth (Bardstown) District. It was settled by the Maryland English Catholics and the first cathedral west of the mountains on United States soil was built there.

Ben Johnson was tall, handsome, a prototype of the Southern aristocrat. As chairman of the House District of Columbia Committee he was engaged in perpetual controversy with District residents and developed a persecution complex. He carried a pistol. He had killed once when his father was "drawn on" in the streets of Bardstown, thrusting his father behind him and making himself the target. Of course, he was promptly acquitted.

He suffered all his life under another complex. During Johnson's lifetime it was accepted as impossible that a Catholic could be elected Governor or Senator. The Governorship was Johnson's aspiration; he was descended from the Maryland-born pioneers in Nelson County who had sheltered Louis Philippe when he was a fugitive from France. Later when he became the "citizen-king," Louis sent gifts purporting to be Murillos and the works of other famous artists to the cathedral in Bardstown, together with a silver service for the altar. Johnson was defeated in the Democratic gubernatorial primary; he knew that his Catholic faith was the reason; and he died an embittered man.

In this period the Kentucky members of the House, with one exception, were above the average in forensic ability. They drank heartily, but all except Representative R. Y. Thomas, Jr., could hold their liquor. They included James's Democratic successor as member of the National House of Representatives, Alben W. Barkley, later U.S. Senate majority leader and Vice-President of the United States, and J. Campbell Cantrill, who was vice-chairman of the Democratic National Committee that conducted the presidential campaign of James M. Cox in 1920.

When I began my service as a Washington correspondent the tiger of the House was Representative James H. Mann of Illinois, author of the celebrated and now somnolent act that bears his name, forbidding interstate transportation of women "for immoral purposes," an expression of the mores of the time. To every challenge of Mann's authority as Republican floor leader he responded ferociously, his beard bristling with resentment. One day, stimulated by his usual refreshment, Representative Thomas of Kentucky rose to attack Mann for an action of the Rules Committee. "I will not," cried Thomas, "be intimidated by the *be-whiskered* gentleman from Illinois." "Nor will I be," replied Mann, "by the *be-whiskeyed* gentleman from Kentucky."

[16]

This same Kentucky paladin was long engaged in a feud with two reporters — John Kirby of *The World* and Gerald Egan of the *New York Tribune* — whose audacity and ingenious devices for retaliation were so well known that Thomas should never have ventured to take them on. But he did, with these results:

In the course of this noisy feud Thomas one day pursued Kirby and Egan down a corridor in the Capitol. As he charged, Kirby stepped aside and neatly tripped up the onrushing terror of the Kentucky "Pennyrile" who fell on his back. Whereupon the two journalists sat on the round, recumbent belly of the Representative and pinned him to the floor long enough for the spectacle to make the newspaper picture-pages.

Another time, learning that the legislator was lying asleep on the steps of his hotel, overcome no doubt by something he had eaten, Kirby and Egan summoned an ambulance that bore the comatose statesman to the morgue (to which they had directed it). Awakening, Thomas swore to avenge the insult by armed force on the grounds of justifiable homicide. But all three of the principals died of natural causes years afterward.

2

Power and Its Germinals

Power in washington is a Janus. Its two aspects are the visible and the invisible, and the latter is the greater. It often is exercised subterraneously in the Executive and legislative branches: only in the judicial arm of the Federal government is the exercise wholly open, though sometimes in the negative form of a Federal court's refusal to try a case or consider an appeal from the judgment of the court below.

The same negative exercise constantly occurs, of course, at the President's desk; among the chairmen of congressional committees, and their hand-picked chairmen of the multiplying subcommittees, who keep legislation indefinitely in the deep freeze or give it unwarranted priority; and among the bureaucrats in the higher departmental echelons. But such abuses of power in these quarters enjoy low visibility unless or until spotlighted by vigilant journalism or members of Congress with a grievance.

Power in Washington has these and the following general origins:

1. Officials seeking reelection derive it from the fact that little more than half of the eligibles usually take the trouble to vote in primaries and elections, a condition favoring the incumbents.

2. Government bureaucrats derive it from civil service en-

trenchment in their jobs, or from statutory authority, or from departmental chiefs too busy, too recreant, too lazy, or too mentally inadequate to check the basic information on which high policy decisions are made. One grave consequence is that a new President, even of the party in power, inherits a bureaucracy beholden to an immediate or remote predecessor and manned by the authors of the policy errors of the past.

3. The power of trade unions flows from the legal immunities that permit strikes, including tolerated and illegal strikes by tax-paid government employees, to paralyze the essential facilities of the people, to frighten the courts and local and national authorities from enforcing the laws assuring public health and security, and in effect to establish a picket line as the supreme law of the land.

4. The power of the industrial-financial management sector is generated by the inherent power of merged capital, by lax enforcement of the antitrust laws, by accommodating management contracts with labor that assure maintained production at the vast expense of uncontrolled price inflation to the consumer, and by indirect purchase of congressmen who pass on legislation in which the purchaser has a direct financial interest.

5. Organized crime acquires and holds power by employment of the instruments of terror and official corruption, and by the leniency and almost illimitable delay of the judicial process.

6. The handful of members of the House and Senate who vastly influence the flow and nature of legislation, whatever the will of the majority, owe their power to the seniority system by which long tenure decides who shall be the committee chairmen; and to the rules, procedures and log-rolling that enable these chairmen and their chosen heads of sub-

committees to decide whether or when there shall be action on legislation or investigations.

7. The ultimate Federal power derives from the assumption, without constitutional warrant, of supremacy over the other two branches by a Federal judiciary whose recent rulings have been more than less influenced by political partisanship and doctrinal considerations.

8. The media of publication — the printed and electronic press, the official government handouts, etc. — are, of course, an enormous source of power in the United States. In every newspaper or other printed form of communication, and in every electronic network or local station, what news and comment shall be selected for what degree of display, or ignored entirely, are choices necessarily made by individuals. Therefore in a few hands is concentrated the power to focus the public mind and eye on certain events, and the interpretation of these, to the subordination of others which in different hands would be the ones selected. Only where professionalism prevails over the personal interests or doctrines do the media meet the standard of responsibility and mental integrity which is the presumptive ideal of the grant of constitutional freedom of the press. But, though the presumption is fulfilled in far larger measure than when I entered the craft, Vice-President Agnew had sound and ample basis for finding this standard wanting in large segments of the media.

9. The official party organizations — Federal, state, and local committees — whose officers and workers are in constant touch with the voters are a basic factor in the power complex because of the vital function they perform. This is to get to the polls the highest possible percentage of eligible voters believed to be more or less favorable to the party nominees. This job can only be done by working at it every day, watching for popular trends, exploiting them when they

are leaning toward the party the organization represents, and seeking out and remedying the causes of surmised or tangible defection.

It is no trade for amateurs and intermittent volunteers, such as has frequently been demonstrated by the failure of independent movements ranging from local to state and national to break slates of candidates chosen by the official party organizations. A key to these failures is provided by contrasting the "Princeton Plan," whereby undergraduates were released from studies for two weeks before the 1970 congressional elections to engage in political activities, with the working programs of professional party organizers that require this concentration every day in the year.

The task of an official party organization was best described by the late Will H. Hays, chairman of the Republican National Committee: "to ee-lect, not see-lect." And the surest route to this is to bring to the voting booth all the eligibles among the voters who are or may be disposed to support the party ticket. Thus minorities can and often have done the electing over inert or craftily divided majorities.

Whether this task will change, and in what respects and degrees, as a consequence of the Supreme Court decision validating that part of the Act of Congress which lowered voting eligibility in Federal elections of citizens who have attained the age of eighteen years, is a matter of speculation which will not be resolved until the returns are in from the presidential contest of 1972. Thus far, in the two states — Kentucky and Georgia — which have lowered the voting age qualification, no appreciable change in the electoral trend has been registered. But youth in this country has become politically activist in a measure never before disclosed. And, since the Supreme Court decision adds more than fourteen million to the voting roll in Federal elections, there is no doubt that presidential and congressional aspirants will concentrate heavily on attracting their activity and allegiance.

The decision itself, like the Act of Congress which it sustained in part, was one of the shoddiest examples of rewriting the Constitution in the history of American government. Justice Black, who was the swing-man in the five to four division which left the age of twenty-one as the minimum *qualification* for state and local voting but advanced it to eighteen in Federal voting, could find no colleagues who would subscribe to the rest of his opinion.

The Constitution, in Article I, Section 2, "unalterably" (in the words of Alexander Hamilton) forbade Congress from making any change in the *qualifications* for voting (one of which was a minimum age of twenty-one), giving Congress authority only over "the time, place and manner" of holding Federal elections. Federal and state assizes were bound together in the same package, with state legislatures free, however, to prescribe age qualifications in *state* elections. But Justice Black, his position effecting both the Court majority that sanctioned congressional power to lower the qualifying age to eighteen in Federal elections but not in state elections, untied this package by judicial fiat. Yet in so doing, he weirdly reversed his own opinion by holding that Congress may not reject "other parts" of the Constitution and validating legislation which did just that.

Thus a proposal which clearly required an amendment to the Constitution was, in the phrase of the late Judge Learned Hand, "bootlegged" by the Court majority of one into the national Charter and thereby plunged into chaos the electoral process in all the states.

But whatever may be the new trends in electoral and other political action that the age reduction to eighteen will set in motion, the power that is latent in organized

[25]

party workers must continue to be reckoned with as one of the high determinant factors in checking or advancing the trends.

10. Militant groups, whose unpunished violence in pressing what are always non-negotiable "demands," no sooner granted than expanded, are increasing as a source of power. They seek to subject the majority to tyranny by a minority composed of an unsavory mixture of "elites" that range from the dark alleys to the college faculty and classrooms, from the campuses to the abodes where the penitent rich drive to demonstrations in chauffeured limousines.

But these sources of power all depend for their strength on public toleration. And the weakness of restraints on the power thus derived is indicated by the percentage of citizens who do not use their high privilege of suffrage. In a nation where a turnout of 60 percent of the eligibles at national elections is unusual, this degree of tolerance of the abuse of power is seen to be very high indeed.

Theoretically, we are governed by the Federal Constitution and a group of statutes — national, state, and local. But the quality, efficiency, and moral character of government are subject to innumerable depletions. *How* the Constitution and the laws, whatever the clarity of their text, are interpreted and administered, and at what rate of adjudication, has much more impact on the American society than what they *prescribe*. By Executive orders national commitments can be and have been firmly woven into domestic laws and foreign compacts that neither their congressional drafters intended nor their subjects, the people, desired. By regulations (those of the Internal Revenue Service are a shining example) drawn up by bureaucrats, a standard of taxable liability can be and is imposed reasonably or unreasonably, according to the mental flexibility of the drafters of the regulations. Or, as in the turnabout of the I.R.S. that subjected segregated private schools to the loss of their tax-exempt status, by a sudden reversal of high Administration policy.

Despite the accusatory dissents of as many as four of the nine members of the Supreme Court, the high tribunal has repeatedly supervened the legislative power of Congress and the designated authorities of the states, and has turned rulings into actual amendments of the Constitution.

In the less than a dozen states where the bulk of the population is centered, and solid blocs of ethnic or self-serving groups can determine the winners of elections, national public policies and administrative actions can be imposed, even punitively — thus reversing the objective of the Bill of Rights — on a popular minority almost as large as the majority itself. And, because politics is the daily business of party organizations, in contrast to the public mass that concerns itself with politics only a few weeks of each year, power can be concentrated in a group of individuals virtually invisible to the general public.

Of the various means by which power can be diverted from the sources designed to exercise it, several are especially ingenious. In the Federal government there are, for instance, the "Indians," the bureaucrats on the lower departmental levels. They have been described as the subordinates who accompany their chiefs to policy-making meetings and, armed with the informative documents their chiefs need for reference, and that the Indians themselves have prepared, sit beside and behind their superiors; make notes on the proceedings; record the decisions reached; and then set out collectively to undermine these decisions according to their views of what the decisions *should* have been.

The Indians accomplish this by keeping in touch with one another as an inner circle, and unite in presenting their superiors with the decisions made in the form the Indians *wish* them to have been made — often quite contrary to their chiefs' understanding of what they had decided. This tactic is executed with the highest skill by the Indians of the Department of Health, Education and Welfare who lately have been emulated by their colleagues in most of the other departments. The results have baffled Presidents and the members of Cabinets who head the Executive departments.

The distribution of power in Congress exemplifies how — though violent change to the point of destruction of the American democratic system has attracted an increasing number of active advocates among students, their professors, and the blacks — outmoded rules and customs in the Capitol successfully resist needful change. Long ago Woodrow Wilson, in *Congressional Government,* placed the locus of power over legislation in the committee chairmanships. And, while one-man rule of the House by the Speaker ended in 1910 when Speaker Joseph Cannon was shorn of the power to appoint all committee members and the Senate no longer is controlled by a small oligarchy, there has been no substantial shift of power from the committee chairmen.

But the almost unvarying fact that these posts nearly always go automatically to the committee member with the longest tenure is not the basic reason for the chairmanship tyranny. Seniority, it is true, is prone to elevate the elderly, from whom time has taken its inevitable toll, over more gifted committee members. But, as Winston Churchill said of democracy, seniority is probably the worst form of chairmanship selection except for any other. This conclusion is strongly supported by an examination of the most favored alternate proposal, which is:

A committee chairman should be chosen by a free secret

vote of the committee membership and subject to replacement by the same procedure at any time.

The anarchic disorder this method would inflict on the legislative process is obvious. The nature of politics and politicians would assure a continuous effort to shift power that would demoralize any committee. And, though the fundamental principle of the Constitution — the separation of powers — has been periodically subverted by each of the three Federal branches in the course of our history, the adoption of this proposal would enable an incoming President with a congressional majority to make Congress an inseparable part of the White House machinery. For the committee chairmen would be the President's hand-picked servitors — at least as long as public opinion approved or tolerated this.

It is also a demonstrated fallacy that the adoption of this substitute for the seniority system would prevent a chairman, as at present, from exercising arbitrary rule over his committee colleagues, including the vital authority to name the heads of subcommittees. President Kennedy's successful effort to pack the House Rules Committee, successful only because enough Republicans defected to accomplish it, was falsely represented as a reform whereby the Rules Committee would be checked in the exercise of its special power to pigeonhole bills demanded by a large congressional majority and the general public. But, as was soon apparent, the change left the committee in possession of its general capacity to blockade. The only change was that the packing lifted this blockade for some of the measures sought by the President.

By the time this book appears one modification of the House rules that the "liberals" are pressing may have been adopted. It would allow an *open* vote by committee members to elect their chairman and ranking minority party representative every two years, and thus be the first step ever taken toward relaxing the rigidity of the seniority system. But, although such a chairman as Representative John L. McMillan (Democrat, S.C.) of the District of Columbia Committee may have been replaced on the ground that he is antagonistic to the concerns of the Negro majority of his constituency, seniority will, I think, continue to be the determining factor in choosing House chairmen; and also those in the Senate, if it has made the same modification of its rules.

But even under its archaic rules, and the reciprocal back scratching which requires adherence to the ordinance that one good turn deserves another, members with special parliamentary talent, personal force, new and constructive ideas, intellect or industry, can soon acquire prominence and influence in Congress. Some examples:

J. William Fulbright was elected to the House in 1942. He had been a Rhodes scholar and president of the University of Arkansas. A year after taking his seat he concentrated his energies on an idea that foreshadowed a revolution in United States foreign policy. The idea, marked for development by President Roosevelt when the political atmosphere was favorable, was simply that the contraction of the oceans by the airplane, plus its combat function as developed by Hitler and the Japanese, had leveled the water bastions which had protected the United States from attack and invasion from abroad, and had permitted this nation to retire securely into isolationism in the period between the First and Second World Wars. On this sound reasoning the young Representative from Arkansas introduced the Fulbright Resolution which forecast the revolution in United States foreign policy that eventually took form in the North Atlantic Alliance, the Greek-Turkish aid bill, the Marshall Plan — and the grand design of the collective world peacekeeping organization, the United Nations, which has foundered so lamentably in practice. And, though the United Nations has fallen far short of the goals enumerated in its Charter, and even constantly has violated it, the Fulbright Resolution was one of the forces that speeded the isolationist foreign policy of the United States into history.

John J. Williams of Delaware was elected in 1946 to a Senate with a bare Republican majority that endured only briefly. But in and out of the majority he proceeded to establish himself as an enemy in Congress of government prodigality, waste, and official misfeasance, becoming their most effective enemy on the death of Senator Harry F. Byrd, Sr., of Virginia. He attained this status by incessant homework (he always knew more than any colleague the facts of the matter in hand), a merited reputation for absolute integrity, impartiality toward the individuals or political parties involved, and personal courage that made him indifferent to reprisals in the Senate or at the polls. With one of the smallest constituencies in the Union, Williams acquired more power in his legislative field than a herd of Senators from the most populous states.

George D. Aiken of Vermont came to the Senate in 1940 with the background of a professional politician: he had been Speaker of the Vermont House and Governor. Like Williams, his constituency was minuscule in comparison with that of a Senator from New York, for instance. But, while his influence with both Republican and Democratic colleagues grew with seniority — he leads the Republican list — its basic derivations are character, the Yankee gift of pithy comment, civility in dealing with others, demonstrated personal and political integrity, and a homespun vocabulary that emanates common sense. Presidents and his fellow Senators listen to Aiken with unusual respect and his position on a complicated issue has at times been decisive.

The population of Kensett, Arkansas, has not expanded much from the 905 persons who were recorded in the 1960 census. Yet in November 1938, a citizen of Kensett was promoted from county judge to member of Congress who at this writing, and for some years past, has been the most influential legislator in the vital areas of taxation and revenue. This is the long-standing chairman of the Committee on Ways and Means, Wilbur D. Mills.

He is perhaps the most nearly perfect combination of the politician and the statesman that exists in the American governing system. Warm and amiable, with no trace of the professionalism that is the source of this behavior by most politicians; brilliant in his analyses of the convoluted statistics on which his judgment must greatly depend; firm but always open to well-documented questioning of his conclusions; industrious in doing his homework to the point where he forsakes all diversions until the homework has been wholly absorbed in his mind and consciousness — these are some of the attributes that help to account for the bipartisan respect and confidence in which Mills is held by the whole Congress and the Executive.

Numerous other instances could be cited to prove that both the House and the Senate quickly recognize the qualities which distinguish the members listed above and permit their possessors soon to emerge in influence from the impeding webs of seniority and short tenure. But these examples, I hope, suffice to make the point that Mr. Bumble's law, which Oliver Twist violated when he asked for "more," can successfully and usefully be breached in Congress by members who disclose one or more of the qualities enumerated above.

It is very helpful, however, to "catch the eye of the Speaker" early in one's career. For the Speaker's power of recognition, while many are clamoring for it, is one of the least noted and most effective in the legislative process.

3

The Presidency

THE LOOSE LANGUAGE of Article II of the Constitution, which both specifies presidential power and leaves its scope open to each President's measurement, was deliberately written in that murky form by its authors in 1787. The Article begins, "The Executive power shall be vested in a President of the United States," but, soon departing from this generality, enumerates a number of acts that fall within presidential authority. And, to add to the confusion, the President is made a partner in the legislative process by granting him the veto function, which can only be overrridden by two-thirds of both houses of Congress.

In consequence, some Presidents are historically characterized as "weak," Washington curiously among them, because they have confined themselves to exercising the powers that are enumerated, and Congress has been the dominant government branch in their time. Others, labeled "strong" Presidents, have continually expanded Executive power by reading "inherent" authorities into the text of their oath and the opening sentence of Article II. The Supreme Court attempted to dodge the unresolvable issue in *Mississippi* v. *Johnson*, in 1867 during the term of Andrew Johnson. Professing inability to enjoin a President from exceeding his constitutional powers, even when convinced of the validity of the charge, the Court expressed the view that in such instances the Chief Executive was "accountable" only "to the country and to his conscience." In the instance of President Truman's seizure of the steel industry the Court reversed this end-run by enjoining the Secretary of Commerce from carrying out the President's order.

But generally speaking, and particularly in foreign policy and action, the extent of presidential power, its function and its use, depend on who is President. Thus, whatever Congress or the courts may attempt by way of limitation — except in the most unlikely event of successful impeachment — the American people in the end will make the determination of his conduct whenever they make full use of the electoral process. But meanwhile he will be able, through error or intent, to involve the nation in war or crisis — military or domestic — at any second of any hour of his term.

The first President to take full advantage of the latitude left him by the loose language of Article II was Andrew Jackson. The clearest statement of his concept of this latitude was made in his veto of Henry Clay's bill to recharter the second Bank of the United States. The Constitution, wrote Jackson, (a) authorized each of the three Federal branches to act or withhold action according to its interpretation of its powers; (b) the Supreme Court has only such influence as the force of its reasoning may deserve; and (c), by the oath he takes, the President is sworn to do what he thinks best in time of emergencies involving the national interest, as he sees it, when the other two branches have failed to take the necessary step (the definition of "necessary" being the President's) or cannot take it with the immediacy required.

The episode of the Louisiana Purchase might lead readers of history to fix on Jefferson, not Jackson, as the first to expound this concept. But the Purchase was an exception:

otherwise Jefferson regularly deferred to Congress and made a broad measurement of its share in Federal power. Since he was the undisputed leader of the Republican (Democratic) party, with an overwhelming majority of congressional followers, this attitude involved no weakening of Jefferson as *President*. However, it did weaken the *presidency*, and it was Jackson who asserted and expanded both the explicit and implicit authority of the office.

But, after Jackson, Congress reassumed domination of the Federal system until the advent of a President who carried Jackson's thesis even further in concept and in practice. This was Abraham Lincoln, whose unilateral suspension of the writ of habeas corpus was only one of many examples of his assertion of presidential supremacy. In a fine study of the constitutional conflict, *The President: Office and Powers*, by the late Professor Edward S. Corwin of Princeton University, Lincoln is described as "a solitary genius who valued the opportunity for reflection above that of counsel" (p. 23).

Although the intra-Federal dispute over the assertion of "inherent" presidential power has often concerned domestic matters, the quarrel has mostly been between Congress and the Executive over a President's use of the military abroad without explicit congressional sanction in advance.

The issue arose in a very limited way when President Polk during the Mexican War ordered the Navy to occupy the port of Tampico. Ruling on a challenge of this action, the Supreme Court held that the President "as Commander-in-Chief . . . is authorized to direct the movements of the naval and military forces placed by law at his command, and to employ them in the manner he may deem most effective . . . to conquer . . . the enemy." But the issue came to full maturity, with pertinence to the current phase, when Lincoln, between the firing on Ft. Sumter and the opening of the special session of Congress on July 4, 1861 — linking the commander-in-chief clause to the requirement in the same Constitution that the President "take care that the laws be faithfully executed" — took the following actions under a claim of inherent "war power":

Federalized the state militias as ninety-day volunteers; called for 40,000 volunteers for three years' service; increased the regular Army and Navy by 23,000 and 18,000 respectively; and disbursed $2 million of Treasury funds to persons legally ineligible as recipients.

Within a month after assembling, Congress approved these acts, took no position on the suspension of the writ (in March 1863 it got around to authorizing this also), and in general reflected Lincoln's judgment that in time of emergency the President had the power to "lay the Constitution on the shelf" — Alfred E. Smith's recommendation, in those very words, during the Great Depression more than seventy years later. But Lincoln was dealing with an internal rebellion, including armed secession. And it was not until the time of Theodore Roosevelt that the issue of inherent presidential power as commander-in-chief to employ the armed forces outside the United States — this time in Latin America under invocation of the Monroe Doctrine — without advance sanction of Congress, became a permanent though spasmodic legislative-Executive conflict.

In Article I it was thought sufficient, as a curb on too liberal a concept of a President's power in the role of commander-in-chief, to reserve to Congress the function "to declare war," and "to raise and support armies." And the power to establish a complete control over the economy, mobilize all the nation's resources, establish priorities in industrial production and its uses, and fix wages and prices, still cannot be employed by the commander-in-chief except by express congressional delegation — as in the War Powers Acts of the First and Second World Wars.

But, citing a national "emergency," and in the absence of a formal declaration of war, Presidents can and have dispatched the armed forces abroad — in the Caribbean, for instance — on their discretionary judgment of what is required for national security, and successfully counted on Congress to foot the bill. Months before Pearl Harbor and the formal congressional declaration of war against Japan and the Central Powers, President Franklin Roosevelt took the following steps on his own to make the United States a virtual cobelligerent with the Allies in World War II:

Seized a California plant of the North American Aviation Company, where a strike had halted production. Ordered the arming of United States merchant vessels carrying supplies of war to the Allies, and instructed their commanders to fire in event of any attempted interception. "Loaned" to the United Kingdom fifty overage, reconditioned destroyers in exchange for American naval bases in Britain's West Indian possessions.

For the latter action there was no statutory nor specific constitutional warrant; and Admiral Stark, the then Chief of Naval Operations, remarked to me that the Navy could not afford, and had no constitutional warrant, to "turn over a single rowboat." It was probably remarks like this, reported to the ever active electronic ear at the White House, that induced Stark's replacement as C.N.O. and his transfer to London for the duration of World War II.

These actions by FDR not only represented an expansion of the role of commander-in-chief in time of formal peace: they were linked to the "stewardship theory" as expanded by the first President Roosevelt: that the President could do anything he deemed in the public interest, in both foreign and domestic affairs, provided only neither the Constitution nor any statute had specifically prohibited it; and, so far as any constitutional restraint was concerned, the President was, and had to be, the sole judge of this. As a result Congress and the Supreme Court would find these actions *faits accomplis* if and when they got around to considering them.

FDR did submit to Congress for approval the Lend-Lease Act more than eight months before Pearl Harbor. But this delegation of power to the President by Congress was enacted only by gross deception on the part of the Administration. Congress and the public were assured, on the highest Executive word, that the measure was a means to keep the United States from becoming involved abroad, on land, sea and in the air, in World War II. Whereas, it was obvious — and so pointed out repeatedly at the time by this writer and others — that militant reaction by the Central Powers and Japan was a certainty; hence the Lend-Lease Act would inevitably change the position of the United States from a disguised cobelligerent — a status previously reached by presidential "Executive orders" — to an active one.

Under the same definition of the role of the President as commander-in-chief in peace and war ("accountable" only "to the country and to his conscience") and, as T. R. put it, "steward" of national security:

President Wilson invaded Mexico with troops in reprisal for invasion of United States territory by Pancho Villa's banditti. President Truman ordered the Air Force and the Navy into combat in Korea when the North Koreans invaded it (on the basis that a treaty — the United Nations compact — is the supreme law of the land), before the U.N. affirmed his request to associate itself with this war on the authority of the Charter. President Kennedy approved the government's continued training, financing, and then transport, of the anti-Castro invaders in the Bay of Pigs affair, sent a vastly increased number of military advisers to South Vietnam and thence to the combat areas. President Johnson ordered military intervention in the Dominican Republic; and, before the dubious sanction of the Tonkin Resolution, multiplied many times the United States combat forces in Southeast Asia. President Nixon — on the original ground of the need to protect U.S. troops in Vietnam, a ground he shifted in later versions — ordered the military expedition temporarily into Cambodia to wipe out sanctuaries of North Vietnamese and Viet Cong armed forces which had long since invaded Cambodia on a permanent basis.

All these episodes, in my judgment, establish the abiding truth of the following summation by Professor Corwin, in the book previously noted: "Taken by and large, the history of the Presidency has been a history of aggrandizement."

This aggrandizement began nearly a century and a half ago in the first term of Andrew Jackson. It expanded with the development and use of the nuclear bomb by the United States, and became inevitable when two potential enemies — Soviet Russia and Communist China — dedicated to the overthrow of the American system became nuclear powers with steadily expanding weapons. Hence the President of a nation, committed against initiating nuclear war and under the threat of physical destruction by nations not so committed, can be depended on to protect it, on his own concept of the need, without waiting for the sanction of Congress, or the response of the Supreme Court to a challenge of constitutionality.

The built-in confusions between Articles I and II are somewhat modified by a broad division between Congress's power of the purse and the President's power of the sword. But not until an inept and cowardly President occupies the White House, or a Congress withdraws the financial support of armies thereby left vulnerable to massacre by an enemy on foreign soil, will the "aggrandizement" of the presidency, in the meaning employed by Corwin, be vitally reduced.

The Ninety-first Congress, near the end of its tenure, did go to unprecedented length in specifically forbidding any use of the appropriation for the Department of Defense for the financing of United States combat troops and military advisers in Cambodia. But, in my judgment, if circumstances arise where, citing his constitutional duty to protect American troops wherever they are stationed (a duty acknowledged in the text of the appropriation measure itself), a President will execute it despite the statutory ban, and whether or not Congress simultaneously or thereafter will — as I believe it would — give the action its approval.

Every four years, and indirectly every two, the voting population of the United States has the only opportunity there is to resolve the immediate issue created by deliberately embedded and continuous conflict between the presidency and the other coordinate arms of the Federal government. The nature of such a confrontation depends on the kind of President who is occupying the White House. There is no viable check on the Executive other than the electoral that can be substantially effective, assuming the Federal bureaucracy is not permitted to obstruct the mandate of the voters in presidential elections.

Considerations of practical politics are the guidelines on which many Presidents have decided whether or not to claim certain "inherent" constitutional powers. For, generally speaking, popular congressional or judicial support for such a claim is essential to its effectiveness.

To protect the Constitution's deepest foundation, the principle of the separation of powers among the three Federal branches, the craftsmen of the national charter built a wall so high and so broad that trespass by any of the three on the premises of another was designed to be the occasion either of limited or all-out fratricidal war. In practice this arrangement has produced the following consequences:

When public opinion, strong enough to be readily transferable into votes, is on the side of the President in a contest with Congress, it is normally Congress that does the substantial compromising, and vice versa.

When there is strong public support for both sides on an Executive-legislative conflict, the swapping of legislative particulars is generally about even.

When, despite a visibly large public division, the President or Congress declines to yield on basic provisions of legislation, the shadow of the President's veto power is likely to gain him the major points in a Congress with a dependable majority of his own party or a bipartisan coalition, but, if neither exists, to inflict on him the damage of having his vetoes overridden.

Even though party lines on domestic matters, especially those dealing with socio-economics, are being increasingly weakened by defections, firm and bold national leadership is usually the factor which determines whether Congress will yield the most important concessions. Congressional leaders of the opposition, even when it is in control at the Capitol, hesitate to venture a certain or probable presidential veto unless they are reasonably certain they can muster the two-thirds in both branches required to override.

For example, on only one occasion was Congress — though Democratic except for the first two years of President Eisenhower's eight-year tenure — able to override his veto. And this was of a "pork-barrel" bill, the kind for which members vote strictly in the interests of their reelection, producing a stampede in which party lines are trampled in the assault on the Treasury.

In addition to the enormous advantage of the veto power

(only forty-seven of seven hundred and fifty were overridden from Washington's first inaugural to FDR's second) in one of those conflicts with Congress that the writers of the Constitution carefully assured, the President has these others:

The moral leadership of the nation if he has the will, quality, and public appeal to exert it.

The power to paralyze congressional resistance by declaring a state or threat of "emergency," and prolonging the status beyond any probable necessity.

The power of patronage (even though circumscribed by an entrenched bureaucracy under civil service protection) by which a President can bestow high-paying offices outside the civil service among the faithful.

A vast, well-paid propaganda machine whose spokesman to the entire nation through all the media, particularly the electronic, can be the President's any time he requests it.

The symbol of government and the people that only *he* can be, standing in respect of Congress like a pillar in a lonely plain.

But, despite these assets of the Executive in the endless struggle between the two branches for the domination of government acts and policies — when both have not been supervened by the Federal courts on the illegitimate doctrine of judicial supremacy — even popular Presidents with party majorities in the Capitol have been forced by Congress into courses they opposed, or denied approval of legislation to which they brought the powerful pressures inherent in their office and the will to exert these pressures to the fullest. Henry Clay and his followers forced a most unwilling President Madison into the War of 1812. Congressional war hawks, exploiting jingo popular sentiment, literally dragged President McKinley into the war with Spain in 1898.

Among the other "deceits" which (as the title of this

book suggests) have become embedded in the language of politics is the illusion that Congress still can be firmly identified as "Democratic" or "Republican." It remains true that the operating machinery of Congress is in the hands of a majority listed under one or the other major party label. It remains true that the possession of this machinery enables the majority leaders to determine what legislation shall be advanced, impeded, or pigeonholed; and gives their party the chairmanships and committee majorities. But the real test of the outcome of a congressional election is whether the majority of members, however affiliated, will support or oppose the major programs of the Executive. So the true description of the outcome of each election is that it promises to be pro- or anti-Administration, partisan or bipartisan, because party defections and bipartisan coalitions are now standard events.

This accounts for the efforts of Presidents to assure, by various means, that the voters will return pro-Administration majorities at the congressional elections, regardless of which party had the more members under its label. By failing to make clear that his objective was a Congress which, regardless of its nominal party majority, would support him on war emergency legislation, President Wilson, in 1918, left himself vulnerable to the charge that he was asking for a Congress composed entirely of Democrats. President Roosevelt, in 1938, invoked the process by attempting to deny the party nominations to anti-Administration Democrats which exposed him to the rising charge of total "dictatorship." President Nixon, by not trying to tell the Republican party whom to nominate, but appealing instead to the whole electorate to return whichever party candidates he could depend on to support him on his fundamental legislative propositions — nonpartisan in nature — was seeking to avoid the procedural errors of both Wilson and Roosevelt and yet attain the same objective as theirs.

In the isolation period of the Twenties and Thirties, when the United States again was seeking to keep out of Europe's troubles, having reaped only a harvest of scorpions from its participation in World War I, public opinion ran with the Republicans who were the champions of the effort. Both parties supported the Neutrality Act which prevented the United States from rendering aid to the Allies in the visibly approaching Second World War. This support was so strong that President Franklin Roosevelt and Secretary Hull, who were both against maintaining the Act, did not venture for some years to propose repeal.

But during this period of politically motivated laissez-faire, President Roosevelt moved in divers ways to induce public acceptance as a fact of the argument that isolation had become dangerous to the security of the United States. And, as Fulbright did among the Democrats in Congress, three Republicans inspired and led a similar movement in their own party. These were Thomas E. Dewey, the Republican presidential nominee in 1944 and 1948, Wendell L. Willkie, the nominee in 1940, and Senator Arthur H. Vandenberg, an isolationist who had honestly, publicly, and courageously changed his mind. They were instrumental in summoning the conference at Mackinac Island, Michigan, from which the new party position of internationalism emerged. This policy had been strongly opposed in the country until the collapse of France in 1940 dramatized that the danger to the American government system was "clear and present."

Vandenberg acquired great public stature by an honest confession of his change of viewpoint and the candor of the reasons he gave for it. As chairman of the Committee on Foreign Relations, and its ranking minority member when the

Democrats recaptured control of Congress in 1948, Vandenberg was the most effective champion of an internationalist position by the United States. But important spadework in converting the party had been done by Willkie and Dewey at the Mackinac conference.

Without their pioneering, the nation might not even have been as prepared for war as it was when the Japanese attacked Pearl Harbor. The preparation was inadequate, as demonstrated in the early stages of American participation. And when Senator Vandenberg, on the floor, asked Senator Truman where lay the responsibility, Truman with customary honesty and bluntness placed it on the Administration of his own party, speaking as chairman of a Senate committee on preparedness.

Even as late as May 1940, in a speech on preparedness, President Roosevelt had assured the people that the military arsenal had all the capacity that might be required by any event. By listing materiel as either in hand or "on order" he glossed over the fact that most of it was in the latter category, many months away from delivery to the armed forces.

The great war machine ultimately went into high gear, but not before the cost of inadequate preparation had been thousands of lives ("one hundred thousand at least," B. M. Baruch once said to me). Despite this experience, the swift postwar demobilization wasted the fruits of victory in World War II and generated the cold war. Therefore it was natural that the political victims of these errors of government should be the party in power and that a trend toward isolationism reappeared in the United States.

Though President Truman had gone to war in Korea under the flag of the United Nations, whose charter pledged protection of South Korea from the aggression of North Korea that had occurred, it was soon evident that the United States would have to supply 95 percent of the manpower and materiel; also that the United Nations would not support the steps necessary to military victory. And the American people began to realize that, contrary to expectations when the United Nations was organized in 1945, this international body was shot through with weaknesses of structure.

The Charter provision that minor members (in population and in the state of their economy), would have the same voting strength in the General Assembly as the major powers, exposed the United Nations in practice to the rule of a wholly unrepresentative majority consisting of immature, anti-American, so-called nations who defaulted on their obligations under the Charter without penalty of any kind. Moreover, foreign aid in the sum of many billions had made the United States no friends in this group but instead a collection of blackmailers. And whenever a charge derogatory to this country was made anywhere, these recipients of American bounty, many existing only because American military power was their shield against Communist take-overs, could be counted on to ventilate and support the accusation — Nehru's India being a perfect example.

Furthermore, the veto power possessed by members of the Security Council was being steadily abused by Soviet Russia at the expense of legitimate American interests, and of the advance of world peace that the United Nations was formed to assure. (The irony was that the United States Senate had insisted on the embodiment of the veto power as the price for approving the Charter.)

In consequence of these flaws in the U.N. structure, there is now a Republican President who owes his election in great part to a pledge to review and diminish our world commitments. But like the nose of the camel, once in the tent it is a long and difficult labor to keep out the whole animal.

This review and diminution of commitments is not, however, entirely a Republican enterprise. Senate Democrats, including the majority leader, Mike Mansfield, and Chairman Fulbright of the Committee on Foreign Relations, have been urging these since the war in Vietnam became a major American conflict. In the congressional elections of 1970 the candidates of both parties claimed that each had the better formula for disengagement.

A good example of distortion of the purpose of an international policy is provided by the SEATO alliance, whose architect was a Republican Secretary of State, John Foster Dulles, and which was later employed by a Democratic successor, Dean Rusk, to justify the military intervention in Vietnam. This treaty, when it came before the Senate, was represented by Chairman Walter George of the Foreign Relations Committee, on Dulles's assurance, as "committing" us to nothing — neither to intervene in Vietnam nor automatically to base similar action in Southeast Asia on the "domino theory." The text of the treaty merely commits the United States Executive to decide what our course should be in the event of aggression in the area, and proceed upon it only in line with constitutional practices.

The Senate accepted this as meaning that not again would the Chief Executive commit the military on his own, as Truman did when he intervened in Korea even before asking the United Nations to assume the responsibility for it, and never requesting the sanction of Congress. But President Kennedy involved the U.S. military more deeply in Vietnam, by sending the advisers to the combat zones, before Johnson came to Congress with the Tonkin Gulf resolution. On this ex post facto procedure, justified by a dubious claim that North Vietnam naval forces had twice attacked

American warships in international waters, he vastly expanded American combat forces in Vietnam.

The drift away from President F. D. Roosevelt's domination of the other two branches and of popular opinion, which was first registered by severe Democratic losses in the congressional elections of 1938, and checked by the progress of the United States into World War II, that began with Hitler's invasion of Poland, was conspicuously renewed by three negative actions by Congress at the height of the war. It repealed his order limiting Federal salaries to $25,000 a year; legislated the War Labor Disputes Act over his veto, and denied him his insistent attempt to increase his already vast authority with a third War Powers Act. To obtain this, he, as the saying is, had "gone to the wall."

The most recent examples of trading with Congress that is forced on a President were provided by (a) the give-and-take of the tax legislation of 1969 — aptly dubbed "the Christmas Tree" because it scattered largesse to all claimants for special favors who controlled a strategic bloc of supporters in Congress; and (b) by the tariff bill of 1970. In the Executive-legislative-lobbyist bartering over that bill, Washington for months resembled a Middle East bazaar — except that it lacked the grace, talent, and craftiness of the Levantine vendors.

Many other instances of trading within the Capitol, and between it and the White House, are provided by history. But their root and necessity, as previously noted, are the built-in conflicts derived from the deliberate structuring of the Constitution. The demands and counterproposals that are rituals of negotiations in the private sector between employers and employees bear only a partial resemblance to what goes on in the government. This is because one-sided, pro-union legislation has put the unions in the driver's seat before negotiations have even begun to begin.

Thomas Jefferson was the first President who was also a master politician, as we now understand the term. Washington was above the battle. John Adams was inept at practical politics. But Jefferson, in addition to being a consummate practitioner of the trade, never overlooked the important fact that government *is* politics; hence only a politician could govern effectively and establish his philosophy of government during his own tenure and beyond. With this ever in mind, he laid the firm foundation of the Jeffersonian dynasty composed of Madison, Monroe, and John Quincy Adams.

The chain of command was not broken until the advent of Andrew Jackson, whom Jefferson described as a "most unfit" man for the presidency, who had "very little respect for laws or constitutions," and whose "passions are terrible" to behold. But Jefferson was dead when Jackson became President, and, though Old Hickory governed with none of the subtlety of the Sage of Monticello, he applied Jefferson's political philosophy of the rigid separation of powers, while keeping pace with the expansion of Federal authority required by the changed social conditions created by the settlement of the new frontier. And Jackson's buildup of the party system controverted Jefferson's expressed fear that the victor of New Orleans would govern "without regard to party."

Also like Jefferson, Jackson founded a presidential dynasty, though briefer and interrupted — Van Buren, Polk, Pierce, and Buchanan. But none of these had Jackson's talent in the political arena.

With a technique that was later to be employed by F. D. Roosevelt in his maneuvering for a third nomination (1939–40), Lincoln pretended, until the Republican convention at Chicago had begun in 1860, that he did not seek the presidential nomination, at the same time doing everything a good politician knows how to do to assure it. And during the War Between the States, Lincoln devised the masterly political gambit of the Emancipation Proclamation.

That this document should have been so entitled is one of the great frauds of American history. It is accepted by every schoolboy as having "freed the slaves," but it was not even a sociological measure, since it freed only those slaves behind the Confederate lines. It was, instead, a stroke of political and military strategy, and even in that status only reluctantly adopted by the President, who had replaced General Fremont for freeing the slaves in Missouri. Slaves in the North remained slaves, and not until slavery was outlawed by a constitutional amendment were all slaves truly freedmen.

Cleveland was a successful politician overall, yet he scrupulously kept his word, once given, and never compromised his clear philosophy of government, which was in the mold of classic nineteenth-century liberalism. In 1888, he was barely defeated for reelection by his own greatness, and even then he carried the popular majority. In 1892 Cleveland was renominated and elected despite his inflexible stand against bimetalism which had begun to acquire a large following in his party. But he was the rock on which the Democrats split, not to regain the presidency again until the election of 1912 when the Republican party was fragmented as the Democrats had been twenty years previously, though on a different issue.

Theodore Roosevelt was simultaneously a natural politician and an idealist. He managed to fuse these opposites by knowing and playing the game of politics. He played it with state leaders, with Congress, and with the American people. He was so adept at the trade that, though William Howard Taft was his hand-picked successor in 1908, T.R. got more

Republican votes than Taft did in 1912 when Roosevelt repudiated his protégé and, by his independent candidacy, assured Taft's defeat for reelection.

He did not achieve what I believe he thought he also could do — defeat Wilson as well at the same assizes. But he remained actively in politics, and so successfully that he was instrumental in reuniting under Charles E. Hughes the party he had split. And in the very year of Roosevelt's sudden death, the political community was largely convinced he would be nominated and elected for a third term in 1920.

Coolidge was as shrewd a politician for his times as this country has produced. His successful technique was to pretend he had no political ambitions, while grasping each rung of the ladder by which he ascended to the White House. He realized that, after the scandals of the Harding Administration, the Republicans in 1924 could retain their voter majority, and the Democrats be defeated, only by intense accent on the Republican nominee as a man of impeccable and simple virtue, and that physically as well as tactically he could be molded into the embodiment of that image. Though others deserved a share of the credit that came entirely to Coolidge for his timing in breaking the Boston police strike (this made him Vice-President) he obscured them by delaying repressive action until time's forelock was within his grasp.

Despite the fact that by Coolidge's total reliance on the economic and monetary counsels of Secretary of Treasury Andrew W. Mellon he invited the deluge of 1929, the onus fell on his successor, Herbert Hoover. It has been contended that Coolidge did not foresee the economic crash, so complete was his acceptance of Mellon's confidence that the great boom of the Twenties was on solid ground. This supports the interpretation of his "I do not choose to run in 1928" — that he was an eagerly receptive candidate for reelection. Others insist that Coolidge saw what was coming and his words were a firm abdication. I am of the school which believes in the first theory.

President Hoover didn't understand practical politics; he didn't enjoy the company of its practitioners and he thought he could govern by engineering efficiency. He did not cater to state leaders or to members of Congress. He thought that not playing politics by the rules was the most successful method, and that in normal circumstances he could have demonstrated this. I am rather inclined to agree with him on that; for, if he hadn't lost Congress to the Democrats in 1930 by reason of the abnormal economic circumstances, I believe he could have pulled the nation out of the Depression and served two terms in the White House.

John J. Raskob and Jouett Shouse, respectively the Democratic National Chairman and chairman of its Executive Committee, launched (on the keys of Charles Michaelson's typewriter) a ceaseless publicity assault on Hoover, blaming him personally for all the ills of the era. In his first campaign FDR attributed to Hoover the full causes of the Depression, but years later in her newspaper column Mrs. Roosevelt blandly observed en passant that Hoover was not responsible for it. Raskob and Shouse turned the whole Democratic party into an anti-Hoover propaganda machine. Its product, widely published and supplying the fabric of innumerable Democratic speeches in and out of Congress, discredited Hoover even before it was known who the Democratic nominee would be.

The effects of this barrage were that the Democrats decided they could beat him with anybody except Al Smith. This was ironical, because both Shouse and Raskob were pro-Smith and were preparing a base for his renomination and election. But, as the convention of 1932 soon disclosed, Smith never had a chance because both the big city and rural party leaders feared his "Bowery accent," Catholic religion, and Tammany background would give the Republicans their only possible means for success. The outcome — Roosevelt's nomination and election on a conservative and "wet" platform — made way for the New Deal, after FDR's brief service to the budget-balancing philosophy of the 1932 platform.

The 1932 platform was written by A. Mitchell Palmer, Wilson's Attorney General. It was a progressive program, but in no way foreshadowed the New Deal; it subscribed to general doctrines which later were distorted into the specific programs of a Welfare State. But though the platform moved the party away from classic conservatism, in recognition of changing conditions, it stopped well short of the state collectivism that was initiated by the New Deal.

Roosevelt overestimated his political strength on at least two notable occasions — the attempts to pack the Supreme Court and his effort to prevent the nomination or renomination by Democratic primary voters of key conservatives as a warning to all. He lost both battles. But with respect to the Court he won the war, for public opinion was mounting against its "strict constructionist" majority. And, though, like other misrepresentations of the real purpose of a Roosevelt proposal to Congress, its slickness varnished over the real objective, the packing plan had a basic justification. Yet, once attained, this was exploited far beyond its warrant after the new Court majority took over.

At the time the packing arrangement was proposed by Roosevelt, the Court docket was overloaded, emphasizing the indisputable merit of FDR's view that there should be an age limit to the active service of Supreme Court Justices. Realizing the weight of these arguments, Chief Justice Hughes set out, before the submission of the packing legislation, to reverse the stand-patism of the Court's majority and had already succeeded in inducing his brethren to backtrack on wholesale nullification of New Deal legislation, in the case of the Washington State minimum wage act.

The next fruit of the Chief Justice's labors was the opinion by which the Wagner Act was upheld. But the effectiveness of Hughes's tactic was best illustrated by the Court's reversal of its original ruling that the Agricultural Adjustment Act was unconstitutional. Owen J. Roberts had written the adverse finding, but the majority was so narrow that, to preserve it, Roberts incorporated in his opinion the contention of Justice Harlan F. Stone that, if the legal issue raised had been over the powers of Congress under the Welfare Clause of the Constitution, the legislation would have been valid.

I called on Stone the afternoon of the day the decision was rendered to ask him to clarify the judgment so that I could accurately report its meaning and effect. "I've got Roberts now," he said. "His concession of vast congressional power through the Welfare Clause opens the way for Congress to make the Act constitutional by changing its base. Then Roberts will have to go along and the purpose of the Act will be achieved."

This forecast proved to be prophetic. But Roberts might still have refused to make up the required Court majority if Hughes had not persuaded him to do this, pointing out that otherwise the public feeling against the Court might rise to the point where serious invasion of its independence by the Executive would quickly follow. (This invasion – the Court packing plan – did not materialize until 1937, when the majority had reverted to striking down New Deal legislation.)

But the Democratic losses in House membership in the 1938 by-election were, I think, due to other reasons than Roosevelt's effort to pack the Court. One, the New Deal's failure to restore a sound economy; two, Roosevelt's effort to induce the state Democratic electorates to retire from Congress, by denying renomination to such distinguished and popular members as Senators Walter George of Georgia and Tydings of Maryland — the so-called purge. He succeeded in eliminating only Representative John J. O'Connor of New York, chairman of the Rules Committee, whom he accused of blocking floor consideration of the legislation of the Second New Deal. During FDR's attempted purge of Democrats in Congress who had opposed certain of his programs, I was an ear- and eye-witness to an instance of a well-used way by which unreported financial aid is covertly sent to candidates in trouble. One evening a friend, who had been a high official in the Roosevelt Administration but left it because of disapproval of the Second New Deal, asked me if he might use the telephone in my apartment in New York. He explained he had a call to make that it was "inadvisable" to transmit over his own, very possibly bugged, line.

The call, it developed, was to another very prominent Democrat in a state bordering on Georgia (where Senator Walter George was a prime object of FDR's purge). The conversation went something like this (with the speakers' names changed):

"That you, Jim? This is Jack. Fine, fine, and you? Good. Listen, Jim, I am sending eleven of those by hand to you tonight to get across the line to help Walter. The messenger will identify himself satisfactorily. . . . You will? Thanks a lot. And give Walter my love."

The "eleven," as it turned out, referred to bank notes of high denominations.

Another perfectly legal but not very admirable method of making cash campaign contributions, is to give money to both major candidates on the prudent theory that, however the contest turns out, the contributor will be in favor. My source of information about one example of this practice was Wendell L. Willkie, the Republican presidential nominee of 1940.

As was his custom after seeing President Roosevelt, he paid me a visit to report on such a conversation in 1941, in which he received FDR's blessing on Willkie's projected tour abroad in the interest of his concept of "One World." "The President," said Willkie, "obviously was trying to make me feel that we were buddies. He told me of plans I had already read about in the press, ending up with 'And I am sending young [Averell] Harriman to be my Minister in London.' When I made no response, he added, 'You know he contributed to my [1940] campaign.' 'How much did he give you?' I inquired, and he named a sum. Then I said, 'Not *your* campaign, Mr. President, *our* campaign. He made the same contribution to me.' "

The long presidential tenure of Franklin D. Roosevelt seems to me to offer support to the impression that a patrician background and the broad "A" have a basic attraction for the voting mass when displayed without a hint of patronage — and Roosevelt was a master of this. At any rate, twice in this century, these attributes appear to have helped to move the so-called average man and woman to repudiate candidates of greater capabilities in statecraft.

In Roosevelt's case this impulse was strengthened by the proliferation of radio sets that brought his compelling, cultivated tones into the living room; in Kennedy's, his special style was projected by the development of home television. It cannot even be guessed how many people less endowed with these superficial lures, viewing and listening, thought to themselves, "I want my President to talk and look like that."

Roosevelt by nature was not a crusading social reformer, nor did he have the dedication. But by word and act he moved the mass of the people as the social reformers could not. He had the same pleasing effect on the masses of other free nations, and perhaps it would have been manifested in Soviet Russia if he had been permitted to tour that nation without the restrictions that autocracy imposes in its own self-interest.

But with the Allied leaders it was a different story. Even Roosevelt's charisma (a new word of the Sixties) and the vast power at his command did not acquit him of the necessity of frequent compromise. He accepted the British pattern for the postwar rezoning of Germany that left Berlin an island deep in Soviet territory, one of the most disastrous arrangements in history, the inevitable precursor of the cold war and the present perils confronting the free world. The price he paid Stalin at Yalta for virtually nothing in exchange has burdened humanity ever since. And in each case he could have averted the damage by playing the trumps that were in his hand, and not erred so grievously in his assessment of the postwar policies of the Soviet Union until just before he died, when it was too late for him to repair the costly miscalculation.

But, though he loved the approving roar of the crowd, for relaxation Roosevelt most enjoyed small intimate sessions with his entourage — listening to Tommy Corcoran's Irish songs to the accompaniment of a guitar, bursting into solos or joining lustily in the choruses; indulging in a game of poker with modest stakes and egregious bluffing; ridiculing persons in public and private life, a pastime in which Harry Hopkins particularly excelled and in which the President, to his delight, was, though warily, included. Such occasions almost visibly lifted from his shoulders the heavy burdens of his office.

Devious means of attaining his goals, such as the packing plan to revise the anti-New Deal bias of the Supreme Court, appealed to him, when frequently a direct and candid approach would have been more effective in enlisting the support of a substantial majority. He denied, for example, over a period of several months, that any material quid pro quo induced him to transfer the overage destroyers to the British, whereas, as it developed, the United States acquired in exchange several military bases in the Caribbean and other British overseas possessions. (This substantial recompense Ambassador Joseph P. Kennedy had urged when the transfer of the destroyers was first proposed.) The result of FDR's deception was to engender a public division over the "loan" of the destroyers that would not have developed to the extent it did if the American people had known it would be compensated.

I believe Roosevelt's denial of the quid pro quo in this instance was prompted to some extent by the same motive that impelled Lyndon Johnson to withdraw or defer decisions the press had anticipated. Roosevelt, too, wanted to be the man who broke the news. He also was wont to suggest the headlines for news he announced — something Johnson never did. He feinted with his left so that he could hit harder with his right. He would even deny news stories there was no point in denying since he knew they soon would be verified.

One of his devices was especially entertaining. To emphasize the wisdom of certain controversial acts or policies he would remark that he had asked a critical visitor to suggest an alternative and the critic had none to offer. I never believed these incidents had occurred, and he never named the vis-à-vis. On one occasion he described the dumb struck visitor as "a big business executive" who complained of the size of the Federal budget but could not, on demand, specify a single item that could be eliminated without irreparable damage to the public interest.

Truman is a political animal, and it was the instinct of the species that enabled him to win the election of 1948, not his strength of character, his humility, and his common sense. His bold though specious assault on the Eightieth Congress (Republican) as a "do nothing" shifted to the opposition the responsibility for a bitter grievance in the farm states (the shortage of crop storage facilities), although this shortage was a product of negligence by his own Administration. In line with this resort to courthouse politics was his charge that his Republican opponent, Thomas E. Dewey, was committed to the Hitler theory of a master race.

But unadmirable as these political tactics were, they were highly professional. And Dewey contributed to their effectiveness by leaving the impression that he accepted the philosophy of the New (Fair) Deal, an impression implied in his claim that he could better redeem its promises.

Once elected in his own right, Truman presided over the revolution in American foreign policy that Roosevelt planned to invoke and of which the North Atlantic Treaty was the keystone. Upon this new base of the "entangling alliances" George Washington had warned the new Republic against, Truman superimposed the Greek-Turk aid bill, the Marshall Plan and proclaimed the "Truman Doctrine." This was a windy pledge that the United States would go to the aid of any nation threatened by "external aggression or internal subversion."

This idealistic rhetoric first materialized in practical and good results of which Point Four (offering diplomatic, scientific, technical, and economic assistance to underdeveloped nations) is an example. But the intent of the doctrine has since been distorted by Truman's successors in the presidency to a global (and in practice, unilateral) military commitment by the United States. In a conversation with Truman he told me what he had in mind was this Point Four type of assistance, and not involvement of the United States in military action wherever nations *outside our national security perimeter* were threatened by "external aggression or internal subversion."

In any form, however, the doctrine was a total break with historic United States foreign policy that derived from Washington's warning against "entangling alliances" and it could not have been approved by Congress without strong support of the opposition party. But part of the groundwork for this support had been laid by some Republicans as early as the fall of France in 1940.

Strong President though he was, Truman made mistakes that could have been politically fatal. Among these were the hurried postwar demobilization of the armed forces; insistence on continuing meat rationing after the wartime spirit of sacrifice had run its course; and the seizure of the strike-crippled steel industry that the Supreme Court later decided, six to three, exceeded the President's statutory and constitutional powers. (In this decision the Court established a landmark precedent which had been set in the Washington trial court by the late District Judge David A. Pine.)

Truman's intense loyalty to his friends, some of whom didn't deserve it, was a fault, in contrast to his reverence for the presidency. But the fault inflicted no irreparable political damage because loyalty, even when misapplied, appeals to the American people. One of two major sacrifices Truman made of a devoted friend was J. Howard McGrath, the Attorney General (the other, of which more later, was of Secretary of Defense Louis A. Johnson).

Truman reluctantly dismissed McGrath because of the Attorney General's abrupt firing of Newbold Morris, a New Yorker whom Truman himself had chosen to investigate charges of corruption in his own Administration. McGrath, himself a professional, eased the President's pain by assuring him that he would continue to give Truman the full measure of devotion. And McGrath was as good as his word.

Although I don't think Truman would have been reelected in 1952, I believe he was sincere in the belief that a tenure of seven years in the White House was all the time such power should be in one man's hands. He was excluded from the mandate of the Twenty-second Amendment, which limited presidential tenure to two terms, but Truman had a sense and knowledge of history that linked him to Jefferson's principle.

Truman liked to relax with a small group of jovial companions, political types. He played poker, drank in moderation, and enjoyed jokes. He didn't mind how coarse those jokes were unless they were about sex. He disliked the latter and people rarely if ever ventured to tell him any. But he reveled in the earthy kind. He had no personal vanity but, where his office was concerned, his dignity was worthy of it.

When he concluded that even a close companion was overstepping the bounds of familiarity with a President of the United States, Truman made this abundantly and harshly clear. He had read deeply in American history before it befell him to become a maker of it. A favorite study was the art of war and the technique of the generalship in all the crucial battles ever fought.

Chafing under the restraint of beginning to govern with subordinates chosen by, and devoted to, FDR, a handicap imposed by the circumstances of his accession to the presidency, Truman patiently bided his time before building an Administration of his own. The process began with the reluctant resignations of Secretaries Harold Ickes and Henry Morgenthau, Jr., from the Interior and Treasury portfolios. Truman felt no confidence in Ickes's loyalty, and distaste for his abrasive self-righteousness. As for Morgenthau, the President's appraisal, having as a Senator observed Morgenthau's dependence at hearings on a flock of assistants to provide answers to even easy questions, was the same as Al Smith's: "Henry is just an echo." Smith's reference was to Morgenthau's relation to FDR. But Truman did not want subordinates of whom the same could be said.

I never believed Truman would seek or accept more than seven years in the White House, however great the pressures upon him to do so. The best alternative he could find in 1952 was to support Adlai E. Stevenson as his successor, though he was doubtful Stevenson had what it takes for the campaign or for making and standing firm on the momentous decisions that would confront the next President.

Eisenhower, the amateur, was a successful politician because he had acquired the prestige of a national military hero before he entered the White House and because his personality made him beloved by the people. He was their ideal of a regular guy whom power could not corrupt nor make arrogant. Thus Eisenhower was able, though sometimes highly partisan, to seem to stand aloof from politics.

He accepted the fact that a President was obliged to practice now and then the politics he despised. But his permanent endowment of glory enabled him to take or leave partisanship as he chose, and to stress his dislike for the trade at no danger of reprisal for the offense this gave the professionals of both parties — his own in particular. In this attitude Eisenhower resembled his greatest hero, General Washington, his model for emulation in both domestic and military activities. Second perhaps he esteemed General William Tecumseh Sherman as a war commander and exemplary private citizen. Knowing this from conversations with the President, I told him a story about Sherman he had not heard, and only a few others have.

It was related at a gathering of the Sherman family (to which my wife belongs) after the funeral service in New York City for Lady Lindsay, a member of the clan and the widow of a British Ambassador to Washington. The narrator was Lady Lindsay's brother, Sherman Hoyt:

One sunny morning, in the period when the W. T. Shermans and the Hoyts were both residents of New York City, the General asked young Hoyt if he would enjoy a ride. Enthusiastically accepting the invitation, Hoyt (aged about ten) got into Sherman's shiny new stanhope behind the General's favorite carriage horse, and the pair proceeded up Riverside Drive with the General at the reins. They were having a most agreeable conversation until Sherman suddenly pulled up and began to loose a torrent of barrack-room language at the bewildered child. "I only knew a few of the words," said the narrator, "but I guessed the rest were equally condemnatory of me, and I didn't know why." The General calmed down after a couple of minutes and then, pointing out to the terrified boy a structure they had just passed, said: "You see that building? Next time and every time you pass it take off your hat. They said he was a drunkard and I was crazy. But by God between us we won the War."

The building was Grant's Tomb.

Eisenhower's unique combination of prestige and a winning personality spared him the vituperation that darkened the last years of Washington's presidency. This combination awed the Senate and intimidated the Democrats. Lyndon Johnson, Senate majority leader, and Speaker Rayburn thought it politically advisable to find common ground with Eisenhower, partly because they would have lost any major conflict with him, and also because Executive-congressional unity was in the national interest in a time when the nuclear threat of the USSR was increasing.

In my opinion, if John Kennedy had not been so much more photogenic on television than Nixon, he would have been defeated in 1960. The age of television had arrived, and TV was a perfect medium for the projection of an unusual grace and charm that appealed particularly to the young and to women. On the screen the contrast with Nixon's personality was heavily emphasized.

Such were Kennedy's wit, grace and youthful good looks that some representatives of the press, radio and television succumbed to it, and virtually fell in love with him; objectivity and even fairness toward his competitor went out the window; and pro-Kennedy coloration crept into the reporting of the campaign. One of the effects of his "charisma" was highly visible in the TV debates — the excessive caution on Nixon's part in challenging Kennedy in person. Nixon's "I concur with the Senator from Massachusetts" made it difficult for viewers to isolate the issues on which to base a decision to vote for Nixon against his challenger.

Kennedy's father, the late Joseph P. Kennedy, was a very astute politician. He knew the power of money in politics and used it generously and effectively to further his son's ambition to be President. Through intensive testing of the public mood he became convinced that the time was ripe for a reaction against the ancient exclusion of an appealing presidential candidate merely because he was a Catholic. The elder saw to it also that Nixon's vulnerability on certain points was fully exploited — for example, the proposal Nixon made in 1954 to send military aid to the French in Vietnam.

On the practical, professional front, Joe Kennedy made it his paramount business to develop close personal relations with the Democratic leaders in the states and large cities. Also he took full advantage of the fact that the law does not require accounting of moneys received, or from what sources, by "nonpartisan" or certain other committees working in behalf of a candidate. The number and immunity of these committees, he anticipated, would provoke Hubert Humphrey, his son's chief contender for the Democratic presidential nomination, into making the personal attacks that the American people estimate as a last resort of a candidate desperately trying to avert clearly impending defeat.

Humphrey obliged (in the West Virginia primary) by angrily remarking he was not seeking votes with a "satchel full of money" — an implicit charge that the Democrats of West Virginia were purchasable. Yet, despite the powerful factors in his favor, Kennedy won the presidency by a margin no greater than was produced by a dubious unanimity of Democratic voters on the South Side of Chicago.

The new young President took office in the glow of a fine inaugural speech in which he outlined a far-seeing program that would revive the interrupted march of the Roosevelt-Truman Administrations toward a moderate form of the Welfare State. But it was not long before Kennedy made his first major mistake — the approval of the invasion of Cuba, which Eisenhower had refused to give, by anti-Castro Cubans the CIA had trained for the project. This error he compounded by canceling the second U.S. airstrike that, in evaluating the military prospect of success of the invasion, the Chiefs of Staff (so one of them indignantly told me) had understood would be forthcoming, if required to establish the invaders on the island at the Bay of Pigs.

Another blunder, I think, was Kennedy's active military support of the Congo general government in the civil war with President Tshombe of Katanga. Though the Congo has since become a stable state under "benevolent" dictatorship, this intervention set a pattern for the military involvements of the United States abroad of which the bitterest fruit is the ground war in Vietnam. Eisenhower, while supplying the Leopoldville government with war-making materials, had refused to permit the Air Force to carry these cargoes to the fighting front. He placed the same restriction on the military advisers to the South Vietnamese armed forces: they must confine their activities to Saigon.

Kennedy reversed this policy by authorizing these advisers to operate in the combat zones, a step that led inevitably to the deep United States ensnarement in ground war in Asia against a client state of the USSR. But, on the same argument used to justify the Congo intervention — that it was essential to avoid "confrontation" with world Communism anywhere and the USSR would not tolerate an anti-Communist independent Katanga — President Kennedy yielded to Sukarno's military blackmail, a clear violation of the United Nations Charter, and applied the pressure that forced the Dutch to abandon their province of West New Guinea.

The disposal of the Cuban missile crisis was represented, and widely accepted, as a total "victory" for the United States. But Kennedy had declared that this government would not tolerate a Communist regime in the Caribbean; that on-the-spot inspection to determine whether the Russian missile sites had really been removed from Cuba was a *sine qua non* of lifting the naval blockade. Yet the episode ended with such concessions by the United States to the USSR as these: we would never invade Cuba and we would abandon the requirement of on-the-spot inspection. Thus the "victory" was a compromise in which the USSR won major points.

The subversive activities of Castro have since expanded throughout the western hemisphere and his dictatorship is more strongly entrenched than it was before the missile crisis. Moreover, the United States does not positively know whether Cuba has Russian missiles (if so, of what types) or launching pads, and if so, in what state of activation.

Like FDR, John F. Kennedy, when not engaged in his official duties, liked to have clever, attractive and amusing people around him. But Kennedy, who had, I think, absorbed more of the education Harvard offered than FDR, and had a higher I.Q., had more intellectuals among his favored companions.

It is now common knowledge that Lyndon Johnson's vice-presidency was, contrary to Nixon's, a constantly unhappy tenure. Though Kennedy assigned to him important missions, there was always an atmosphere of contrivance in the action. Johnson was never meant to be a Number Two but Kennedy and his people made him acutely aware that he was. The inner Kennedy circle ridiculed him and he heard of it, heard of their exaggerated imitation of his Southwest country accent, knew they accounted him a "vulgar" person. I once heard Kennedy say, "I wish I could find something to *keep* Lyndon happy." But Kennedy, in the nature of the case, never did — nor could.

It is generally acknowledged by the professionals in politics and the press that the 1960 Democratic national ticket would have been defeated without Johnson as the vice-presidential nominee. But I do not believe Johnson, before the 1960 convention, ever contemplated the project of becoming a submissive Number Two to John F. Kennedy. I think he went to the convention absolutely determined that if he failed to win first prize he would not accept the second. And any hope he may have had of the presidential nomination was obviously shaken after he and Kennedy appeared before the Texas and Massachusetts delegations to present their separate qualifications.

I was with him just before this confrontation with a rival whose superiority in hand-to-hand encounter he suddenly seemed to realize. In a reasoned exposition of a legislative issue Johnson knew he was the master, but in this kind of competition the risk of coming off second best appeared to have struck him with its full potential at the last minute before the debate. Even when the confrontation was over, and Kennedy's triumph was clear to observers, I do not think Johnson considered settling for the vice-presidency.

But the time came when Kennedy, first by messenger and then personally, showed he realized the ticket would be defeated by Southern Democratic defections at the polls and a resentful majority leader in the Senate (it was only in recess), and Nixon would become President unless Johnson was his running mate. Kennedy assured Johnson he would be a full partner in the Administration and not a cipher, a Throttlebottom, as Vice-President. Yet Johnson accepted the offer only after Speaker Sam Rayburn, convinced at last that the election of Nixon was the certain alternative to a Kennedy-Johnson ticket, finally approved the proposal.

Johnson had other reasons than the support of the South and the friendly attitudes of some big city bosses to hope to head the ticket in 1960. There was a segment of the Old New Dealers who saw in Johnson the legitimate heir of President Roosevelt and hence, as it proved, far more of a New Dealer than Kennedy. These people not only were political pros, but pros with influence in the party.

As early as 1956, Johnson had begun to prepare the ground for a presidential nomination in 1960. This seems inherent in his approach to Adlai E. Stevenson at the 1956 Democratic convention. Through John Connally and E. B. Hardeman (Rayburn's closest aide) Johnson sent word to Stevenson that, if the freshly nominated Stevenson thought Rayburn or himself would strengthen the national ticket, either was available. For in the strong prospect that Stevenson could not win over Eisenhower in 1956, the way to the Democratic presidential nomination would be open to his 1956 running mate in the convention of 1960. But Stevenson reacted coldly, and a new path to Johnson's goal, the White House, was required. This Johnson began to blaze with the powerful ax he wielded as Senate majority leader.

Assaying FDR as a total political success, Lyndon Johnson took his tactics as his guide. (Johnson also was personally devoted to Roosevelt, a sort of son-and-father relationship.) As majority leader of the Senate, Lyndon Johnson showed a mastery of men, of difficult situations, and of professional politics unsurpassed by any predecessor and matched by only one or two. But once in the White House these talents withered in the blinding glare of the place and the office and the personality change that seems to attend the acquisition of the vast presidential power. Perhaps the withering process began with the sharp shock of finding himself as Vice-President shorn of power, after exercising so much of it in the Senate. Anyhow, when as President he had regained this power and much more, it shortly became evident he had lost the sure touch he daily disclosed as Senate leader.

The 1964 landslide on which Johnson rode into the presidency in his own right enabled him to expand and put through Congress the social-economic programs which Kennedy proposed but was unable to induce Congress to legislate. But this same landslide victory seemed to have numbed his once infallible political instinct and caused him to fall into errors of policy and administration that Johnson had never made before. Paramount among these was the huge manpower expansion of the war in Vietnam that proved to be his downfall.

In her diary Mrs. Johnson has confirmed my belief at the time of Johnson's abdication that he acted not because he concluded he could not be reelected in 1968 but because he decided he would be unable to unify, or even govern, a people rent by the deep division over Vietnam and staggering under the burden of constantly rising, war-abetted price inflation. The Republicans were prepared to lay on him the responsibility for both conditions if he was again a candidate. His great enlargement of the war — the cost of which his experts underestimated by at least 50 percent — called for a tax increase in 1966 to pay for it, but the President shrank from facing the clear necessity that the Johnson I knew as majority Senate leader would not have hesitated to confront head on. "The liberals put a price tag on everything" was his frequent criticism of their reliance on increased spending as the solution of all domestic problems.

Nixon is perhaps the most politically imbued President, even including Johnson, since Franklin Roosevelt's time. He understands politics; he likes politics; with extraordinary deftness and perfect timing he yields the fewest concessions that the "art of the possible" requires. And when he makes a tactical blunder, as he did in choosing and personalizing the issues he believed were best calculated to produce a Republican sweep in the 1970 elections, he not only recognizes where he went wrong. Also he can be depended on to profit by his error. This is why I do not as yet share the conviction of many political observers that Nixon will be a one-term President.

He made firm promises in the 1968 campaign that he knew he would be able to deliver only in part, but this is normal political practice. And Nixon understood better than anybody, except, ironically, Barry Goldwater, that to work hard for your party when it is out of power and out of luck is the surest way to promote a personal ambition for a presidential nomination.

But the President also recognizes that there are some campaign promises that must be redeemed in full. With respect to deflating the Vietnam war, he is doing that, with the effect that Vietnam disappeared as an adverse factor in the campaign of 1970. However, on inflation, his long refusal to bite the bullet of active government interference was so successfully exploited by the Democrats as responsible for the then current steady rise in prices, and unemployment, and the drop in stock market values, that he was confronted with the necessity to review his policy fundamentally.

Richard M. Nixon has also revealed the same presidential need for the lively entertainment that Roosevelt and Kennedy found so necessary, and Truman and Eisenhower so conspicuously did not. On the job, however, Nixon is a loner, confiding in and trusting few. His is not the open door of Roosevelt, Truman, Eisenhower, and Kennedy. In this respect, surprisingly, Nixon is more like Lyndon Johnson. But on the other hand Johnson was regularly accessible to his staff and to a small number of reporters and commentators, and Nixon is not. Despite his incredible gaffe at Denver in August 1970 in commenting on the Manson murder trial and its heavy press coverage, he is perhaps overly aware of the potentially adverse effects of his slightest word or even intonation. These at any time can set the whispering galleries going and find their way into the press and onto the television screen, distorting or magnifying a chance presidential observation into a matter of serious intent.

My impression of Nixon as Vice-President was that he was happy in his job and the outside presidential assignments until General Eisenhower suggested to him that it might enhance Nixon's political future if he transferred to the Cabinet at the top level. It was possible to read into this odd suggestion a desire on the President's part to groom another as his successor in 1960 — a desire affirmed by the revelation of his interest in Robert B. Anderson as a replacement. But the suggestion was eventually classified as another display of the General's political naiveté, and Nixon accepted it as such after the President denied he had anything in mind except to help Nixon attain his ambition to be President.

The Vice-President is one of the only two nationally elected officials of the United States, a fact which seems never fully to have entered public comprehension. Though he owes his nomination to the presidential candidate in nearly all cases, the Vice-President nevertheless has received as many popular and electoral votes as his chief. And there are no constitutional limitations on his political use of the office, even if it takes the form of opposition to presidential policies, actions, and legislative programs.

The only restraints a President can impose on a Vice-President in this field, in addition to disowning him as spokesman for the Administration, arise from the obligations the latter has contracted by the President's choice of him as running mate, a question of purely personal gratitude and loyalty. Thus when in 1970 there were far-ranging appeals to President Nixon to "muzzle" Vice-President Agnew, it was clear that some were based on an assumption that Nixon had the constitutional or some other legal power to do this. It is singular that, despite all that has been written and said about the Constitution, the simple fact which totally disposes of the assumption — that the Vice-President has been nationally elected, too — should be so little understood, even in academic and legal circles.

The inexorable laws of the book-publishing trade require that this book go to the printers long before the social, political, military, and economic effects of the 1970 elections can be soundly assayed. And even for the political experts of the media, the immediate intervention of a lame-duck session of Congress — notoriously impeded in constructive action by the bitterness of the election casualties — will defer the process until the new Congress takes over.

But on the superficial evidence of the returns it would appear that the following balance sheet may be ventured:

Because of the victories of the Independent Harry F. Byrd, Jr., in Virginia, and the Conservative James L. Buckley in New York, the overall gain of two or three Senate seats with the Republican label will have more weight in terms of the Administration's foreign policy and national security than is measured by the statistics of the Senate major party division.

But the reduction of Republican Governors by eleven, giving the Democrats a majority in the state houses where previously there were thirty-two Republicans to the Democrats' eighteen, casts a shadow over President Nixon's reelection prospects and his hope for a pro-Administration Congress in 1972. This shadow is darkened by the facts that new Democratic Governors, as in the key state of Pennsylvania, carried party majorities into the legislatures, and that Democrats elected majorities in both branches of the California legislature.

This will give Democrats control over the process of redistricting in favor of party candidates, especially important in states — particularly California — entitled by the 1970 census to additional seats in Congress.

The loss of less than a dozen House seats, in a midterm election, by the party to which the incumbent President belongs was much below the average overturn. But this good news for the Republicans was tempered by the fact that they failed to win a majority in the 1968 elections and thus had few to lose in the circumstances.

The revived Democratic strength in the congressional, state, and local elections in the South, especially in Florida, South Carolina, and Arkansas, and in the normally Republican farm belt, poses another threat to the President's prospects for reelection. The so-called Southern Strategy — despite the President's reliance on his nomination of two Southern "strict constructionists" to the Supreme Court and his attack on the Senate liberals who opposed them as anti-Southern — did not succeed. And, in the Middle West, discontent over the state of the economy resisted the intensive efforts of the President and the Vice-President to hold the state offices occupied by Republicans.

The Republican losses in the Middle West, as well as the Democratic capture of the legislatures in Pennsylvania, Ohio, and California, are strong evidence that this economic discontent finally prevailed over the law-and-order issue on which the Republicans laid great store. One reason was that Vice-President Agnew started too early to link liberal Democrats with, and castigate them for, tolerance of the several violences that afflicted the nation, giving his targets the time to shake off the image and hammer on the inflation which, with the continuous rise in prices and losses of stock market values, was a grievance that struck home in many more households than violence did.

By putting miniature American flags in their lapels, and almost out-Agnewing Agnew in their denunciations of crime and student violence, many Democratic candidates had by election day removed the curse which the October polls revealed was very real for the party liberals. Since the voters are disposed to blame inflation on the occupant of the White

House, even though he inherited it from preceding Presidents of the other party, and Nixon could show no short-term progress in his anti-inflation policies, law-and-order was supplanted as the paramount issue in their consciousness. This accounts for the failure of the hardhats and other blue-collar workers to deliver the support the Republicans expected.

The belief that the candidate with the most money to spend on TV would most surely be elected was badly damaged by the many results that demonstrated the contrary.

But of far greater importance than these transient factors are the effects on the country and the world of the nature of the preelection campaign of 1970. And these effects will not be wholly clear for two years or more. They must resolve the following questions:

Were the Senate gains in support of the President's foreign policy and national defense programs worth his gamble in laying his prestige and national leadership on the line in the twenty-two states? Were these Senate gains reduced or even canceled by the aggressiveness of his presentations, and was an angrily divided people made angrier and more divided in a most critical period of history? Were Nixon's encouragement and endorsement of the militant campaigning of Vice-President Agnew mistakes, not only politically, but in terms of a popular reaction which could impair the Administration's ability to govern in the next two years? And what course will the George Wallace voters and their champion take?

The answers will not fully emerge until 1972. But another reason why I think they may well be resolved in favor of another term for Nixon, with the opportunities that are ever available to the incumbent of the White House, arises from this fact of political history: when the presidential chances of the party out of power change from dubious to excellent as a result of midterm elections, the rivalry for its nomination begins at once, and usually becomes dangerously divisive.

On occasion the office has indeed sought the man rather than the man the office. George Washington, for instance. But the only other real presidential draft known to me was that of Adlai Stevenson at the Democratic national convention of 1952, which I reported. Not only did he flee from the gathering prospect: he attempted to elude it by suggesting privately that he might be incapacitated by ill health while in the White House. (X rays, he informed me, on the Saturday night before the convention, had disclosed "shadows in my kidney.") However, in the end he had no choice but to accept the nomination.

Franklin D. Roosevelt was never drafted unless a draft can correctly be defined as applying to such automatic actions as his first renomination in 1936. I was not convinced for a moment that Roosevelt was sincere in looking for another presidential candidate in 1940. He was certain our involvement in World War II was inevitable, necessary to the security of the United States and the American system, and he was confident that no one else could deal with the emergency and align the country behind him. So with one voice he encouraged aspirants to his office and with another he cut them down. It was a very deliberate process and its objective — to create the *appearance* of being drafted for a third nomination in 1940 — was obvious to the political and press community.

There are and were some believers in his own representation that he was sincerely seeking a successor he deemed could meet the grave test invoked by the threat and then the fact of global war. But, after the Democrats almost lost control of Congress in the 1938 elections, and Hitler invaded Poland, it is not difficult, nor disparaging, to conclude that he feared turning over the government to new and inexperienced hands. Once again, it was merely the deviousness by which he attained his ends that embittered his victims — Cordell Hull, James A. Farley, Paul McNutt, and Burton K. Wheeler.

Eisenhower was induced to be a presidential candidate in 1952 — he was not, as he had hoped, truly drafted — by the argument that Taft would be nominated if he abstained, and reestablish party and national policies of isolation. This argument was verified by a division of the delegates so close that, had it not been for the blunders of Taft's managers in the matter of the contested Texas and Georgia delegates, the nominee might not have been Eisenhower.

In 1956, in contrast with his attitude four years before, Stevenson sought the nomination. He went into the primaries because only by a showing of strength in these could he overcome the powerful opposition to giving a second try to a candidate who, those opposed felt, had flunked his first.

So, by and large, a true draft is a myth. Wendell Willkie was the beneficiary of a cleverly induced, lavishly financed movement, organized in key states by persons with great financial and industrial influence. The convention battle was hard-fought and close. But artful direction, made more effective by Willkie's public display of honest ignorance of the machinery of conventions, gave the support for Willkie the simulation of a popular draft. However, the balloting statistics show that it was not; as also do subsequent revelations of the pressures brought on the large delegations by corporate forces, among whose most effective agents at Philadelphia were John W. Hanes, Harold Talbott, Samuel F. Pryor, and Winthrop Aldrich.

And true drafts will probably remain the myth spun by political bosses and peddled by gullible journalists because the political convention system is unlikely to be changed in form. The effort to involve party registrants more directly in the selection of delegates, now moving ahead in the Democratic party, could change it materially in substance unless, as happens so often in politics, local and state bosses manage by evasion to maintain the old method. Thereby they choose the delegates themselves, confining the choices to slates they prepare for the local conventions and the primaries; and, by splitting each delegate's vote into fractions, crowding the convention floor beyond the point where the opposition can coalesce.

Under the prevailing system individual or small interior blocs of state or national convention delegates rarely swing from the candidates to whom they have been committed by their party machines until they get the word to do so from the organization bosses. And uncommitted delegations, which usually operate behind the shield of a "favorite son," awaiting the situation where their votes will break a deadlock between the leading candidates, are generally bound by instructions from boss-controlled local conventions that leave to the machine the timing of the shift and the choice of its beneficiary.

Since the 1936 national Democratic convention abolished the two-third requirement for the nomination of a presidential candidate, and a simple majority is now sufficient in both parties, the impact of a shift by a large uncommitted or "favorite son" delegation has become conclusive.

This was strikingly demonstrated at the Republican gathering of 1952 and the Democratic of 1960. In 1952 the timing of Minnesota's calculated break from "favorite son" Harold E. Stassen to Dwight D. Eisenhower clinched the General's nomination on the first ballot. In 1960 enough Wyoming delegates swung to John F. Kennedy to assure his choice during the tabulation of the first ballot.

The design of the reform program for the Democrats formulated under the leadership of Senator George McGovern of South Dakota is to remove the control of the bosses and their machines in the selection of delegates and transfer this directly to the registered party voters. If this design is fully successful in the practice of Democratic national conventions — where the native volubility of the party is traditional — they will more nearly resemble town meetings, every eligible speaking his piece, and voting according to his views as an individual. It remains to be seen how this system can be established along with the orderly procedures such large bodies require for definite and binding decisions.

The Democratic national convention of 1972 will provide the first test of the reform, if meanwhile it has been adopted by the party authorities and sanctioned by statutes. If so, my belief is either that the new arrangements for having delegates chosen by direct popular action, with full independence, will make a mob scene of the gathering, or the state and national bosses will have found some way of reinvoking their control of majorities of the delegations.

For politics is a trade that can be mastered only by working at it every day and only the professionals have the time for that. Hence the few weeks a year that the nonprofessionals devote to the field — before the primaries and the elections — are not sufficient to effect the organization and the direction that success at the polls inexorably requires. The professionals *can* be buried under landslides, but this occurs only when the voting population is swept by a self-generated emotion that invests a large majority with a clear purpose which side issues cannot divert.

I believe that in the two preelection weeks some colleges suspend their classes, the undergraduates released to devote their full time to electioneering will discover in the long run they are no match for the workaday professionals except when the popular mass is already committed to their particular objectives of policy and to the candidates of their fervent choice.

Meanwhile, television has restricted what spontaneity there was in national conventions by prescribing timetables when and by whom speeches will be screened. Delegates who are scheduled to appear on the tube are always under the threat of cancellation by sudden developments the networks find more newsworthy.

But on the whole, TV coverage of the conventions has been an improvement over the old press practice of publishing almost every speech. And to see a convention in action instead of merely reading about it is welcomed by the bulk of the viewers, most of whom are bored by detailed analyses of the intricacies of political maneuvering. Convention coverage has also been expanded and dramatized by turning the cameras on related activities outside the hall, such as the demonstrations that marked the Democratic gathering at Chicago in 1968, on the floor, in the streets, and in the hotels.

My first convention was the 1908 Democratic in Denver. The feud between William J. Connors of Buffalo and Charles F. Murphy, boss of Tammany, materialized on the floor. The two competitors for political domination in New York State bitterly disliked each other. Connors, by calling for a public poll of the New York delegation, forced the embarrassed Murphy to vote aloud for William Jennings Bryan who to him was anathema. This spotlighted Tammany's failure to make the New York delegation a holdout against Bryan's renomination, as Murphy had endeavored to do. Instead, the Tammany delegates, one by one, sheepishly arose to respond "Bryan" (Murphy pronounced it "Brine") when their names were called. When Murphy's turn came, and he stood, his head hanging, to bite the bullet, Connors exclaimed "ah ha" and pointed his finger at his captive rival. (This is how Connors got his nickname of "Fingy.") What a TV show this would have been! But neither TV nor radio had been invented.

The 1912 conventions were endlessly dramatic for the spectators. At the Republican gathering the adherents of Theodore Roosevelt provided the element by moving to "purge the roll" of the Taft delegates whom they asserted were corruptly or illegally chosen. That produced a pro-Roosevelt uproar on the floor and in the galleries. But, calmly ignoring the tumult, the permanent chairman, Elihu Root, declared the motion rejected, though to us in the press section a voice vote seemed to be to the contrary.

When Root gaveled down the motion to purge the roll, and the Taft supporters cheered, I was watching the running account my seatmate, Henry L. Mencken, was writing for the *Baltimore Evening Sun*. It read, "At this point the aristocracy of the abattoir and the rolling-mill . . ." In other words, the rich and prominent of Chicago.

Having failed in the effort to "purge the roll," and after it was established that Theodore Roosevelt could not accomplish his purpose in coming to Chicago — to prevent the renomination of Taft — the Colonel did not return at once to Oyster Bay as everyone expected. The unanswered question was "why," and Don Martin of the *New York Herald* and I asked T.R.'s close newspaper friend, George E. Miller of the *Detroit News*, to try to get an explanation from Roosevelt in person. The extraordinary reply T.R. gave Miller was, "To make sure that Mr. Taft will be renominated."

The astonishing clarification of that remark soon followed the adjournment of the convention. Roosevelt mounted a raised platform in the Florentine Room of the Congress Hotel and launched an attack on the convention procedures that left no doubt the sequel would be the formation of the Bull Moose party and his nomination on its platform as an independent candidate for President.

In the November election T.R. got more votes than Taft, the regular Republican nominee, assuring the election of Woodrow Wilson by a voting minority.

In Baltimore in 1912, at the Democratic national convention, Bryan made his famous speech charging that J. P. Morgan, Sr., Thomas F. Ryan, and August Belmont, three New York multimillionaires who were Tammany backers, were in control of the New York delegation and the source of its support of Speaker Champ Clark, whom Bryan had first favored and then opposed. This evoked a violent response, pro and con, among the delegates and the occupants of the galleries. The Tammany contingent chose, to respond to Bryan, a celebrated Wall Street lawyer, John B. Stanchfield. He fed the fire by assailing Bryan personally, calling him "the marplot from Nebraska."

The turbulence on the floor this phrase renewed was gleefully augmented by the galleries, crowded with Princeton undergraduates shouting "We want Wilson." After a recess, required to restore order, the convention reassembled for the balloting. The drama reached a new climax when Roger Sullivan, the Illinois Democratic boss, announced for Wilson, and Rep. Oscar Underwood of Alabama, with a solid bloc of one hundred delegates, released them to Wilson, foreshadowing his nomination. Wilson responded by sending a message of acceptance, adding he would not accept renomination and recommending a six-year term for Presidents. But his manager, William J. McCombs of Arkansas, deleted this part of Wilson's message.

McCombs had done his job brilliantly. It was he who

arranged for and timed Sullivan's announcement and the abdication of Underwood. Sullivan's move was quickly followed by other big city bosses, except for New York's. And, though Clark had been voted for by a majority, and party tradition called for two-thirds of the delegates to do likewise, Bryan's speech had broken the tradition, and Wilson received the necessary two-thirds. (The Republicans have nominated by a majority from the formation of their party.)

James A. Farley tried to abolish the two-thirds rule at the 1932 Democratic convention, with the open assistance of Senator Huey Long, at the secret instance of Governor F. D. Roosevelt, operating from Albany. When there existed an immovable minority of one-third plus one, Long viewed this power as negative minority rule, which it is. But private polls of the delegates established that the party was not yet willing to alter the full two-thirds requirement. And Roosevelt, when he learned the convention would reject the proposal, telephoned Farley and Howe to cease and desist. In 1936, however, the reform was adopted by the Democratic delegates, the party machinery now being wholly controlled by Roosevelt.

The 1916 Republican convention was notable largely because Theodore Roosevelt rejoined the party when it seemed the liberals had gained control and he could count on the nomination of Charles Evans Hughes instead of a vestigial Taft conservative. But at the Democratic gathering at St. Louis that year there were fireworks in plenty. They were alighted by the speeches of Governor Martin Glenn of New York, the keynoter, and Senator Ollie M. James of Kentucky, the permanent chairman.

The Democrats aspired to present their party to the voters as the guardians of peace, and the Republicans as the advocates of United States entrance into World War I. "He kept us out of war," cried Glenn, and James expanded on the theme in old-fashioned oratorical style, deliberately conveying the belief that Wilson was unalterably resolved on nonparticipation and would succeed. But less than a year later, after von Tirpitz's submarines had sunk a large percentage of American supply shipping to the Allies, Wilson drove to the Capitol and asked Congress to declare war on the Central Powers.

A bitter contest marked the Republican convention of 1920, intensified by a carefully planned Democratic intrusion. Before and while the Republicans were meeting, Senator James A. Reed of Missouri, a Democrat, conducted an inquiry into alleged Republican primary frauds and delegate-buying involving backers of the two leading aspirants to the Republican nomination — Governor Frank Lowden of Illinois and General Leonard Wood. The result was to eliminate both, although they were innocent of the corrupt practices of their workers that Reed exposed.

But the convention was unable to unite on any other of the candidates for the nomination, and as the fruitless maneuvering continued, reports of every move were given over the telephone to Senator Boies Penrose of Pennsylvania lying in Washington on the sickbed from which he was not to arise. He held almost hourly conversations with members of the Republican national establishment in Chicago, who eventually assembled in the celebrated "smoke-filled room," to remain there until they agreed on a choice.

According to an account given me by the late Dr. Harry Kerr, of Washington, who was Penrose's physician-surgeon, the Senator, after a series of telephoned reports of what was happening at the conference, decided the matter with these words to his informant at the other end of the wire: "Harding's the man. Nominate him." And it was done, as the powerful Pennsylvania boss and the inner Republican circle had planned from the beginning.

The 1920 Democratic convention, at San Francisco, was remarkable only for the numerous ballots required before a presidential nominee emerged from the deadlock. Governor James M. Cox of Ohio and William G. McAdoo, Wilson's Secretary of the Treasury, were the chief contestants, and the party's stand on national prohibition was the gut issue — the "wets" were opposed to McAdoo; the "drys" to Cox — while below the surface was a probing operation to determine whether Wilson could be nominated for a third term. But, though the ailing President was suspected of nurturing this ambition, the movement never acquired the power to surface.

Cox decided on Franklin D. Roosevelt as his running mate, and the convention agreed, as is the custom. But the action was less than enthusiastic. For instance, Boss Murphy of Tammany Hall made this comment to Cox: "Roosevelt's no good, but if you want him you can have him." Murphy's adverse judgment derived from Roosevelt's opposition to Tammany Hall when he was in the New York Senate, and also from personal experiences with FDR that persuaded him Roosevelt could not be relied on to keep a promise — the worst sin against the code of professional politicians.

An unusual aspect of the 1920 convention was that both presidential nominees were from Ohio. Cox had successfully run for Governor three times. Harding had unsuccessfully run for Governor once but was an incumbent Senator. Cox was publisher of two Ohio newspapers — in Dayton and Springfield. Harding was a publisher in Marion.

Realizing the odds against him — the backwash of World War I and the unpopularity of Wilson's effort to make the U.S. a member of the League of Nations — Cox believed Roosevelt would help restore a popular balance to the Democratic ticket. FDR was young, handsome, in perfect health, and the bearer of a name that Cox hoped would, but did not, attract to the ticket those Republicans, internationalists and independents, who disapproved of the party's retreat from the League of Nations and the nomination of Harding.

The 1924 Democratic convention staged that form of theater called melodrama. In the fading memories of those who were delegates or spectators during this frenzied tournament of politics, among the firm recollections include:

The incessant answer, on every roll call but the last, by the chairman of the Alabama delegation, "Alabama casts twenty-four votes for Oscar W. Underwood."

The perfervid oratory over whether the Ku Klux Klan should be denounced by name in the platform plank that assailed bias and vigilantes. (Southern and some Midwestern delegates were opposed to naming the Klan, many with highly personal reasons.)

The attack on the proposal to "name" the Klan made in a speech by Bryan that reached a boiling point of political oratory and, though but barely, prevailed.

Franklin D. Roosevelt's "Happy Warrior" speech for Al Smith (after having been carried to the platform), leaning on the podium, his legs in braces, a cane by his side. In ordinary circumstances the "Happy Warrior" speech could have nominated its hero. But the "drys," the Klan, and the anti-Catholics were too strong a combination to overcome.

The passionate, literate, unsuccessful, but remarkably prophetic speech by Newton D. Baker, Wilson's political heir, urging support and endorsement of American membership in the League of Nations. Speaking without a note, Baker again displayed the extraordinary command of memory and orderly logic that made him one of the great lawyers and public speakers of his time.

After the protracted Smith-McAdoo deadlock, the convention nominated for President the eminent former Solicitor General and Ambassador to the Court of St. James's, John W. Davis who, by the time of his selection, was Wall Street's foremost lawyer. Though he had long left his native state, political custom decreed he be designated as "of West Virginia" instead of New York State where, in Nassau County, he dwelt in a most fashionable neighborhood. It was this tribal convention rite of accrediting presidential candidates to the states of their nativity that inspired Henry L. Mencken to write: "And then they nominated John W. Davis, of Piping Rock, West Virginia." (For the readers who may not know, the Piping Rock Club near Davis's country house was at the time a symbol of wealth and exclusiveness.)

Summarizing the self-destructive urge that had characterized the Democratic party at the 1924 convention, I wrote an article for Mencken's *American Mercury* entitled "The Damn Fool Democrats." To this day I would not change a word of it.

Perhaps the only contribution to history that was made by the Madison Square convention was the reintroduction of Franklin Roosevelt to national politics. Except for his "Happy Warrior" speech he would not have recaptured the party's attention, persuaded the Democrats that his crippling illness was no handicap to his political potential, and gone on to become Governor of New York and victor in four successive presidential elections.

Among the duller conventions was the 1928 Republican affair in Kansas City that nominated Herbert Hoover. The only stir, and it never became more than a ripple, was made by Andrew W. Mellon, President Coolidge's Secretary of the Treasury. He, like some other Republicans in high finance and big business, wanted the convention to renominate the

President. Into Coolidge's "I do not choose to run in 1928," they read only that he would not be an active candidate but was a receptive one.

Accordingly, Mellon, while the Pennsylvania delegation was on its way by train to Houston, arranged a test of sentiment for Coolidge's renomination. But the boss of Philadelphia, James Vare, who later became Senator, easily destroyed the plan in embryo, and the delegation reached the convention site committed to Hoover.

When the Republicans assembled for their 1932 convention, both realism and necessity made Hoover's renomination a foregone conclusion. The only room for a contest was on the issue of national prohibition — should the party's stand for the Eighteenth (prohibition) Amendment and the Volstead (enforcement) Act be inflexible or slightly eased? Secretary of the Treasury Ogden L. Mills, a hardy soul and a "wet," attempted to induce the President at least to mention repeal in the platform, while not endorsing it. But the best concession he was able to gain was a platform proposal for a national referendum, with the party committed in advance to support retention of the Amendment and the Act.

The issue of repeal of the Eighteenth Amendment and the hot battles it engendered, enabled the Democrats in 1932 at Chicago to make the prior Republican convention seem like a town meeting in Dullsville. Al Smith, in a powerful speech, carried the votes for repeal over the opposition of a known and respected Roosevelt supporter, a "dry," Senator (later Secretary of State) Cordell Hull of Tennessee.

In the contest for the nomination the identity of the victor depended, after three fruitless ballots, on which of the leading contestants — Roosevelt, Baker, and Governor Albert C. Ritchie of Maryland — would get the vote of the Texas delegation (committed to John N. Garner) and of the California delegation (also committed to Garner, but controlled by William R. Hearst). Warned by Joseph P. Kennedy and Farley — Kennedy through an intermediary, John Neylan, Hearst's attorney and number one counselor; Farley direct — that Baker (Hearst's favorite bête noire) would be nominated unless Texas and California swung to Roosevelt, Hearst released California to FDR on the arrangement that Garner would be nominated for Vice-President.

Speaker Sam Rayburn always insisted there was no "deal," that the outcome was a natural fission of the factors of the convention majority. This in a literal sense may have been true, for Garner, like Roosevelt, was considered cut from the pattern of conservative reform, with accent on economy in government and monetary stability. Garner remained steadfast to those principles throughout his two terms as Vice-President and his lifetime. But Roosevelt, early in his first Administration, reversed the economic pledges of the platform.

A large contributor to the dramatic quality of the Republican convention of 1952 was Senator Everett M. Dirksen of Illinois, a supporter of the candidacy of Senator Robert A. Taft. Looking down from the podium at Thomas E. Dewey, who had captured the New York delegation for General Eisenhower, Dirksen pointed his finger at the presidential nominee of 1944 and 1948, and with great deliberation said, "Twice you have led us down the garden path [to defeat]."

A survey of the influence of presidential wives over their husband's administrative actions begins with a negative. Illness, congenital acerbity, and indiscretion of speech made Mrs. Lincoln a public and private burden to her spouse. An unhappy home life adds to the torment of the wheel of Ixion to which a President is already bound by his responsibilities.

When these include conducting a war, as in Lincoln's case, the strain must be almost unendurable, even for the stoutest of heart and spirit.

The powerful influence of the second Mrs. Wilson arose because illness long rendered the President incompetent to govern. Being both self-confident and aggressive, and convinced the national interest depended on perpetuating the myth that Wilson was at the helm of government, his wife secretly took on the role of regent, with his personal physician, Rear Admiral Cary T. Grayson, as her closest adviser.

Mrs. Wilson was perhaps the first President's wife in history to issue, in the President's name, announcements of which he knew nothing, including active decisions. This secret regency governed the nation for many months.

But had the President not been stricken in brain, limb, and speech, I doubt that Mrs. Wilson would have had prevailing influence over act and policy. Nor do I believe her inherent wish was for such power. Her assumption was an extreme act of wifely devotion, but it was taken in circumstances that had no precedent. Yet the contrast with the open and responsible conduct of the interregnum, when President Eisenhower was stricken, by Vice-President Nixon, the top White House staff aides, and the Cabinet, provided a precedent since buttressed by the Twenty-fifth Amendment to the Constitution.

During Mrs. Wilson's "regency" there was, of course, great uneasiness in the Cabinet and Congress over the current and potential state of a nation whose Chief Executive lay in an indefinite condition of incompetence to perform his "powers and duties." Whenever two persons in public office came together the subject arose, but also the dilemma of what should or could be done about it. The Cabinet, prompted by Secretary of State Robert Lansing, asked for counsel on how the Executive government should function from Rear Admiral

Grayson. When Wilson heard of this inquiry he was highly displeased. And even a message from Secretary of War Baker — whose loyalty the invalid never questioned — that Cabinet meetings were strictly confined to departmental business did not assuage Wilson's resentment of Lansing's initiative that ended with the Secretary's replacement.

In October 1919, Lansing read to the Cabinet the section of the Constitution providing that the Vice-President (Thomas R. Marshall in this period) should assume the presidential "powers and duties" when the President was unable to perform them. But Marshall would have no part of it.

He firmly declined proposals of any intervention or assumption on his part. To the small group in the White House who were acting as presidential deputies, to the concerned members of the Cabinet and congressional leaders, Marshall was the invisible man. I was posted in Louisville in this period, but I made frequent visits to Washington and on one such occasion, presuming on a long friendship with the Vice-President, I brought up the subject of his deliberate inaction in the grave premises.

His reply was that constitutionally he had no warrant to act as President until or unless the incumbent in person certified his temporary incapacity; that Wilson apparently was unable to perform this physical act, even if he wanted to (of which Marshall said he was more than dubious); that to earn the President's hostility in such circumstances, and the resentment "of a woman," would make the situation worse for the country; and that, finally, he had no authoritative medical evidence to challenge the official White House report that the President was steadily on the mend.

On these grounds the Wilson interregnum was preserved from effective supervention by the only national officer with even arguably inherent rights and duties so to act (this was before the Constitution was amended to deal with such a situation, but still by a process — see the Twenty-fifth Amendment — vulnerable to blockade by a President unwilling to concede his incompetency).

I doubt Franklin Roosevelt had any strong, specific sociological concerns beyond a compassion for underprivileged groups when their plight was brought to his attention. But Mrs. Roosevelt was deeply aware of these defects in the American democratic system — the privation and grave working hazards of miners, the discriminations, legal and rooted in old prejudices, whose victims were ethnic and economic minority groups. She explored and inveighed against these publicly and with the President, and her influence for remedial action grew constantly greater.

Sometimes she forced a breach in security regulations that were accepted as necessary at the time. For example, Mrs. Earl Browder, whose husband was the leader of the Communist party in this country, went to Canada to obtain a return visa into the United States because she was foreign-born and her expired visitor's visa had to be renewed to qualify for permanent citizenship. When she applied to the American Consul in Toronto, he, believing the regulations forbade such action in behalf of an active member of the Communist party, asked for instructions from Secretary of State Hull. The message never reached Hull personally and the department automatically instructed the Consul to refuse the visa. Mrs. Browder appealed to Mrs. Roosevelt. Mrs. Roosevelt took up the matter with the President on the ground that Mrs. Browder's constitutional rights were denied, and urged him to convey this view to Secretary Hull, who had firmly supported the Consul's interpretation of the laws.

Mrs. Roosevelt persisted until she had induced the President to request Hull directly to order the issuance of the visa.

Hull asked why. "The Missus," Roosevelt explained, "is giving me trouble over this. I've got other things to think about, so if you could take this one off my back I would appreciate it." Hull returned to his office, sent for a subordinate, Edward Travis, and directed him to prepare instructions for the Consul in Toronto to readmit Mrs. Browder.

"Sir," Travis responded, "I will, of course, draw up the instructions but I cannot possibly sign the message." (The form in such cases requires that under the name of the Secretary the signatory deputy must add his own.)

"This is insubordination, Mr. Travis," said Hull sternly.

"Yes, sir," agreed Travis miserably.

"Well," said Hull, "anyhow it must be done. You draw up the directive and take it down the hall to [Adolph] Berle [an assistant Secretary of State]. He likes to sign my name."

Berle signed and Travis returned to his office, certain the ax would soon fall. He had just begun packing his personal effects when Hull's messenger appeared. The messenger bore a box of cigars, accompanied by a photograph of the Secretary on which was written, "With my deep admiration, Cordell Hull."

Mrs. Roosevelt's protégés were usually members of the left, sometimes extremists, and through her influence a number joined the Executive Department. I considered some of them highly undesirable as public servants — I was not by any means alone in this estimate — and I think the President was not enthusiastic about his wife's activities in this field. But he wanted to keep peace in his household, and this was one way of doing it.

And in a way the scale of these activities amused him, as indicated by a remark the President made to Commissar Maxim Litvinov when that Soviet official came to the United States to execute the agreement by which the United States gave diplomatic recognition to the government of the USSR and restored diplomatic relations, a total reversal of long-standing U.S. policy. In greeting the Commissar the President said, "Mr. Litvinov, my wife and I regret very much that Madame Litvinov did not come with you." "Ah," answered Litvinov, "so do I, but, you see, my wife has separate career. Lectures; organizes; takes positions on public issues; reluctantly decided could not spare the time."

"I *think* I understand," said Roosevelt with a grin.

A White House hostess who ideally met the general concept of how a First Lady should conduct herself was Mrs. Truman. She kept completely aloof from any activity related to the presidency. I suppose at times, in the privacy of their home life, he asked her judgment on a problem and that she supplied it. But to the people she was only the gracious hostess of the White House.

Mrs. Eisenhower was very much the same sort of First Lady. She lobbied with her husband for no special causes. Mrs. Kennedy confined her role largely to redecoration of the White House and other cultural matters that had no connection with politics or policy. Nevertheless she had one concern with public affairs and worked at it — the President's relations with the press. As a loyal, admiring wife she did what she could to sweeten them.

One day after I had lunched with Kennedy, the guard at the gate I was exiting from informed me the President wanted me to return to the mansion. When I reached the third-floor family quarters, however, I was received by Mrs. Kennedy, who explained that the President was having a nap and the summons had come from her. "If you have anything critical to write," she said, "don't pin it on the poor President; pin it on me." At that moment the door of the Lincoln bedroom opened and out came Kennedy, tousled, unshod, with his braces hanging down. "What's this?" he inquired. I falsely replied that Mrs. Kennedy merely wanted to speak to me about a mutual friend she and I had been discussing while I was waiting for him to come to lunch.

On a previous occasion, at a party during the preconvention period in the spring of 1960 when the then Senator Kennedy was a candidate for the presidential nomination, she brought up the same subject lightly and in another context. We were sitting at a table off the dance floor at the Sulgrave Club. "I think," she said, "it is so unfair for Jack to be opposed because he is a Catholic. After all, he's such a *poor* Catholic. Now if it were Bobby: he never misses mass and prays all the time." She laughed as she said it. And when she laughs the privilege of being among those present is very special indeed.

Johnson's published recollections have established the fact that Mrs. Johnson had great influence in shaping his most important decisions, a fact known only to a few of his intimates when he was President. But her most visible identification with public affairs was with beautification of the environment, particularly in Washington, a legitimate and most constructive way to use the prestige of a First Lady. The revelation of her very substantial participation in his historic decision not to seek reelection came as a surprise to the press and the public, so great was her discretion and so completely did she appear to be detached from essentially political activism.

Mrs. Nixon at first conformed to the precedent Mrs. Truman followed. But in the changing times the people appear to expect and want more exposure of the First Lady in a quasi-official capacity: at any rate, Mrs. Nixon yielded to this expectation and became a familiar political presence. But my impression formed during the years I saw something of the Nixons, in small informal gatherings, is that she would if she could remain a wholly private person.

4

Advisers —
Official and Unofficial

Constitutionally, there is no Cabinet. There are only heads of departments. The departments have grown enormously since George Washington's time. It depends on the President what and how much influence a Cabinet member has. In Washington's tenure those who influenced him the most were acutely divided on political philosophy. Alexander Hamilton was a Federalist and Thomas Jefferson was what was then called a Republican, later a Democrat, head of the rival party. Hamilton had Washington's ear on fiscal and monetary policy as Secretary of the Treasury, but the President relied on Jefferson for foreign policy, such as there was at that time. Hamilton was a Centralist and Jefferson a De-Centralist with respect to the situs of governmental functions and power, and Washington largely left his Cabinet members to work out their departmental problems.

The most influential members of Jefferson's Cabinet were James Madison and Albert Gallatin, head of the Treasury. Gallatin built substantially on Hamilton's program to eliminate the national debt. Madison, the Secretary of State, was chief interpreter of the limitations and permissions of the Constitution. He enjoyed close and confidential relations with the Diplomatic Corps and skillfully steered the young Republic through the Atlantic minefields sown by the wars between Great Britain and Napoleon. When Madison succeeded his mentor in the White House, James Monroe was his most influential Cabinet member, but Jefferson, in technical retirement at Monticello, continued to be the President's chief counselor.

Monroe, last President in the Jefferson dynasty, chose John Quincy Adams as his right-hand man in the Cabinet, and their close personal relations enabled Adams to acquire the influence that Cabinet members are supposed to have but rarely do. This influence was reflected in the formulation of the understanding between Adams and George Canning, the British Foreign Minister, that led to the proclamation of the British-supported Monroe Doctrine. This shielded the western hemisphere from European aggression and subversion as long as the British fleet was dominant on the seas, allowing the United States to count on its security in the Atlantic areas.

Andrew Jackson was his own chief adviser. He knew what he wanted to do and did it. He was an agrarian reformer, a strict Union man, and once emphasized his attachment to the concept of the separation of powers by refusing to enforce a Supreme Court decision, a position Jefferson also had indicated but never supported by official action.

Among Jackson's successors up to the time of the War of the States, all except James K. Polk were greatly guided by the prevailing counsels of their Cabinets. Polk, like Lincoln after him, sought this counsel regularly and respectfully, but proceeded to count himself as a Cabinet majority, though the subsequent policy or act may have been supported by the President alone.

President Andrew Johnson, a Union Democrat, was rendered so helpless politically and administratively by the Republican radicals in Congress that it is difficult to identify a member of his Cabinet who was influential as an adviser.

President U. S. Grant fell victim to his trust in some Cabinet members who proved unworthy of it, generating scandals which have obscured the historical fact that he was well served by some of the foremost men in public life — Hamilton Fish, William Tecumseh Sherman and Alphonso Taft. President Hayes relied on such distinguished Cabinet advisers as John Sherman and Carl Schurz; Cleveland on Walter Q. Gresham and Richard Olney; and Harrison's Cabinet was illuminated by the brilliance of James G. Blaine. But none of the above can be confidently identified as the *most* influential with the President he served. And the same is true of the Cabinets of Garfield and Arthur.

Secretaries John Sherman, John Hay, Elihu Root, and Philander C. Knox all had the ear of President McKinley and their contributions are outstanding in the record of his two Administrations. But though Theodore Roosevelt frequently disregarded the majority counsel of his Cabinet, he met with it regularly and it is hardly conceivable that he was wholly inattentive to the judgments of Secretaries Root and Robert Bacon. However, evidence exists in plenty that, whatever the Cabinet may have advised him to do, he did not follow the counsel unless it fitted his own preconception.

On the other hand, William H. Taft was a Cabinet-type President. He listened to and was influenced by his official advisers, often yielding his own initial position to such strongminded heads of the Federal departments as Knox, Henry L. Stimson, and George W. Wickersham. He was also persuaded, partly by T.R.'s challenge to his renomination, to align himself with the conservative Republican leaders in Congress. It was James A. Tawney, chairman of the Appropriations Committee, who persuaded the President to make the fatal speech (in Tawney's hometown of Winona, Minnesota) that defended the Payne-Aldrich tariff bill. This legislation was bitterly opposed by the growing band of liberal Senate Republicans who later joined with T.R. in forming the independent Bull Moose party and made Taft a one-termer.

Wilson took the Cabinet seriously as an essential guide to wise policy. But for the early part of his first Administration he found his Secretary of State a roadblock, not a pathfinder. Wilson had appointed William Jennings Bryan as a political expedient, because, as a minority President, it was necessary to seek Democratic solidarity and Bryan had a large party following. Also Wilson was in deep debt to Bryan for inducing the Baltimore convention to deny the nomination to Speaker Champ Clark after Clark had polled a majority of the delegates.

But as Secretary of State, when Europe plunged into World War I, Bryan's pacifist views led him to oppose loans to the Allies and advocate peace at any price, in and out of Cabinet meetings, to the point where his presence in the government became untenable. Wilson must have accepted his resignation with a mixture of feelings — relief that he was rid of Bryan as his foreign policy deputy, concern lest Bryan's pro-pacifist activities as a private citizen would complicate the President's determination to stay out of World War I, but not, as it proved, at the expense of German command of the seas.

With Bryan gone, his successors — Robert Lansing and Brainbridge Colby — did precisely what they were told. When Wilson entrusted Colonel Edward M. House of Texas with foreign policy missions and responsibilities normally conducted by the Secretary of State, Lansing kept his feelings to himself and served the President loyally in the minor role Wilson assigned to him. Eventually Wilson decided that House had taken too much on himself and in Wilson's name had made unauthorized commitments to the Allies. This ended House's influence with the President, and he was "banished from Court" for life.

But throughout Wilson's terms there were four members of the Cabinet who had his special confidence and on whose counsel he heavily depended — Franklin K. Lane, Secretary of the Interior, William G. McAdoo, Secretary of the Treasury, David F. Houston, Secretary of Agriculture, and Newton D. Baker, Secretary of War. Nor did they fail him in loyalty. Throughout his disability, and after his death — except for McAdoo's embrace of national prohibition in the interest of his presidential ambition — they were the champions of his policies in a party that deserted them.

Blindness to his betrayal by friends who put the stigma of corruption on his Administration was the weakness that obscured the constructive progressivism of Warren G. Harding. Yet the premier of his Cabinet was the incorruptible Charles Evans Hughes. And in the adverse appraisal of Harding's official choices, the evidence that the President's foreign minister played another major role — awakening Harding to the realization that he was being exploited by rascals — has not been given the counterbalancing weight it merits.

When Coolidge became President on Harding's death in office it was soon obvious that he was disposed to give his Cabinet a free rein in its departments, and involve himself in only a minimum percentage of departmental problems. But, though Coolidge's chief interest in sustaining the boom economy automatically elevated the presidential influence of the Secretary of the Treasury, Andrew W. Mellon, this member of the Cabinet became Coolidge's principal mentor on all matters. That relationship fixed the Executive policies which led directly to the crash of the stock market in 1929 and the Great Depression.

Herbert Hoover's influence with President Coolidge was

limited to his field as Secretary of Commerce and in planning the reorganization of the Federal establishment to attain greater efficiency and functional consolidation. But neither was drawn to the other as an individual and Hoover's ambition to succeed Coolidge was the target of private presidential remarks that had a tinge of actual unfriendliness and indicated, at least to me, that the only successor who entirely appealed to Coolidge was the one he saw in the mirror.

President Hoover's relations to the members of his Cabinet, and his dependence on their counsels, are obscured by the early arrival in his Administration of the economic hurricane. Amid its lightnings his was the figure the public saw, standing alone and beleaguered. There were excellent men around him — Secretary of State Henry L. Stimson; Ogden L. Mills, who became Secretary of the Treasury when Mellon was sent off to the Court of St. James's; and several others. Stimson's protracted and varied official experience was with the problems of diplomacy and national defense. Mills was popular in Congress even after the Democrats captured control of the House in 1930. Moreover, Mills and his chief aides, Arthur Ballantine and James H. Douglas, had fashioned the tools which, if Hoover had possessed the political power to use them in 1931–32, would, I believe, have checked and then routed the Depression. But only with Speaker Garner's consent was he able to employ even one of these anti-Depression tools, the Reconstruction Finance Corporation.

After Franklin Roosevelt became President, he made use of those very tools, but without giving any credit to Hoover or his aides for having themselves designed them. They bought the time FDR needed before Congress could be induced to accept, in the form of the First New Deal, the legislation that jettisoned the platform of 1932 on which Roosevelt was elected.

In the Roosevelt Cabinet there was a tendency of some members to linger behind after a Cabinet session to press their own points of view, but they always risked the displeasure of the President in so doing. Sometimes he showed it. Other times he would ask, as all Presidents have asked, a member of the Cabinet to wait over, not necessarily to expand his argument on a problem that had been surveyed during the meeting, but to consult him in private on another matter.

The Cabinet, nonetheless, became even more of a living institution under Franklin D. Roosevelt than it had been for some years previously. He restored it to the status of a top-level advisory group from which he sought and found useful ideas and guidance, often by encouraging open rivalries among its members in the belief, that, in the washdown of contention, the nugget of truth would more surely emerge. He stood aloof, for example, when Harry Hopkins and Harold Ickes fought out their differences in public; also in other inter-Administration conflicts.

Whether or not this was his way to make an appraisal of their strengths and weaknesses, in Hopkins the President found the right-hand man he was seeking. The outbreak of war in Europe and the Pacific raised new, difficult, and delicate problems, and Hopkins's discharge of the major assignments the President entrusted to him confirmed Roosevelt in the wisdom of his choice. After the war General Marshall expressed to me the judgment that Hopkins's skill in dealing with temperamental Allied statesmen and military commanders had "shortened the conflict by at least a year."

The Secretary of Agriculture, Henry A. Wallace, was popular with those groups whose political support was important — the antiwar and radical elements of the left. Hence, though Hopkins's presidential aspirations had to be sacrificed in the process, Roosevelt chose Wallace as his running mate in 1940. The choice was made easier because Garner, disillusioned by FDR's turn to paternal Federalism (socialism in Garner's book), and opposed to the third term, had removed himself from consideration for renomination as Vice-President after toying briefly with the urging of friends that he should actively seek the presidential nomination in 1940.

But when war impended Roosevelt found a new use for his Cabinet, despite its decline with the rise of Hopkins. He opened its membership to prominent Republicans as a move in unifying the nation against the time when, FDR was certain, the United States would enter World War II on the Allied side. On the argument of patriotic duty he induced Stimson to join the Cabinet as Secretary of War and Frank Knox as Secretary of the Navy. (Alf M. Landon, the Republican nominee in 1936, declined the latter post because he felt he was wanted chiefly as bipartisan window dressing.)

The choice of Cordell Hull, Secretary of State for the greater part of Roosevelt's long tenure in the White House, was dictated by necessitous party politics, as was Wilson's of Bryan. A Senate leader, Hull, as chairman of the committee on arrangements for the Democratic national convention of 1932, had given FDR a considerable edge in setting up the convention machinery. Hull was an aspirant for Secretary of State who could not safely be bypassed, though an effort was made in the President's camp to fob off Hull with the chairmanship of the Tariff Commission. But the President and Hull were never on the close personal terms so desirable between the Chief Executive and his foreign minister; this relationship was with Under Secretary Sumner Welles instead, to a point where Hull's resignation, which FDR could not politically afford, was averted only by Welles's reluctant removal by the President.

Hull's caution, cold reserve, stubbornness, and obsession

with the conviction that removing tariff barriers cleared the straightest road to world peace, bored FDR. And, finding the Secretary an obstacle to many of Winston Churchill's efforts to take primary control of the war strategy, the British Embassy in Washington encouraged Roosevelt to deal directly and secretly with Welles, whom the British considered more sympathetic with their interests.

To Roosevelt this was an agreeable procedure. He and Welles both were alumni of Groton School and they belonged to the same Harvard elite, which the Tennessee hillman definitely did not. But inevitably there were "leaks" to Hull of this undercover relationship, and eventually the Secretary indicated to the President that he found the situation intolerable. This hint of resignation, in the midst of war, so alarmed Roosevelt that Welles was sent on a foreign mission and then to Coventry.

Associate Justice Felix Frankfurter, before and after he joined the Court, was a talent scout for President Franklin Roosevelt. His contributions consisted of inducing young men who had been his students at Harvard Law School, and other talented lawyers and executives, to come to Washington. They became influential in the formulation and administration of policy and in drafting legislation relevant thereto. These "hot dogs," as Frankfurter's protégés were flippantly named, were never in the Cabinet and most of them were not even official members of the White House staff. But they enjoyed constant access to the President until the imminence of war and then war itself established Hopkins as Number One, with aides of his own selection.

The President regularly consulted Justice Frankfurter on many matters, both men relaxing the canon of the separation of powers. But even before his elevation to the Court Frankfurter's influence was so great that when the NRA was challenged as unconstitutional, Frankfurter selected as the legal test what became known as the "sick chicken [Schecter] case." Donald Richberg, Under Secretary of Commerce, had proposed litigation arising in Alabama in the lumber industry as a more promising vehicle and urged that the weakest was *Schecter*.

Convinced that Richberg was right, I wrote an article after the Administration lost the case in the Supreme Court, saying as much and identifying Frankfurter as responsible for the choice. Whether or not this was the reason for his display of lifelong personal enmity to me I do not know. But after the article appeared Frankfurter pretended not to recognize me at parties where we were fellow guests, and once asked my wife, when he read her name on a place card, to point me out and tell him what I did for a living.

Soon after Harry S. Truman became Roosevelt's successor he began to weed out prudently, but with mounting acceleration, the Cabinet he inherited. The first to be handed their congés were Morgenthau and Ickes, as previously noted. The Secretary of State, E. R. Stettinius, Jr., although deserving recognition for achievements in other government posts, owed his selection to Hopkins, whose suzerainty of the department Stettinius maintained by doing nothing without Hopkins's imprimatur or initiative, and by keeping Hopkins fully informed of the activities of the department's entrenched bureaucracy. Truman, soon after Stettinius headed the U.S. delegation to the San Francisco conference where the United Nations was created, replaced him with James F. Byrnes, to whom the President was bound by ties of admiration and fealty from the days in the Senate where Byrnes was Truman's party leader.

The new Secretary of State also had been FDR's Director of Mobilization, virtually functioning (and known) as "the Assistant President." As Secretary of State he acted as the new, inexperienced President's mentor at the Potsdam Conference, and at home as Truman's adviser in all things. But once again in the history of the presidency, a Chief Executive came to feel that a subordinate was "getting too big for his britches," making statements and commitments without advance consultation with the President. This led to Byrnes's resignation and a rift with Truman that exists to this day. Yet Byrnes laid the foundations of the United States policies that replaced with realism Roosevelt's long-enduring mistaken appraisal of the USSR as a prospective, constructive partner of this government in the postwar effort to restore international peace and order. I think had he, perhaps, been able to adjust himself to being Truman's subordinate, Byrnes would have continued to wield the influence with the President that Dean G. Acheson did when he became Secretary. Acheson was sedulous in his show of deference to the President and the presidency and was rewarded by the free hand Truman gave him in the formalization and unhampered conduct of foreign policy.

The incident that began the alienation of Truman and Byrnes put the President in an embarrassing position, the more so because Truman was responsible for it. Secretary of Commerce Henry A. Wallace, in 1946, brought to the President the text of a foreign policy speech he was to make that night in New York City. It was in direct conflict with the international policy that Byrnes, with Truman's specific backing, was expounding in Paris at the time.

The President glanced at Wallace's text, missed its significance and offered no objection. Byrnes, when he read in the newspapers the gist of the Wallace speech, promptly sent a teletyped message to the President to the effect that Truman must now choose between them as the spokesman of United States foreign policy. Necessarily, Truman publicly disavowed Wallace's presentation. Wallace at once resigned from the Cabinet, and, seizing the opportunity to cozen the gullible Wallace into becoming the anti-Administration leader, Communists and others on the extreme left began the movement that culminated in Wallace's independent presidential candidacy in 1948.

For Byrnes's successor the President selected the soldier-statesman he admired and respected above all Americans, General George C. Marshall. Fortunately for the national interest and the General's eventual rating in the conduct of an office to which he brought no direct experience, the new Secretary induced Robert A. Lovett, one of the ablest and wisest public servants ever to appear in Washington, to serve as Under Secretary.

They had known each other intimately since Lovett was Assistant Secretary of War for Air in World War II. Marshall's estimate that Lovett was indispensable was formed at that time, and at State Lovett fully justified the General's reliance on him. When, therefore, the President decided that a greater need for Marshall had arisen in the area of national military security and transferred him to the Department of Defense, Marshall's condition was that Lovett should go with him as Deputy Secretary. There the team worked as successfully as at State, where Acheson, whom the President had come extravagantly to admire, was available as Marshall's replacement. His proved competence in the field allayed any concern Truman may have had over shifting Marshall to a post where rebuilding of the Department of Defense had to be centered.

Marshall's original predecessor at Defense was James V.

Forrestal. Ironically, he became the victim of one of the most foresighted moves any member of the government has ever made. Granting as a *possibility* that Dewey might be elected in 1948, an estimate implicit in all the polls and other portents, Forrestal felt it would be disastrous if an Administration came into office without knowledge of the inner and vital operations of the government and of the acute state of the military problems confronting the United States. He therefore proposed that Dewey be asked to designate several representatives for a comprehensive and confidential briefing so that Dewey could take over rapidly and informatively if elected President.

At the White House, several aides regarded this as an act of treachery by Forrestal. They accepted the conclusion of fervent Truman loyalists that Forrestal really wanted Dewey elected, and they fed the suspicion into the President's mind. But Forrestal had already revealed some of the indecision and recurrent melancholy which, reported to the President, helped to support the argument of other members of the White House staff that he was verging upon a nervous breakdown. In combination these two contentions induced the President to replace the Secretary after the 1948 elections with Louis A. Johnson, his campaign fund raiser in 1948.

The Forrestal tragedy culminated in his suicide while under psychiatric treatment at the Naval Hospital at Bethesda. Yet the President later, by the appointment of the Hoover Commission, authorized the same preparations Forrestal had proposed against the event of the transfer of control of the government from one party to the other, or to a Vice-President as uninformed as Truman had been when he succeeded. Forrestal's general objective was to equip a new President, either in the line of succession or of the opposition, with the information on which he could soundly and promptly base urgent decisions instead of having to postpone them for months while being briefed on the facts.

Of the intra-Administration disputes that characterized the Roosevelt Administration none was more bitter than that between Henry A. Wallace and Jesse H. Jones, which the President permitted to reach a critical status. Their ideas differed fundamentally on economic policy and Allied aid during the war and on foreign aid in the postwar period. As chairman of the RFC, Jones had made a remarkable record in salvaging the financial and industrial communities from the ravages of the Great Depression, while Wallace's administration of economic warfare had been plagued by inefficiency and weird ideology.

When the important work of the RFC had been accomplished and its dissolution could safely be turned over to minor officers, Jones, after Harry Hopkins died in office, was appointed to the high and critical post of Secretary of Commerce. In this office he quickly fell into conflict with Vice-President Wallace on economic policy. But it was not until 1945 that Jones was suddenly removed from the Cabinet in the final phase of their personal conflict. To stem the anger of the left affiliates of the Democratic party at the rejection of Wallace for renomination as Vice-President by the Democratic convention of 1944, Roosevelt summarily notified Jones that Wallace would replace him at Commerce. Smoldering with anger at the special indignity from a President he had served so notably, Jones returned to his extensive business interests at Houston. Eventually he gave vent to his resentment by authorizing a biography in which the documented facts revealed the shabbiness and crude political expediency of his treatment by Roosevelt.

The short tenure of Louis Johnson at Defense was another

effect of personal conflict within the Administration. Johnson
had clashed with Under Secretary of State Acheson on
matters growing out of the war in Korea; and by that time
Acheson stood high in President Truman's favor. For a while
he did nothing to allay the Johnson-Acheson rift, but in the
end he removed Johnson as suddenly as Roosevelt had removed Jesse Jones.

By way of temporary digression, no Cabinet member of
recent history has drawn such a hostile press as Louis Johnson. And the durability of this attitude was demonstrated as
late as October 18–19, 1970, in two successive comments in
the *Washington Post* dealing with the 1971–72 military
budget. In 1949–50, wrote one, Johnson "slashed the Pentagon budget with such a consummate lack of skill and finesse
that two service Secretaries resigned in disgust. . . ." And the
second commentator categorized Johnson as an "evil" man.

When Johnson cut the Pentagon budget to thirteen billion
dollars, he was following the instructions of President Truman. And much earlier, in 1939, when, as the Assistant
Secretary of War, Johnson exercised certain powers of that
office reserved to it by law, I found him most forcefully
engaged in building up the feeble national defense. In the
course of this activity Johnson arranged for me to meet with
Army Chief of Staff George C. Marshall and himself in the
interest of laying before the country the acute need for a
standing army build-up to two million men — a figure that,
when I used it in an article for the *Times* Sunday Magazine,
was hotly attacked by the dominant isolationist group of that
time.

After the passage of the National Security Act and its
amendments (1947–49), each armed service — the Army, the
Navy, and the Air Force — had a Secretary under Johnson as
Secretary of Defense. The incumbents at one period were

Gordon Gray (Army), John L. Sullivan (Navy), and Stuart Symington (Air Force). Sullivan resigned because the slash included a decision not to proceed with the construction of a new carrier, and he did this in dramatic fashion. Symington retired in March 1950, because of the overall slash in the budget of the Air Force. Johnson and Dean Acheson, the Secretary of State, were in a running feud over the status of diplomatic, as related to military, policy in Korea. But Gray did not leave his post for any of these reasons. In the following memorandum, dated May 6, 1970, he relates the actual circumstances that caused him to resign:

I was sworn in as Assistant Secretary of the Army on September 24, 1947. This was immediately after the President signed the National Security Act of 1947.

In accordance with the instructions of President Truman that civilian officials in the Defense Department should not become involved in the Presidential campaign of 1948, I took absolutely no public part. As I recall it, Louis Johnson was in charge of certain aspects of fund-raising for the Democratic party, and I somehow received word from him requesting financial activity on my part. I declined this request, and it was known to me that at least in this context, Louis Johnson could not have been said to be exactly fond of me.

(I think Louis Johnson probably never knew about a contribution I actually made to the Democratic party in connection with the 1948 campaign. Furthermore, information of this fact is known to really few, if any, other living persons. If documentation were ever required, one could examine my tax returns, Federal and State, for 1948. I am certain that I reported this gift on gift tax returns and that I paid some North Carolina gift tax in connection with the contribution. At the time of the 1948 campaign, the Treasurer of the National

*Democratic Committee was an old friend of mine named Joe
Blythe with whom I had served at least twice in the North
Carolina Senate. The records will show that he died unex-
pectedly towards the end of the 1948 campaign. Recorded
now for the first time is the fact that the night before Joe
Blythe died, he and I had some drinks together in the Mayflower Hotel in one of the downstairs' public rooms. In the
course of this meeting, which I had asked for, I handed to Joe
an envelope containing $5,000.00 in cash but without any
identification whatsoever. He put it in his pocket, and although I never inquired, I would have no doubt it was found
in his Mayflower apartment after his death was discovered. As
I recall it, he died within a very few hours of my meeting
with him and before he could have begun the business of the
succeeding day.)*

*Kenneth Royall, who had been the last Secretary of War
and the first Secretary of the Army, resigned about April 15,
1949. The Under Secretary, William H. Draper, Jr., had re-
signed about six weeks earlier. At this time I was the Assistant
Secretary of the Army and Tracy Voorhees was Assistant
Secretary. As a result of these resignations, as senior Assistant
Secretary, I became Acting Secretary (and, if it mattered,
Acting Under Secretary) and continued to serve as the Assis-
tant Secretary, with the competent and loyal help of Tracy
Voorhees.*

*It was known to me that Kenneth Royall had not recom-
mended to Louis Johnson that he suggest my name to the
President as Royall's successor. The understanding that I had
at the time was that Kenneth Royall felt that I was not "force-
ful" enough. The fact is in any case that I was not ambitious
to be Secretary of the Army and had planned to return to
North Carolina.*

In the same time frame, John Sullivan had resigned in a

public disagreement with Louis Johnson with respect to the question of construction of Navy carriers. One day, in early May, while I was, of course, still Acting Secretary of the Army, Louis Johnson called me and asked me to come to his office. When I entered, he asked me to go into his dining room and talk with a man who was waiting there. It turned out to be Frank Matthews, whom I had never met before nor had I heard of him. We had a very pleasant conversation, but I did not know its purpose. Later, when the conversation was finished, I returned to Louis Johnson's office. He asked me what I thought of this individual. I said I thought he was very pleasant and personable. Louis then asked me if I thought he would be a good Secretary of the Navy. My response was something to the effect that I had no basis for forming a competent judgment.

Very soon thereafter I was asked by the President to come to his office. He asked me if I would accept appointment as Under Secretary of the Army. He knew from earlier conversations that I wished to return to North Carolina, and I reminded him of this fact. He said he well understood that, but that he was about to appoint a new Secretary of the Navy. He was aware of the fact that the two top spots in the Army were vacant, and he could hardly take care of the Navy problem without doing something about the Army, and, therefore, he wanted me to take the Under Secretaryship for a reasonable period; and he would relieve me to go back to North Carolina when I wished to do so.

Naturally I acceded to the President's wishes, and I was appointed (on May 13 — at the same time Frank Matthews was appointed to the Navy Secretaryship) and then confirmed on May 19 as Under Secretary of the Army. In early June, I went to see Louis Johnson one day to tell him that the Army lawyers had advised me that I should cease taking official action with respect to important parts of Army business. They had pointed out that there was an old Federal statute, never clearly tested in the courts, which cast some doubt on the validity of actions taken by an acting head of a department when the statutory top spot had been vacant for more than 30 days. This was then the case in the Army.

I said to Louis Johnson that he should get about the business of getting his Secretary of the Army appointed because the Army was suffering in a legal sense as well as a public relations sense. This latter was the subject of some press reports at the time. I knew that he had offered the post to a man named Curtis Calder, a public utilities executive in New York City. Louis said, "I will call Curtis Calder today. Will you come back to see me this afternoon?" This was on the morning of June 6. I responded that I could not because I was going to Chapel Hill, North Carolina, that afternoon to receive an Honorary Degree from the University of Chapel Hill that night. He said, "Well, come in to see me tomorrow morning." I said, "Louis, I cannot come in to see you tomorrow morning because I will be leaving early to make the commencement address at West Point." He said, "Well, telephone me before you depart." I replied that it would be very early, and he said, "That's all right. I'm up early." So, that afternoon I flew to Chapel Hill. I remember that among others on my plane with me was Jim Webb, then Under Secretary of State, who was also to receive an Honorary Degree. While in Chapel Hill, I met with a Committee from the Business School, which formally offered me the post of Dean of the Business School which had been the subject of earlier discussions. I agreed to take on this post at a time to be determined later, largely depending upon my Washington commitments. After the commencement exercises, we flew back to Washington.

The next morning, before I took off for West Point to make the commencement address, I called Louis Johnson as he had requested. He said that he had been unable to reach Curtis Calder. He then said, "What do you think about my sending your name to the President?" I said, "Louis, I do not want the job. I wish to return to North Carolina. The President understands this very well. So please dismiss my name from any thoughts of yours." He then said, "Well, come in to see me this afternoon when you get back from West Point."

I flew to West Point, made the commencement address, returned to Washington and upon arrival at the Washington airport was met by Tracy Voorhees, who got aboard the plane before I could get off. He had left an important meeting and said he wanted to talk to me before the press got to me. He reported, "In your absence, while you have been out of Washington, the President sent your name to the Senate this morning and placed it in nomination for Secretary of the Army." (I learned later that the idea of doing it hastily like this had come out of a conversation between Louis Johnson and Steve Early, who was Louis's deputy. Steve had the notion that it would be a good thing if the news came out while I was still at West Point. This, indeed, actually did not happen.)

In any event, I went back to my Pentagon office in a rage and as I entered everyone was saying "Congratulations, Mr. Secretary." I had already told Tracy Voorhees I would not accept the position, and I told my closest associates. Among the first things I did was to call Matt Connolly, the President's appointment secretary. He said, "Congratulations, Mr. Secretary." I said, "Congratulations, Hell. I'm not going to take it." He was shocked, of course, but when I explained the circumstances to him, and said I wanted to see the President, he said, "Indeed, you must see the President," and he gave me the first open appointment in the afternoon. Before I went to the White House, there began to be a parade of people into my office telling me that it was vital that I accept the appointment. I remember particularly General Omar Bradley and Jack McCloy, both of whom happened to be in the building at the time and had got some word of the situation from Tracy Voorhees.

When I went in to see the President, he was his usual cordial self. I explained the situation to him reminding him of our conversation in May when he asked me to become Under Secretary of the Army. He was somewhat flabbergasted. He said, "You know, Louis Johnson told me this morning that you wanted this job so bad you could taste it." He said, "Of course we are in some trouble, and I will take the rap." I said, "Mr. President, what does that mean?" He said, "I will send a message up to the Senate, withdraw your name, and tell them that I had made a mistake." Suddenly, it dawned on me that one doesn't do that to the President of the United States. I said to the President that I would accept it if he would understand that I would stay in the post only for a respectable period. I told him of my acceptance of the Business School post the night before and pointed out to him the extreme embarrassments this situation would cause.

As a matter of fact, I was deeply embarrassed with the people in Chapel Hill but, more importantly, deeply embarrassed in my own family. My wife, Jane, heard on the radio that I was to become Secretary of the Army. She knew nothing of it from me and was deeply hurt. Of course, I knew nothing myself, and it was on the radio before I could ever get in touch with her upon my return from West Point.

Because of Louis Johnson's own ambitions to become

Secretary of War in earlier years, I suppose, and always felt, that he simply didn't believe me when I said that I did not want to be Secretary of the Army.

Now, to relationships. I was not entirely fond of Louis Johnson's method of operations in the performance of his duties as Secretary of Defense.

However, there is one point that I wish to make very strongly. My resignation as Secretary of the Army had nothing to do with Louis Johnson as a man or as Secretary of Defense.

There is a long story behind my election as President of the University of North Carolina. Suffice it to say for this memorandum, I was elected in about January or February of 1950 subject to my release from the Government service. In about late March or early April, 1950, the President asked me to become his Special Assistant for a study of the Foreign Economic Policy of the United States, and I left the Department of the Army to undertake this assignment. When that was completed, and in the fall, I proceeded to Chapel Hill.

Louis Johnson did not interfere with my administration of the Department of the Army and, except as he issued Pentagonwide directives which affected all of the services, I had no problems with him. It will be recalled that during his tenure the Air Force and the Navy were in a constant quarrel which I tried to keep the Army out of, successfully I believe. The specific disagreements we had largely concerned themselves with personnel matters.

Given the circumstances of my appointment as Secretary of the Army, I think the later sequence of events would have been the same, no matter who had been Secretary of Defense. In other words, I would have accepted the position at the University of North Carolina at the time I did, in any event.

Gray subsequently added a footnote to this memorandum:

I do recall one instance in which he [Johnson] *asked me to promote to brigadier general an individual who was a colonel in the Army Reserve. After investigating the matter, I informed him that I would make the promotion only if ordered to do so. The order was given, and it was a clear instance of political promotion. I think in fairness to Louis Johnson, he acknowledged to me in later years that he had lived to regret this action which turned out to serve neither the Army's nor his interests.*

As a detailed example of one of the characteristics that led to Johnson's downfall, and as an insight into how fully President Truman lived up to the obligation he expressed in the words "the buck stops here," the memorandum is a valuable contribution to the history of the feud-ridden Truman Administration and a rare view of the inner workings of government that are concealed in the official handouts.

Truman, in dire need of informed counsel, turned to the Cabinet. He met with it frequently and more often with a Cabinet committee on national security. This informal group preceded the National Security Council established by the National Security Act and included such Cabinet-rank officials as the director of the CIA. But the President continued to be sensitive to the problems of the departments whose chiefs constituted the formal Cabinet.

Truman, innately one of the most modest of the Presidents, had the greatest respect for the institutions of government, the Cabinet as one of them. But no Chief Executive respected the office of the presidency more than he, or assumed fuller responsibility to the people for all policies and actions. "The buck stops here," a perfectly chosen use of the vernacular, summed up his sense of the President's accountability.

Eisenhower, as President-elect, chose an advisory group, headed by Sherman Adams, to assist him in selecting a Cabinet. Adams and Secretary of State John Foster Dulles had immediate access to the President when the new Administration took over, but Eisenhower found another tower of strength in George M. Humphrey, Secretary of the Treasury — a relationship he continued with Robert B. Anderson when Anderson succeeded Humphrey at the Treasury. These favorites, particularly Adams, Dulles, Humphrey, and Anderson, were the filters through which as few problems as possible were passed on to the President for decision.

But the screening procedure became visible in enough instances to arouse resentment in Congress and the Cabinet and engendered a rising crop of political analysts who projected the image of a President too lazy to attend to his responsibilities. This image was sharpened when Adams was discovered to have committed imprudences — a fact he belatedly realized and acted upon in Eisenhower's interest by resigning despite the President's expressed determination to retain his White House chief of staff with the simple explanation, "I need him."

The realism of Adams's conclusion that he had become an embarrassment to the President, and, as an act of supreme loyalty, should resign was typical of this arrogant but coldly practical man. He had been Governor of New Hampshire; he knew politics, its way and its works, and in the campaign of 1952 he came to know its principal practitioners throughout the nation.

The same quality of arrogance that was Adams's undoing led another important member of the Eisenhower Administration, Secretary of the Air Force Harold E. Talbott, into committing an act of imprudence, and it cost him his official head. Talbott had also been a talent scout for the new Administration. In that role the President found him indispensable, and so was his rating as a campaign fund raiser in the Republican party. But the revelation that Talbott had solicited business for a company in which he had a personal interest — and on Air Force stationery — persuaded the reluctant President that the Secretary had become a political burden to an Administration vociferously dedicated to "hound's tooth" cleanliness.

This was another personal tragedy because Talbott was an outstanding Secretary of the Air Force. The College at Colorado Springs was his idea. Also, he built up our striking and retaliatory air power to the highest point of effectiveness by then attained. Like Adams, it never occurred to Talbott that anything he did could be wrong or thought to be. He had found the company of efficiency engineers he was recommending in his letters of such value to him in his private capacity as a financier that he conceived he was doing his correspondents a great favor. He never gave a thought to what stationery his letters were typed on.

George Humphrey's tremendous influence on Eisenhower in all matters of policy had its origin in the fact that the President had neither experience nor natural aptitude for dealing with monetary and fiscal problems. Except for Arthur Burns, the members of his Council of Economic Advisers were remote from Eisenhower's preoccupations, as were the members of the Federal Reserve Board. Congress had made this agency independent of the Executive, and the President was a strict respecter of the statutes. Moreover, Humphrey was a man of great personal charm. But the time came when the President listened to counselors whose approach to the economy was made with an eye fixed on vote-getting. Humphrey, alarmed at what he conceived to be potentially disastrous consequences of a tax bill Eisenhower had not criticized, told a congressional committee at a public hearing, "If you approve this legislation you will see a depression that will curl your hair." But the President did not reveal the embarrassment the incident surely caused him, and his relations with Humphrey seemed to be unchanged. Nor is there any conclusive evidence that Humphrey's resignation was linked with what he said to the congressional committee.

The Cabinet, or an individual member, can embarrass the President and has done so, but usually this has not been a deliberate act. Eisenhower wanted his Cabinet members to have full opportunity to expound their attitudes toward a problem in camera, and then either give full support to the President's conclusion or be silent. This formula failed in the case of Martin Durkin, a trade-union official whom President Eisenhower appointed Secretary of Labor in the hope that Durkin would serve as a balance to the pro-industry position of Secretary of Commerce Sinclair Weeks. But when Durkin proposed legislation that would weaken the Taft-Hartley Act, and Weeks made that effect clear to the President, Eisenhower sided with Weeks. Durkin found his membership in the Cabinet untenable, and resigned. Yet, Durkin was not at any time a "natural enemy" of the President. He was merely trying to induce Eisenhower to adopt his own concept of what the labor policy of the Administration should be, and almost succeeded until Weeks persuaded the President that this policy would augment the already vast power of organized labor over the economy.

Durkin's successor, James Mitchell of New Jersey, made a similar effort with respect to the Taft-Hartley Act, but once again Weeks successfully interposed. Mitchell, also not as an "enemy" in the Cabinet, but as the President's friend, was seeking to make organized labor a dependable political ally of the Administration. And Weeks, in frustrating Mitchell's and Durkin's legislative proposals, was acting in the same capacity. For he was aware that Eisenhower would not consciously increase the powers and statutory immunities of the labor unions.

President Kennedy, by contrast, dominated his Cabinet, and there were recurrent periods when he did not meet with it for weeks. His principal advisers on Far East policy were McGeorge Bundy, Averell Harriman, and Walt Rostow, who, with General Maxwell Taylor, influenced him to increase the number of military advisers in South Vietnam, and extend their activities to the combat zones. These actions led directly to the deep involvement of the United States in the war in Vietnam, with the full concurrence — publicly at least — of Robert McNamara, the Secretary of Defense. McNamara also had great influence with the President in shaping overall military policy and the military budget.

Senator J. William Fulbright had been under serious consideration for Secretary of State, and might have been chosen had it not been for his opposition to civil rights legislation — the price of a Senate seat from Arkansas. With Fulbright out of the running, Dean Acheson suggested Dean Rusk. The President-elect was assured — correctly as it developed — that Rusk would do what he was told and the President would find no obstacles in acting as his own Secretary of State.

Douglas Dillon, Secretary of the Treasury, who easily transferred to Kennedy the allegiance he bore to President Eisenhower and the Republican party as Under Secretary of State, was the new President's most trusted adviser in fiscal and monetary policy. Arthur Goldberg, Secretary of Labor, was Kennedy's very serviceable liaison with organized labor, Goldberg's ancient client, whose support in Congress and at the polls often made the difference between the success and failure of the President's programs. The quid pro quo, as always, was government favoritism to labor at the expense of the people as a whole. But Goldberg saw to it that the price was paid.

The Cabinet member on whom Kennedy most relied for counsel was his younger brother Robert F. After considerable reflection the President had appointed Robert Attorney General, his decision to do this finally formed by his father's insistence and by his sense of need for someone in the Cabinet to whom he could give unquestioning confidence and receive selfless loyalty.

But President Kennedy also relied for counsel on men outside the government, often at the disregard of the views of his Cabinet. Some were newspapermen, the principal among whom was Charles L. Bartlett. Often when not otherwise engaged, and weather permitting, Kennedy would pick up Bartlett at his home for a long walk during which the President would talk of his problems, of the options of act and policy available to him, and of the probable effect of each choice on the President's political fortunes and the state of the nation.

Kennedy also discussed all important decisions with his father until the elder's power of speech was almost totally impaired by a stroke. But the President continued to lay his problems before his sire, watching for reactions as expressed by his father's eyes or indicated by a nod, affirmative or negative.

On certain issues the two differed substantively: for example, on interventionist foreign policy as the best containment of world Communism, and on the building of the Welfare State. But the President had such respect for the senior's judgment that I think he always felt dubious when his decision ran counter to it.

Before and after becoming President, especially during his tenure as Senate majority leader, Lyndon Johnson relied heavily, for common sense and technical advice, on a number of non-officials. His trusted counselor on personal affairs was and is Judge W. A. Moresund of Texas. But so highly does Johnson rate Moresund's judgment that I suspect their consultations have also involved great affairs of politics and state. Among other preferred counselors were Edward Weisl (New York politics and congressional relations), Abe Fortas (end-running around legal obstacles on delicate ground), and Clark M. Clifford (general policy, legal authorization of contemplated acts, unique experience in the operation of the Truman presidency and public relations). After Clifford had retired from the White House staff to the private practice of law Presidents Truman, and later Kennedy and Johnson, constantly consulted him.

Except for his rejection by the Senate as Chief Justice of the United States, I think what Fortas wanted, he got — influence in the highest official quarters, fame, and money. But Fortas's influence suffered from an exposure that Clifford's did not, for the simple reason that the lure of publicity does not attract Clifford. He knows its price, that Fortas eventually paid, and kept secret the constancy of his role as the adviser of Presidents. The American people did not fully realize Clifford's profound association with the power structure of the government, even after his appointment as Secretary of Defense, until after leaving office he wrote the celebrated *Foreign Affairs* article. In this he traced the reasons for his change from an earlier view in favor of intensive bombing of North Vietnam and proposed a fixed phase-out that would remove U.S. troops by the end of 1970. President Nixon then stated publicly he hoped to beat Clifford's timetable.

As lawyers, both Fortas and Clifford, of course, benefited

materially by the attraction the repute of close relations with Presidents has for corporations doing business with the Federal establishment. For the corporate community firmly believes that even to get a fair deal from government it must have, if only in an advisory capacity, a lawyer in Washington with "connections," especially with the entrenched bureaucracy.

On this belief, supported by considerable experience, corporations seek to augment their legal representation in the capital, however competent professionally, with such lawyers. Clifford — in a familiar posture, gazing skyward with his fingers tented under his chin — makes it a point to assure such applicants for his advisory service that they do not need him, that he would not approach any official from the President down on a personal basis in behalf of their interest. But seldom, regardless of the amount of the fee set for merely acting "of counsel," are corporate clients dissuaded from the conviction that a former official and personal association with the establishment of government will win more favorable consideration of their interest than would otherwise be given.

Lyndon Johnson fully recognized the political and public relations value that would accrue from making a visible ally of a popular predecessor of the other major party. By constantly seeking counsel of General Eisenhower, often on occasions with attendant publicity which identified the approaches as plainly show business, Johnson pleased the millions of citizens whose respect and devotion to the General endured to the day of his death. And to the end of his life, Eisenhower seemed unaware that some of this solicitude had the aspect of a snow job.

Unlike the hostile relationship that existed between Hoover and Roosevelt, President Truman made constructive use of the former President of the opposition party, but not as a political tactic. Hoover was the best-qualified man in the country to head the commission to reorganize the government, and Truman drafted him for the task for this sole and excellent reason. Snow jobs were not in Truman's line. And, though President Nixon has shown deference to Truman — visiting him on his birthday, for example — he has not exploited such amenities or made them the systematic operation that Johnson employed with Eisenhower.

The General, like Truman, had the deepest respect for the presidential office. And, in succumbing to Johnson's wooing, Eisenhower, the old soldier, was primarily obeying the call to duty of the commander-in-chief. This helps to explain why Eisenhower, in answer to pleas for help from Johnson, unwittingly, it seemed, deviated at times from his own policy on Vietnam. As President, Eisenhower, for example, had steadfastly refused to involve American military personnel in combat on the mainland of Asia. When he sent a handful of military advisers to South Vietnam he limited their activity to Saigon. They were forbidden to go to the front or become in any way associated with combat. But as an ex-President he upheld Johnson's disastrous removal of this restraint.

Kennedy, moreover, had not only greatly increased the number of military advisers, but authorized them to perform their service at the fronts. But, as evidence of the effect of Johnson's cultivating of Eisenhower, which Kennedy never did, it was Kennedy whom the General criticized for reversing his policy as to the number, and zone enlargement, of the activities of the military advisers. And it was Johnson to whom Eisenhower gave support at critical stages in the broadening of United States military involvement in the war.

Of course few advisers are selfless. Joseph Kennedy exacted a price from Roosevelt — to be Ambassador to the Court of

St. James's. When Louis A. Johnson took over the task, from which all others shrank, of raising the campaign funds for Truman in 1948, he made it quite clear that his price was to succeed Forrestal as Secretary of Defense. And the price was duly paid.

President Johnson, because of the circumstances of his succession, felt politically obliged to make Kennedy's Cabinet his own, at least for a period, before he could venture to supplant those who, by his own estimate and reports, neither respected nor liked him and whose driving objective was, and remains, the return of a Kennedy to the White House. But Johnson found indispensable in key positions a larger number of his predecessor's most influential aides than Truman had — Rostow, McGeorge Bundy, Douglas Dillon, Dean Rusk, and Averell Harriman. Thereby he was fated to elevate Kennedy's involvement of the United States in combat in Vietnam. For in continuing to rely on their counsel that arguably was motivated by an unrealized ambition to justify the grave errors in act and policies into which they had led Kennedy, Johnson accomplished his own downfall.

I have always thought that one of President Kennedy's great mistakes was to abolish the Operations Coordinating Board, the OCB, set up by the Eisenhower Administration. Its function, vital to orderly government, was to assure that the policies adopted by the National Security Council were transmitted to each executive unit with such clarity that any infraction had to be committed deliberately or by demonstrable stupidity.

The OCB was first presided over by Herbert Hoover, Jr., and then by Christian A. Herter, each successively the Under Secretary of State. It included a special assistant to the President for Security Operations Coordination, who served as vice-chairman. In 1959 that was Karl D. Harr, Jr. The other members were Donald Quarles, Deputy Secretary of Defense; Allen W. Dulles, Director of the Central Intelligence Agency; George B. Allen, Director of the U.S. Information Agency; the Director of the International Cooperation Association, and Gordon Gray, Special Assistant to the President for National Security Affairs. The Board was established by Executive order and Kennedy abolished it by the same procedure.

After the Board was set up, it soon became evident that it would carry out its function more efficiently if headed by the White House member. Accordingly Gordon Gray was installed as chairman. From that time until the end of Eisenhower's White House tenure there were no more breaks in the transmission of major policy to all the government branches, no more actions incompatible with the decision of the National Security Council and the President. But when President Kennedy came into office, and, following the counsel of Walt Rostow, abolished the Board, the old breaks in the chain of command reappeared and have continued.

Charles Bartlett and I once asked Rostow to explain the reasons on which he based his belief that the Board should be supplanted, and for concrete illustrations why the committee system was not a better method of coordinating policy throughout the government than his substitute of remote control. His explanation satisfied neither Bartlett nor me that the substitute was more productive of cohesive government. And the subsequent conflicts and confusions in the Johnson, Kennedy, and Nixon Administrations in the top-to-bottom execution of National Security Council decisions seem to sustain this judgment.

As Bartlett and I recalled it, the reasons Rostow gave us for his recommendation that the OCB be abolished were:

The group had become a "paper mill," piling up endless

documents recording discussions of minor points, conflicting interpretations of what the policy decisions of the NSC really were, particularly whether the goal of the United States was that this nation be first in space or first among equals, etc. Moreover, argued Rostow, all coordinating should be done directly at the White House and not by an interdepartmental group meeting elsewhere. When thereafter, in the two following Administrations, it so often appeared that the right hand moved one way and the left hand another, I thought I could trace the confusion to the abolition of the OCB as Gordon Gray had refashioned it.

President Johnson preferred the subcommittee method of counseling with the Cabinet and the NSC, excluding from final major policy decisions members who were not directly concerned with the subject matter. Those excluded often were unclear as to settled policy, and therefore how to execute it, with the result that, after the abolition of the OCB, there were continuing instances of administrative ambivalence and confusion, more than came to public notice.

President Nixon has not revived the OCB or reestablished the close communication of the Eisenhower Administration between the White House and the Cabinet as a whole that Kennedy and Johnson dispensed with. Therefore, ambivalence and confusion as to certain presidential policy remain, a condition that reflects what seems at times to be the deliberate intent of the President himself — for example, the apparent day-by-day shift of Administration positions on the timing and scope of public school racial integration. And a number of long, belated discourses by Nixon on Vietnam, racial integration, and overall foreign policy failed to clarify his policies in these sensitive areas.

His Cabinet members freely make announcements in matters of policy that President Johnson restricted to himself and a faceless "White House." Perhaps the principal reason for this unrepressed show of latitude is that Nixon wants to establish a public estimate that his Cabinet is composed of supermen, an estimate he himself sought to project when he introduced them, one by one, on a television program at the outset of his Administration.

But in hard fact, no Cabinet can be other than subordinate if a strong President is in the White House. And Nixon is that. Only a few times in our history has the Cabinet dominated the President, for example, in the Administrations of Taft, Harding, and Coolidge.

The role of the press as internal adviser and external organ of propaganda for the incumbent President or the opposition party began during Washington's first term. Freneau's *National Gazette* was Jefferson's mouthpiece, Fenno's *Gazette of the United States* was Hamilton's, and Frank Blair, in the *Washington Globe*, was Andrew Jackson's. As American journalism has emerged into full independence there now are few newspapers or periodicals which follow the hazy, so-called party line, even most of the time. But in their day, the writers of propaganda sheets in the guise of newspapers wielded more influence than any other unofficial presidential advisers.

It was Franklin Roosevelt who raised the status of roving advisers to institutional level. Though the best known of these, Benjamin Cohen and Thomas G. Corcoran, were not members of the official White House staff, Corcoran was privileged to associate the White House with his lobbying for the President's legislative programs. For example, a member of Congress, at once coming on the line when told "the White House is calling," would find Corcoran on the other end, though often Corcoran would be telephoning from his office at the RFC. The introduction had a magic effect.

Roosevelt's six White House assistants who were committed to reveal and maintain a "passion for anonymity" did not long remain unknown to the public. They appeared at the Capitol regularly, lobbying for presidential programs and were readily available to the press, often identified by name. They did not function as watchdogs of the President's time and accessibility to the degree that Nixon's staff does and as Sherman Adams did more openly in President Eisenhower's terms. Roosevelt did not want them to have even the semblance of authority to isolate the President from the people. But no Chief Executive has been informed by his aides of the names of all who have asked to see him, and why. And probably none has wanted to be, even though errors of selection by his staff have lost him now and then the support of politicians and private citizens he came to need acutely later on.

Yet, while Sherman Adams exercised unmatched powers of exclusion, Eisenhower held a concept of the American democratic system that frequently impelled him to break through the Adams barrier on his own initiative. Reacting to something he heard or read he would summon reporters in whom he had confidence and considered "fair," to private interviews. In these meetings he always displayed the utter candor that was one of his basic attributes.

I think Nixon is being harmed by his own and his staff's restriction of his accessibility, and by the fact that his senior staff watchdogs have a very limited knowledge of who are the local and state political rajahs and other leading citizens. In combination this, I believe, accounts in considerable measure for the major episodes of backing and filling, and the confusions over what the President's policy is toward problems over which the American people are deeply divided.

In the first years of the Johnson Administration Walter Jenkins, as chief of the White House staff, exercised probably as much of this power of selection as Sherman Adams did, but he was more discreet in employing it. And he was not as widely visible to newspapermen as Adams, Henry Kissinger, or Walt Rostow have been. Even expert observers were surprised when they discovered how very influential Jenkins was in affairs of state. His obscurity conformed to Johnson's design for governing, and the reason generally cited by the President's intimates for the fall of Bill Moyers from presidential grace was Johnson's conclusion that Moyers was exploiting his job for personal aggrandizement. But Eisenhower's press secretary, James C. Haggerty, suffered no visible presidential displeasure for making policy announcements in his own name and, in plenipotentiary phraseology, suggesting he was given full authority to decide when to do that.

The mistakes a new Administration can make when manned by political amateurs are illustrated by certain blunders by President Nixon's Attorney General, John Mitchell. A professional in that office would never have recommended the appointment to the Supreme Court of persons as vulnerable to political assassination as were Clement Haynsworth and Harrold Carswell without protective arrangements made in advance. He would either have recommended others or checked the Haynsworth and Carswell records thoroughly and set up an effective defense of any judicial ruling, act, or speech by the nominee that was bound to give material aid to the opposition, however specious its nature. A veteran professional politician in Mitchell's job would have left the opposition Senators hard put to it to rebut the charge that their attack on the nominee was based only on his interpretations of the meaning and intent of the Constitution that did not serve the self-interest of the pressure groups to whom these Senators owe their seats.

But political amateurs, new to office, nearly always make

the mistakes of negligence (which they do not even realize is negligence) that Mitchell made in the above instances. As Mitchell has, some learn by bitter experience; others remain amateurs as long as they are retained in government, and the President who chose them for their jobs pays the price and should — especially when he is the master political pro that Nixon is. But with the upgrading of his liaison staff at the Capitol, and the reorganization that brought George P. Shultz and Robert Finch into the White House, the President has made some good use of the lessons of adversity.

But on taking office Nixon was at once confronted with the task of halting inflation and reversing it without causing a higher percentage of unemployment than Congress has the congenital fortitude to accept over the threats of reprisal by the ethnic blocs and trade unions. That his political future depends on restoring economic stability was proved by the loss of eleven Republican governorships in the 1970 elections. If events in Southeast Asia do not frustrate Nixon's de-escalation program, Vietnam will not dog his heels and trip him as it did Johnson — also demonstrated in the 1970 elections by the subordination of the war as an issue.

Some of the advisers, called by Presidents from the private sector, have exerted such influence on policies that they merit special notice in this context. But the contribution of others has become a matter of historical dispute as to what it was and whether it was taken. Hence the evaluation in their cases must await the disclosure of thus far secret memoirs and records, such as those made by the late Rear Admiral Cary T. Grayson in the Wilson era, or remain forever in the realm of speculation and mystery.

Among the unofficial White House advisers in history the tenure of Bernard M. Baruch was the longest and the most nearly nonpartisan (both Republican and Democratic Presidents sought his opinions). But it also was marked by an uneven mixture of White House regard and disregard of his counsels to Presidents, or, if these counsels were taken, by delay in acting on them until their applicability to the problems involved had become outdated.

For example, Baruch strongly advocated imposing price and wage controls when the shadow of World War II spread and darkened over this country. But the inflation they sought to check had become firmly entrenched by the time the President imposed them.

Until his election in his own right in 1948, President Truman also sought Baruch's advice. But Baruch had refused to make the campaign contribution expected of him and their relations ended with a letter in which the President upbraided Baruch for ingratitude, noting that Truman had appointed his brother as Ambassador to Portugal and the Netherlands.

Overall, however, the record disclosed a preponderance of presidential policies contrary to those Baruch had proposed. So I remarked to him on several occasions that, considering the state of the nation, either he gave lousy advice or nobody paid any attention to it. He enjoyed this kind of ribbing and frequently quoted the jibe in company.

Baruch declined several presidential offers of high government posts. But his avoidance of public office, I think, was considerably motivated by his preference for power without public accountability for its exercise. However, when requested by Presidents to do temporary piecework he was always available and obviously relished the visibility that accrues to the head man.

Dean Acheson was among the many who disliked Baruch personally and indicated the view that self-advertising, sometimes at great personal expense, accounted for the wide acceptance of his reputation as the wisest of presidential advisers. Acheson's pique over Baruch's United Nations assignment by President Truman, to negotiate away the threat of nuclear war, shows clearly in Acheson's memoirs, *Present at the Creation.*

Antecedent to the Baruch-Acheson mutual nonadmiration society was Baruch's distrust of Colonel E. M. House as President Wilson's unofficial but authorized chief emissary in the area of foreign affairs. He felt that House was pre-empting Wilson's postwar options, and warned the President that House virtually was making commitments which Wilson would find embarrassing when he got to the Paris Peace Conference. The events subsequently demonstrated that Baruch's appraisal was sound, and, when Wilson discovered this, the break with House quickly followed.

Baruch first acquired national prestige by virtue of his record as Director of the War Industries Board under Woodrow Wilson. The task to which Wilson assigned Baruch was to mobilize the country's industrial and natural resources for World War I. As a successful administrative performance it set a record that has not been surpassed. And as a new public figure, nature had made him also a prepossessing one. He was well over six feet tall and radiated a high degree of personal charm. To romantics, his patrician air and features suggested descent from the kings of Biblical times. He began his public life with a large fortune, and this made him independent of material lures that have dragged down and destroyed the influence of some persons who had at least as much wisdom in counsel as he.

After the Wilson period he became a volunteer in search of solutions of the economic problems of the nation. In 1920–21 tobacco and cotton farmers were in a desperate plight.

Baruch personally underwrote the entire cotton crop of his native state, South Carolina. He could afford to do it and lost little if anything by it. But this did not detract from the sincerity of his motivation — to save the economy of South Carolina.

The next problem he tackled was the plight of the tobacco farmers in Kentucky. The price of tobacco had fallen so low that violence broke out and was spreading to other tobacco states. Distressed growers who dumped their crops on the market to finance the barest necessities of life were punished by having their barns burned down by the so-called Night Riders — the vigilante growers who were for holding out — and the law enforcement fabric of the state of Kentucky was in tatters.

Baruch was asked by R. W. Bingham, proprietor of the *Courier-Journal* and *Times* of Louisville, to come to the rescue of the state's economy and lawful order. He organized the Kentucky Tobacco Growers Association, a cooperative; provided a brilliant New York lawyer to manage the political and legal aspects of the enterprise; and within months the income of tobacco growers rose substantially and civil peace was restored. Aided by state subsidies, the experiment was highly successful and tobacco was included in the Federal agricultural subsidies that exist today.

Baruch had one of the first fact-finding organizations ever organized and financed privately as a public service. He made its resources available to Presidents and Congress whenever requested to do so, which became more and more frequent. This assistance was, as previously noted, nonpartisan: if a presidential nominee of the opposition party called on Baruch for a factual report he was supplied with it. The shift of Congress to Democratic control in the elections of 1930 had crippled Hoover's ability to govern, and Baruch, a Democrat anyhow, concentrated on the economic counsel requested of him by his party's 1932 nominee, Franklin D. Roosevelt. Baruch's influence as a Roosevelt adviser was maintained in appearance for years, though in substance it declined because Baruch disapproved of many aspects of the First and Second New Deals.

But Roosevelt realized that when it was reported he had conferred with Baruch on a problem, this was useful public relations and helped counteract the charge that the President approached such issues with the main purpose of getting or holding votes. Baruch understood this perfectly but continued to answer presidential summonses to meetings he knew were mere formalities. Nevertheless, some of his advice with respect to mobilizing for this nation's entrance into World War II (which both Baruch and Roosevelt were confident was inevitable) eventually materialized in action such as the belated imposition of wage and price controls.

A most important source of Baruch's political influence, regardless of his status at the White House, was the United States Senate. There was good reason for this, aside from the respect of Senators for his judgment on public problems. As a congressional election approached he compiled a list of candidates for the Senate who were running for reelection (or to replace the incumbent) whose presence in Congress he deemed essential to sound legislation and to the maintenance of a viable two-party system.

At his request I helped him for several years to make this compilation, and as far as I know he never changed or deleted the names I listed. One, for instance, was Senator William Borah of Idaho, a Republican and, from Baruch's standpoint, a radical on certain issues, who was having a hard fight for reelection. To Borah and the others on the list Baruch sent considerable campaign contributions. He never asked any personal favor in return. The natural result was that these Senators sought his counsel and followed much of it. That induced Presidents, especially F. D. Roosevelt, to consult Baruch as a matter of expediency when the Senate was balking on an Executive proposal.

Baruch, of course, was well aware of a constitutional fact which enabled him to effect his purpose with the least expenditure. A friendly Senator from Nevada or Delaware has as much weight on the roll call as one from New York or California, and his campaign expenses are in reverse proportion.

Another of Baruch's public activities was to persuade highly qualified but reluctant citizens to serve the government men such as Alexander Legge of the International Harvester Corporation, John Hancock, Robert S. Brookings, and Robert A. Lovett.

Baruch became an authority on the money market when he was a very young man, beginning with an intensive study of the railroad systems in the United States. He came to know all the facts pertinent to the subject. From this study he proceeded to acquire a general knowledge of industrial economics. For instance, when the rubber shortage in World War II became critical, it was Baruch to whom Roosevelt turned for an investigation and report. When Herbert Hoover was appointed chairman of the Government Reorganization Commission by President Truman, Hoover, and his vice-chairman, Joseph P. Kennedy, Sr., consulted Baruch for assistance in formulating recommendations. This duty brought him frequently to Washington, where — not without a keen sense of what was good publicity — he interrupted a daily walk by sitting on a certain bench in Lafayette Square across from the White House. Newspaper reporters came there to interview him, and, recognizing him, passersby would engage him in friendly conversation. Though he was courteous to all, he was an expert in evading questions he did not choose to answer. One familiar device was his hearing aid which he would detach on such occasions, saying, "I'm off the air," as an amusing substitute for the clumsy evasion usual among politicians — "No comment."

Before his rebuke in 1948 by Truman, Baruch maintained close, though at times superficial, relations with the President. But when Eisenhower replaced Truman these relations were renewed in the degree they had existed when Wilson occupied the White House.

Baruch was a strong supporter of the Marshall Plan and of the original intent of the Truman Doctrine to concentrate on nonmilitary aid to peoples, outside the clear security perimeter of the United States, threatened by "external aggression or internal subversion." When American foreign policy, including what Washington termed "entangling alliances," was totally reversed by the North Atlantic military alliance, Senators who anxiously consulted Baruch about possible consequences found him convinced the treaty was an essential recognition of the changed situation in the world. But on the President's proposal for military and material aid to Greece and Turkey, Baruch protested that the British, whose withdrawal of military and economic assistance had moved the President to assume the burden, were well able to afford the protection they claimed was no longer within their means.

Eisenhower, while Chief of Staff after the war, often sought out Baruch for advice on military problems arising out of the cold war. As president of Columbia University, Ike broadened the topics of consultation to such domestic matters as the trend toward the Welfare State and Southern denial of the right of Negroes to unobstructed voting in all elections.

When Baruch died at ninety-three he was firmly established in the public mind as elder statesman and the adviser of Presidents, though that was to some extent an exaggeration. "Adviser" means to most people one whose advice is generally taken, whereas over a long period in Roosevelt's and Truman's time his advice was not taken at all.

Roosevelt eventually began to refer to him as "Old Bernie," indicating also he was a nuisance, a butter-in who exploited the publicity of summonses to the White House that had become a mere formality. It is quite true that, pretending he shunned publicity, Baruch enjoyed it. This tactic is very effective with the press. If one in the public eye pretends he dislikes the spotlight, the press is more active in turning it on him.

This tactic was, of course, well known to Herbert Bayard Swope who, as Baruch's public relations adviser, made brilliant use of it. When Truman appointed Baruch as spokesman for the United States on atomic energy controls at the United Nations, it was Swope who wrote the dramatic introduction that begins, "The choice we face is between the quick and the dead."

I suppose Baruch at times dreamed of the presidency, but he knew well he never could attain it. He was very rich; he had made his money as a Wall Street speculator; he was a Jew; and he was practical enough to assess all this as three strikes against him before even going to the plate. He could have been Secretary of the Treasury in the Wilson Administration, but he declined the President's proffer of that post because, as a practical and loyal Wilson man, he knew — and so advised Wilson — that the appointment would be politically damaging to the President. He would have liked the opportunity for public service and the prestige the office would give him, and to that extent the self-denial was painful. But he did not aspire to being a Senator or a Governor, being well content with the general public acceptance of him as a leading elder statesman and "the adviser of Presidents."

Joseph E. Davies was a personal friend from the days of the formation of the College Men For Wilson group in 1912. The first time I met him was in Milwaukee where he was practicing law. In those days there were no Gallup polls. Instead, reporters went to a number of key states and talked to people who were in a position to sense the local issues and evaluate which candidates these issues would benefit.

Beginning in 1910 I made this biennial survey for the *Courier-Journal,* traveling with Frank R. Kent of the *Baltimore Sun.* In Milwaukee we checked the usual sources — reporters, professional politicians, editors, etc. — and were told that a lawyer, Joseph E. Davies, was the head of the Wilson collegiate group, with headquarters at the Plankinton Hotel. There, standing on the sidewalk in front of the hotel, was a man in his early thirties garbed in clothes and boots of apparently London craftsmanship, and twirling a malacca cane. Completing this impressive outfit were a homburg, and a black tie embellished with a pearl. And that young man, we were informed, was Davies. He proved to be an accurate forecaster of Wilson's victory in Wisconsin.

Years afterward, he went to Soviet Russia as U.S. Ambassador — he also was our envoy to Belgium in the course of his diplomatic career — to give the Soviets their second acquaintance with American plutocrats. Averell Harriman in his youth was the first. Davies had married a fabulously rich woman, Marjorie Post Close Hutton. And she brought to and bought for the Embassy priceless objets d'art, and Embassy entertaining was lavish. As a diplomat Davies, I think, was taken in by the Soviet professions of devotion to democracy and world peace. But he was a man of good will and a sound patriot.

Yet his success in love and business made him the butt of unkind jests. After the Wilson Administration, during which he was chairman of the Federal Trade Commission, Davies established a law firm with a former Ohio Congressman, a rough diamond sort, Timothy W. Ansberry. They acquired very desirable clients whom they represented successfully with the government. One day John Lord O'Brian, whom I esteem the most distinguished lawyer and classic liberal of our time, returned to the capital from Buffalo to assume one of his many tours of duty in the government. O'Brian had a close friend, Judge William Hitz, of the District Federal Court, celebrated for his saturnine wit. Hitz met O'Brian at the train. O'Brian said, "Hitz, I see that the firm of Davies & Ansberry has dissolved partnership. What happened?" Hitz replied, "Their lawyer died."

Many years later when I had become a member of the famous Table at the Metropolitan Club, among those who always lunched there were Davies and James B. Reynolds. Reynolds, known for his wit, had been an Assistant Secretary of the Treasury under President Coolidge and for years was Secretary of the Republican National Committee. One day he was needling Davies — how rich and important his clients were, how lavish their retainers. Davies, finally nettled, said, "My record at the bar is as clean as a hound's tooth!" Reynolds responded, "When did it come back from the laundry?"

Another time, Reynolds said to Davies, "Joe, I just read your book *Mission to Moscow*. I want to congratulate you on that book. I think you should write another." "You do?" said Davies trustingly. "Yes," answered Reynolds, "and I have a title all ready for it." Davies inquired what it was. Said Reynolds, "Sub*mission to Moscow*."

Davies eventually realized the true nature and aggressive world aspirations of Russian Communism. But he long continued to hope for a peaceful and honorable relation with the West. On retirement from the foreign service he bought Tregoran, a great estate in Washington that he sought to bequeath to the government as a permanent residence for the Vice-President. Congress declined the offer. On this estate Davies built a dacha, a Russian country house, and moved into it from the palatial main house after his marriage to Marjorie Post Close Hutton ended in divorce. He died after protracted illness — a sad old man, living alone among distinguished and well-merited trophies of his political, romantic, and diplomatic career.

In 1951 Davies was sent by President Truman to Paris to sound out General Eisenhower as to whether he would accept Truman's support for the Democratic presidential nomination in 1952. (Later, of course, Truman sounded out Eisenhower himself. The controversy over the factual basis for the story I wrote about those activities is past history but Davies confirmed it later in an article in the *Diplomat*, a Washington magazine.) When Davies returned from this errand he informed the President that not only had Eisenhower reiterated he never would engage in active politics, but he also had cited the Democratic party's alliance with organized labor as a reason he could not affiliate with it. Truman denied my report of his firsthand approach to Eisenhower after it appeared in the *New York Times* on November 7, 1951. But in both his memoirs and Eisenhower's there is ample verification of Truman's approaches to the General. And no denial was made of Davies's account of his mission to Paris at Truman's behest.

Joseph P. Kennedy, Sr., not only dreamed of being President: he once actively promoted efforts to the end that he

would be installed in the White House as the first Roman
Catholic. With the early vanishing of that aspiration, he
transferred it to his sons, first to his eldest and namesake and,
on young Joe's death in a bomb-laden plane in World War II,
to his second son. He had no ambition to be a Senator or
Governor, offices that were easily within his grasp.

He found great satisfaction in his appointment by President
F. D. Roosevelt to be the first chairman of the SEC. This
choice was made on the argument by Baruch and others, that
Kennedy knew all the tricks of the trade, the sins as well as
the virtues of the market, and could be counted on to ad-
minister the office with the integrity, impartiality, and self-
lessness that were required. This prophecy was thoroughly
borne out by the record. Kennedy, because of his intimate
knowledge of the ways of Wall Street, used the powers of his
office with special effectiveness in the institution of reforms
that were long overdue, with the result that he policed the
money markets as they had never been before and never
expected to be; but they are ever delicately probing the
durability of Kennedy's disciplines.

From the standpoint of Roosevelt's political interest, Kennedy was of enormous value. His influence was great with the
Catholic hierarchy; cardinals and even popes sought and
heeded his counsels. He was valuable to Roosevelt also as a
"no" man who would not hesitate to say to the President, "If
you do such-and-such you will live to regret it." And he had a
standing in the business community that served the President
well when, as a candidate for reelection in 1936, Roosevelt
faced an active, well-funded opposition from the financial and
industrial communities.

At the President's request, Kennedy formed an organization
called Businessmen for Roosevelt and wrote a book, *I'm For
Roosevelt*, which set out to prove that FDR had saved

the capitalist system in the First New Deal — as he had — and that his reelection offered the best prospect that business would be restored to a sound, profitable condition and the Depression ended.

Another political asset Kennedy acquired for Roosevelt stemmed from his influence with the big city bosses, many of whom were Irish Catholics. He used it to get their essential help for the President's congressional programs, some of which were saved from defeat thereby.

From the American Revolution forward, beginning with Franklin and Dickinson, Pennsylvania seems to have produced more than its share of colorful characters directly or tangentially aligned with politics, business, statesmanship, and diplomacy. From all four there emerged the justly celebrated Alexander P. Moore, also of Pittsburgh, who was prominent in the pro-T. Roosevelt group in 1912. As Ambassador to Spain, in a later period, he projected the image of a "plain American businessman" to the degree that his remarks to royal Bourbon-Hapsburgs, including King Alphonso XIII, and his Queen, were happily received by Spaniards as conforming to their concept of all Americans as down-to-earth "folks."

One day, while traveling with the King, Moore attended a *fiera* in a large city where Alphonso was greeted with a tumultuously friendly reception. "What do you think of that?" the King asked Moore. "King," he answered, slapping the monarch encouragingly on the back, "I think you'll be elected."

During the 1912 preconvention Republican campaign Moore came into the lobby of the Ritz. It was apparent that his name, much less his importance, was unknown to the reservation clerk, who dithered for a moment about whether a suite was available. "Listen, son," boomed Moore, "I'm expecting some calls, so get me located right away. When Judge Gary [chairman of the U.S. Steel Corporation] calls, put him through. When Colonel Theodore Roosevelt calls, I want to speak to him at once. When Miss Lillian Russell calls, send her up to the suite."

The calls followed according to schedule because: Moore was one of the largest stockholders of U.S. Steel. Moore was one of T.R.'s principal backers and largest contributors to the campaign fund of the Bull Moose party. And Moore was engaged to Miss Russell, whom soon afterward he married.

The rumor that the haughty clerk fainted has not been thoroughly verified. But it could have happened.

Averell Harriman's dual campaign contribution (to FDR and to Willkie) in 1940 came at a time when he was zigzagging along the dividing party line, before he finally became an intensely partisan Democrat. But Harriman already had demonstrated both perceptiveness and ability in various ways. With the late James V. Forrestal, he as Ambassador to the USSR was the first high government official to forecast that postwar Soviet foreign policy would be deliberately inimical to the United States. He had successfully reorganized the Union Pacific Railroad, revealing an administrative talent that gave distinction to his tenure as Secretary of Commerce in Roosevelt's Cabinet.

But after leaving government service when the Nixon Administration took office, Harriman, in reversal of all the rules by which Washington consigns has-beens to oblivion in the press, continued to attract a large share of the headlines. He accomplished this by assiduous attention to his press relations, constantly entertaining reporters and commentators with the lavishness that only a very rich man can afford and being ever available for interviews in the press and on television where the friendly beneficiaries of his hospitality abound. He took full advantage of the reverent publicity that media seem instinctively disposed to accord to the fabulously wealthy, especially to one who possesses good looks and great personal charm.

Yet as a diplomat he never managed a treaty that was enforceable by the United States, and he played a vital part in the Kennedy-Johnson Southeast Asia policy by which the United States was engulfed in the Indochinese adventure. But, despite this record, he sustained his reputation as an oracle on foreign affairs. On one occasion in May 1970, his picture illustrated a *New York Times* news dispatch that made no reference to him whatsoever.

The omission of the paragraph pertinent to Harriman was traceable to the printers, whose deliberate slowdown was creating such oddities in the *Times*'s news report. But whenever he, even tangentially, is mentioned in news reports it is almost a habit of news editors to illustrate the dispatch with his picture — even though in this instance the mention failed to survive the journey from the typewriter to the linotype machine. This is the consequence of a good public relations job indeed.

While opposition to the transfer to the United Kingdom of the overage destroyers was gathering, I received a telephone call from Wendell L. Willkie who was resting at Colorado Springs, preparatory to beginning his 1940 presidential campaign. He informed me that Archibald MacLeish had approached Russell Davenport, Willkie's public relations aide, with a message from President Roosevelt. It was, that, in the interest of national security, Willkie would refrain from making a campaign issue of the transfer plan.

At my request MacLeish clarified the incident in a letter dated October 23, 1968. "Actually," he wrote, "Mr. Willkie was wrong in telling you over the phone that I approached Davenport on Mr. Roosevelt's behalf. On the contrary, what I was trying (presumptuous, no doubt) to do was to prepare myself for one more approach to FDR on the destroyer proposal which Bob Sherwood and I and others had been working on, as you know, for some time previous. I was, in other words, pretty well off-base and your friendliness to the whole project was heartening rather than otherwise."

This reference was to a column I wrote associating Mac-Leish favorably with the proposal, a column I had been told impelled the President to urge MacLeish not even to *seem* to be in company with me, especially on a matter of policy the President was inclined to view with disfavor. MacLeish dismissed this report, writing, "The only impression I recall forming as to Mr. Roosevelt's attitude toward you was that it was very much like your attitude toward him insofar as I could determine it."

Anyhow, in response to Willkie's request for my counsel, I advised him as follows: Whatever your viewpoint may be, do not in any way take a public position for or against the transfer. Merely decline to commit yourself, though I also think you should not oppose the project. If you send or relay a reply, suggest that the matter of the transfer is wholly in the area of the President's sole responsibility as commander-in-chief.

Whether the counsel was good or bad, Willkie followed it.

A full-length biography would be required to enumerate the selfless and eminent services John Lord O'Brian has contributed to the United States. But one is typical of them all. The episode begins with a telephone call to O'Brian from

Attorney General (later Associate Supreme Court Justice) Robert H. Jackson in the Christmas season of 1940.

O'Brian had again returned from a government assignment to his law practice in Buffalo. Jackson informed him that President Roosevelt was about to set up the two-headed Knudsen-Hillman Office of Production Management, the precursor of the War Production Board, and had chosen O'Brian as general counsel. He would not take "no" for an answer.

According to Jackson, the job would pay $15,000 a year (the actual figure turned out to be $9,000) and O'Brian's annual earning from his law practice at this period was about $90,000. On the sole condition that he would be released by the end of 1941 O'Brian bowed to the summons and became general counsel of the WPB when this agency replaced the OPM.

Before his specified service of one year was concluded, however, the Japanese attacked Pearl Harbor and O'Brian remained at his post for five years, or until the mission of the WPB had been brilliantly fulfilled.

5

The Congress

PRIOR TO WORLD WAR II, there were many more colorful characters in Congress than today — some only because they "looked like Senators": Clyde Hoey of North Carolina, tall, gray-haired, frock-coated; James Frazier of Tennessee, tall, frock-coated, with his widow's peak, his right hand ever cradled under his left lapel. But an example of the true color that is bone-deep was Elihu Root. He was of normal height, dynamic neither in speech nor gait, but he possessed a mind and a presence that overawed the Senate, the judges before whom he practiced, and the galleries to which he never cast a glance. When a frown appeared below the bang that terminated his hairdo, Senators who were thinking of "asking him to yield" forsook their intention.

Joseph W. Bailey of Texas was another frock-coated Senator. But he was a titan, a loud and voluble orator, often terrifying his colleagues by his boldness and his brilliance, yet he was less effective than his talents merited because often he had not done his homework. Once Bailey attempted to bully Senator John Sharp Williams of Mississippi, a small man but with the steady gray eyes that in Southern novels and movies of the Old West are standard equipment of characters who are quick on the draw. His rejoinder to Bailey was quietly spoken but so mercilessly devastating that Bailey made no attempt to reply. Williams, a superb analytical orator, relied on satire in controversial debate, Bailey on invective delivered in tones of thunder.

Bailey's colleague was Charles A. Culberson, who by contrast was slight of stature and rarely raised his voice. But his dignity, intellect, and typed Southern gentility captured the Senate's attention whenever he rose to speak.

The appearances of Georgia's two Senators during this same period were even more traditionally senatorial, but in their case this was a wrapping around unusually high intellect and character. One was Augustus Bacon, a huge, bald man with a walrus moustache; the other Alexander Stephens Clay, the father of General Lucius Clay, slender, with a thatch of gray pompadour, reminding one of the portraits of Andrew Jackson. These, with John A. Morgan of Alabama, gave the impression — as years afterward Walter George of Georgia also did — of having been born to match the ideal of what a Senator should look like. McEnery of Louisiana, by the time I knew him, was a small, stooped man with a short white beard, but there was steel beneath, glinting with flashes of his dashing past. He had been a high Confederate officer, credited with daring exploits, and shades of the greatest American tragedy enveloped him. Yet, as was common among such men, McEnery reserved for private association a delightful sense of humor and a gift of wit.

One day Senator Ollie James of Kentucky and I encountered him in the Rotunda of the Capitol. Said James, "Do you think I ought to tell the old man?" to which I replied affirmatively. So, after the customary Southern exchange of amenities, James said, "Senator, your fly is open." "Oh, thank you, Senator," McEnery replied and buttoned up (zippers had not been invented). Completing the repairs he quietly observed, "It may fall out, but it will never jump out again."

But the colorful characteristics of members of Congress in those days were not exclusively the possession of those from the South. There was, for example, an unforgettable Senator from Chicago, James Hamilton Lewis, who, though Georgia-born, had spent most of his life in Washington State and Illinois. He was a brilliant debater and at times a statesman. He was referred to by everyone as "Jim Ham"; he wore an auburn toupee to match a beard and moustache dyed to effect conformity. As he grew older he gradually modified these adornments with a growing tint of gray — a notable triumph of cosmetics.

But to be colorful was and is not a requisite to fame and effectiveness in Congress. A member of the House who was dry as dust in his parliamentary person, but one of the ablest and most influential men ever to sit in Congress, was John J. Fitzgerald of Brooklyn. He was chairman of the Appropriations Committee in the first Wilson Administration. None was more knowledgeable in the procedures and the rules of either branch. Fitzgerald was no orator; he spoke with a rasping Brooklyn accent. But when he took the floor his colleagues listened with utmost respect and his score of attainment was high indeed.

That congressional power and effectiveness could be achieved without the toga which in fancy seemed to drape most of the Southern legislators was proved by some of the Northerners. Representative Sereno E. Payne of New York, chairman of the Ways and Means Committee in several Congresses with Republican majorities, had a bull-like voice, and a massive abdomen that caused him to walk like a duck. He was coauthor, with Senator Nelson W. Aldrich of Rhode Island, of the tariff bill that split the Republican party from 1912 to 1916 and hence was greatly responsible for the election of Woodrow Wilson in 1912.

It was Payne's abdomen that inspired the Washington correspondent of the Memphis *Commercial Appeal* to lend luster to the output of the press gallery in the Taft Administration. This reporter, Robert Gates, described Payne in the heat of the House debate over the fateful tariff bill as follows: "Then, striding down the aisle came Chairman Sereno E. Payne of New York, shaking his bowels at the enemy."

This joyous bit of reporting was of a piece with a famous lead paragraph in a dispatch to the *Philadelphia Record* by its correspondent, Maurice Splain. Its wit and literary quality certainly match any to be found in Washington correspondence today. The Senate had revolted against the despotic rule of Senators Nelson Aldrich, Eugene Hale of Maine, and Boies Penrose of Pennsylvania, the Republican bosses whose word was law, and repudiated them three times in one session. Splain's report of this sensational event began: "A brood of young revolutions hatched explosively in the Senate today. When the repercussions ended there were to be seen, hanging from their political fences, the deflated forms of Boies Penrose, Nelson W. Aldrich and Eugene Hale."

Penrose (a Harvard graduate magna cum laude) was a big, red-faced burly man. He spoke with a curious accent I could not place geographically, but finally discovered it was old, highborn Philadelphian. "I" was pronounced "Oy," "star" became "storr," and the "r's" resounded in every word that included them.

He possessed a bludgeoning wit, and especially enjoyed using it against the Republican Senate Progressives whom Senator George Moses of New Hampshire dubbed "Sons of the Wild Jackass." Foremost among these was the elder Robert LaFollette of Wisconsin. Once, after LaFollette had attacked Penrose for "bossism" with respect to pending legislation, Penrose lumbered to his feet and proceeded gravely to read LaFollette's record of attendance in the Senate, which was practically nil. Since the subject under discussion was a bill on which arduous committee work had been done, Penrose's mocking statistics demolished LaFollette's qualifications to appraise the legislation.

In his private person Penrose was a delightfully congenial companion. Once I was sitting between him and John N. Garner at the Washington Senators' ball park. At the end of the seventh inning, the spectators, according to custom, rose as a body to take the seventh-inning stretch; and the umpire, also according to custom, took a whisk broom from his hip pocket and dusted off home plate. Penrose, ponderously resuming his seat, remarked to Garner, "If we had thought about it in Philadelphia, we would have made that a city job."

Penrose was a lifelong bachelor, a condition which evoked an incident that exemplified both his cynical cunning and his tactics in keeping happy the Pennsylvania political machine he dominated. This incident occurred when certain representatives of the machine called on Penrose to report that gossip about his private life — "of course, unfounded, Senator" — was spreading among the women of Pennsylvania, and suggested it would be advisable if Penrose entered upon matrimonial bliss. The Senator listened gravely and then replied, "I will marry any lady the organization can agree on." Needless to say, this mission impossible was not undertaken.

During the preliminaries of the 1912 presidential campaign, William Flynn, of Pittsburgh, led an intensive and successful effort to capture for Theodore Roosevelt the Republican delegation from Pennsylvania. This effort was accompanied by charges of corruption in the regular Republican organization, which was committed to the renomination of President Taft. Penrose, in ways known to him, acquired a coded telegram signed by Flynn, outlining strategies that fell far short of the ethical standards which the Pittsburgh boss had charged were wholly lacking in the Penrose organization. Arising in the Senate, Penrose, stone-faced as usual, and translating the coded words as he went, began with the first sentence: "Posy does not shout friskiness," which turned out to be a highly ruthless proposition. The Senate followed the translation with delight, the political community similarly responded, and, though T.R. got the delegates, Flynn's claim that a halo encircled the movement in Roosevelt's behalf in Pennsylvania dissolved in gales of laughter.

Henry Watterson used to say that the cavaliers of the North were the people of Maine, that they shared with Kentucky the love of hard liquor (while voting for prohibition), beautiful women, and horse racing. The analogy applied at least to the two Maine Senators of my early newspapers days — William Pierce Frye and Eugene Hale. In appearance and dress Frye suggested an antebellum Southern planter, but his humor and accent were of the down-to-earth Yankee variety, as witness a happening when Frye was in the chair as President pro tem of the Senate.

Senator George Vest of Missouri — annoying but brilliant, a great orator whose organ tones rolled from a height of only four feet eleven inches — addressed an insulting question to the chair. Frye pretended not to see him; Vest repeated his "parliamentary inquiry"; finally Frye leaned down to the clerk on the tier below and in a whisper, audible as far as the galleries, asked, "Is that little son-of-a-bitch standin' up or sittin' down?"

In more recent times Tom Connally of Texas was among the diminishing number of Southern Senators who looked the part. The resemblance did not go much further because Connally was rougher in debate than the old aristocrats, and not as well versed in the complex Senate rules. But he had the respect of his colleagues and firmly exercised the great prestige and power that goes with the office of chairman of the Committee on Foreign Relations.

But not so much as did another Foreign Relations chairman, a Republican, Arthur H. Vandenberg of Michigan. He was foremost among those few leaders who turned his party's foreign policy back from isolation and was largely responsible for such bipartisanship as there can be in that area — limited because, as once noted by Harold E. Stassen, no Administration in power gives the opposition a full share in any success its foreign policy may have, only in its failures. When the Republicans carried Congress in 1946, at the outset of the Truman Administration, Vandenberg, as the new chairman of the FRC, demanded, as Stassen put it, "participation in the take-offs instead of merely in the crash landings." He laid claim to and at times was given partnership in the formulation of foreign policy, an arrangement whereby both the Administration and the Senate would share the credit and/or the blame.

Loud of voice and given to heavy underlining of key words, he was disposed to make the welkin ring — on the Senate floor and on the hustings. He was large of head and frame. He smiled most of the time. He was a good companion at the table (though women were not exactly entranced with his habit of smoking cigars from the soup to the savory). And, next to the practice of the political art and association with lovely ladies, he most enjoyed general conversation. I don't recall a more powerful and effective occupant of his chairmanship when Congress was controlled by one major party and the President belonged to the other.

Vandenberg's romantic impulses led to gossip at Washington hen-parties, where the hens have teeth and the teeth are sharp, that Vandenberg had been "converted" from isolationism by the pretty wife of a West European diplomat, a lady of whom, as the saying goes, he "saw a lot." But in my judgment, based on many private conversations, his shift to internationalism was an honest change of mind and his evangelism for the new internationalist religion a call of conscience.

Senator E. D. ("Cotton Ed") Smith of South Carolina was the archetype of the Southern politician born of humble station who swayed the masses with what John Garner described as "bloviating." He often was unintentionally amusing, but always was craftily parochial, knew all the tricks of demagogy, and was proficient in performing them. He reflected, with klieg lights, the feelings of his community on racial equality, and maintaining a flourishing cotton economy. As a raconteur he could convulse his rural constituency. My longtime *Times* colleague Turner Catledge does an impersonation of Cotton Ed, explaining to his constituents why he walked out of a Democratic national convention, that has become justly famous.

One of the more inspired of the phrases Catledge attributes to the Senator occurs in an account of Smith's comment on the appearance on the platform of a Negro minister to deliver the invocation: "He was as black as melted midnight!" Other immortal passages in the impersonation describe Cotton Ed's consternation as more and more Negroes sat down among the delegates: "Why gentlemen, the Democratic convention looked like a checkerbo'd. . . . I had just come from the funeral of a Senator, a great Senator, a *Southern* Senator. Senator Fletcher of Florida. My feet were sore with walkin' the streets of the convention city. But when I saw that Negro preacher, and those black men on the floor of the Democratic convention, I got up and I began to walk. And I walked and I walked and I kept on walkin' to the door on my pore sore feet, and I walked out the door, and, folks, I never went back."

Smith's type of oratory was compactly described by Samuel G. Blythe in his Washington correspondence to the *Saturday Evening Post:* "His name is Ellison *Du*-rant Smith. That's what he do."

Cotton Ed followed the established pattern of South Carolina politics. But a harbinger of the change in the pattern was his successor Olin Johnston. He managed to seem to preserve the old standard while deviating from it in favor of all New Deal legislation except that dealing with "civil rights." Like Smith, a "walker out" of a Democratic convention, he surprised me in the early Fifties by praising Hubert H. Humphrey whose passionate equal rights speech had been responsible for the exodus of the Southern Democrats from the convention hall in 1948.

Encountering Johnston in the Stephens Hotel lobby during the 1956 convention that renominated Adlai Stevenson, I asked him how he came to speak so approvingly of a Northern liberal with the civil rights views Humphrey had. "He's changing," said Johnston. "You watch. I've converted him and he's changing."

In the light of subsequent events, Johnston may have been right in his conclusion. Nevertheless, I had it on good authority that, though Johnston had a table for ten at a Democratic dinner featuring Humphrey and subsequent to our conversation, he was ostentatiously absent, explaining to a friend, "I was afraid my wife might have to sit next to a Nee-gro."

The political progenitors of the Southern civil rights dissenters were Senators from Mississippi — James K. Vardaman and Theodore Bilbo. I had more respect for the former because it seemed to me that he could and at times did rise above vote-getting expediency, which Bilbo never did. I did not and do not disagree with their opposition to overall compulsory racial integration, but there are worthy and unworthy paths to the same position, and I recall none trod by Bilbo that was not wholly demagogic.

An aspect of the controversy fired by the Supreme Court's 1954 public schools integration order strongly suggests that the most vociferous and militant pro-integrationists are more concerned with getting political power than the human "equality" in all areas of the American society they assert as their true goal. Including the blacks among them, these activists do not attack black separatism — a factually authentic movement — with anything like the vigor they bring to their assault on white separatism. Except for Whitney Young and Roy Wilkins, the black separatism movement, with its inevitable concomitant of bloc voting, has received only a tap on the wrist from black as well as white "liberals." Yet it is as anti-egalitarian as any other kind.

The mention of Vardaman brings to mind two stories of the kind that enliven the dreary round of political reporting. The first was incidental to the Democratic national convention at Denver in 1908. As aforesaid, Senator James Hamilton Lewis of Illinois was a true wit. He and Vardaman had rooms on a court, their windows facing each other, in the Brown Palace Hotel. After a nightlong session of the Resolutions Committee of which both Senators were members they returned to their quarters and prepared for bed. Chancing to glance out of his window across the court Lewis beheld Vardaman, standing before a full-length mirror, wearing only a facial expression of interest in the reflection he beheld. In the mellifluous tones with which he bewitched the Senate and the ladies, Lewis called across to his colleague on the Resolutions Committee, "Senator, do you 'point with pride' or 'view with alarm'?"

The second tale deals with Senator Thomas J. Heflin of

Alabama, a political rogue and demagogue of unusual delin-
quency whose targets were Negroes and the Pope. But like all
country Southern politicians Heflin had a certain outrageous
and winning bravado and he, as a raconteur, was exceptionally gifted. He was loud, narrow, vindictive, not very
brave, but he had enough brass in his construction to supply
all of Caesar's legions with their greaves and breastplates.

These attributes were compactly illustrated by his performance in the Senate Democratic cloakroom just before an
Alabama primary, in which he was a candidate for renomination, as the hour (midnight) drew near for potential competitors to file their entries or thereafter hold their peace. One
Alabama Democrat had threatened to file, and it was established he would be a dangerous opponent. Beginning about
eight o'clock, Heflin began a series of telephone calls to the
State capital from the cloakroom. "Let me know," he said
each time, "if someone files."

No return call came as the clock ticked on, with Heflin's
uneasiness increasing in the full sight of a number of amused
colleagues. A few minutes before the bodeful hour Heflin,
unable longer to endure the suspense, again phoned Montgomery for news, saying he would hold on until the deadline.
When midnight arrived and passed Heflin turned to the
onlookers, now stricken with uncontrollable laughter, and,
naming the citizen whose opposition he obviously feared,
exclaimed, "That's lucky for him. Of course I'd have beat
the ———— out of him."

Another Louisiana Senator of note, who became the Chief
Justice of the United States, was Edward Douglas White. His
physical presence was massively impressive, and he had in
perfection the combination of dignity and courteous manner
that distinguishes the breed. This gives point to an anecdote
involving Charles Evans Hughes when he was Chief Justice.

Hughes restricted his social activities to Saturday night. On this occasion he was the guest of Mrs. Alice Roosevelt Longworth. Among the other guests was Representative Walter Gresham (Ham) Andrews of Buffalo, who was feeling a bit exhilarated. Said Andrews, "Governor, Judge, Mr. Secretary, Mr. Chief Justice — what do I call you anyway?" The great man's bearded lips parted in what some irreverently described as his "wolfish grin," and in a cutting tone he replied: "Someone asked that question once of Chief Justice White, noting that he had been a Confederate general, a Senator from Louisiana, and an Associate Justice of the Supreme Court beforehand. And he replied, 'people who don't know me call me Eddie.'" "Well, hello Charlie," boomed the unabashed Andrews. And with Hughes's forced laugh the horrified group around them unfroze.

On another Saturday night, when Hughes was a dinner guest at the Rumanian legation, he more patently was not amused by a jest at his expense. On the previous Monday he had spoken for the Court in ruling that, though President Roosevelt's repeal by Executive order of the gold clause in government and private contracts was unconstitutional, it conferred no right on the plaintiff to sue the government in the Court of Claims because his financial loss was minimal. In this indirect manner the repeal was sustained. Mrs. Longworth, her eyes sparkling with mischief, said to the Chief Justice, "Oh that gold decision! Pragmatic sanctions!" Hughes was unable to manage even that "wolfish" grin.

Pressures from home necessarily exert powerful influence on a member of Congress. If a constituency sufficiently indicates how it desires him [for "him" hereafter read "him or her"] to vote on a pending bill, the theory of representative government usually yields to his desire to be reelected, and to the self-persuasion that the country needs him in office in the overall national interest.

There are a few notable instances of legislators who have served the concept that they are sworn to represent their constituencies as their principles and consciences dictate, whether or not their constituencies disagree at the time. A celebrated example of this high-mindedness in elective politics was related by John F. Kennedy in the book he published before he became President, *Profiles in Courage.* His principal was Edmond Gibson Ross, a Senator from Kansas, and the issue was whether the Senate should impeach President Andrew Johnson.

Ross was disposed to vote "aye" and thereby oust Johnson from the presidency. But he also felt his oath of office required him to see that the defense was allowed all the facilities for a fair Senate trial of the House's charges on which the impeachment was based, and that evidence offered by the defense which was ruled out by the tribunal should be included in the hearings. When this was taken in Kansas as proof of indecision by Ross as to how he would vote, he was subjected to enormous pressure — by telegrams and letters, growing more and more violent and abusive, by the Kansas press, by constituents who came to Washington, by emotional meetings held in Kansas — to support the impeachment.

Eventually Ross decided that Johnson was not being given a fair trial under the rules that had been adopted in the Senate. He wrote, "I have taken an oath to do impartial justice according to the Constitution and laws, and trust that I shall have the courage to vote according to the dictates of my judgment and for the highest good of the country." And on two motions he voted against the conviction of the President, creating the negative majority of one.

Of those votes, he said, "I almost literally looked down into my open grave. Friendships, position, fortune, everything that makes life desirable . . . were about to be swept away by the breath of my mouth, perhaps forever."

He was excoriated in Kansas and hung in effigy; his name was a hissing and a byword. He left the state for New Mexico, after two unsuccessful contests for office, and was appointed by President Grover Cleveland as Governor of the territory. Before Ross died he was sent a message by the Governor of Kansas and the legislature expressing appreciation of the stand he had taken in the Johnson impeachment trial and praising him for his courage. But it was too late to repair the damage that had been done to him for adhering to the concept that the national interest, as he saw it, must prevail over a current emotion which had seized an overwhelming majority of his constituents.

On a far less tragic level was Senator J. W. Fulbright's break with President Lyndon Johnson over the Vietnamese War. His rising demand that the bombing of North Vietnam be permanently ended and the United States combat forces be rapidly reduced to the point of complete withdrawal, regardless of whether there would be reciprocal action by the enemy, was widely denounced in the press and among the American people, and for a time he was a pariah in the Senate Democratic cloakroom. He found justification for abatement of his demands in President Nixon's announcement of a graduated timetable for withdrawal in Vietnam, though he had proposed getting out faster. But at all times Fulbright showed great political courage, for he had, over a long period, risked his standing as a popular national figure, and attrition of the power he wielded as chairman of the Foreign Relations Committee. And it was a long time before his insurgency against the President of his own party began to attract influential recruits, culminating in the historic 1970 ban by Congress on the use of American combat forces and military advisers in Cambodia. This, despite the fact that it was Fulbright who sponsored the Gulf of Tonkin resolution on which LBJ claimed Senate advance approval of his escalation of the war.

Pressures from constituents which take the form of a deluge of letters and telegrams that plainly are spontaneous, and therefore as plainly not the product of an organized solicitation, are also among the activities that shape the voting record of members of Congress. Communications of this type and magnitude are even more effective than the commercial polls because the latter are shaped by the type of question submitted to the voters and the former are an automatic reaction of individual citizens.

But any catalogue of the persuasions applied to legislators must include two which at times have proved to be the most effective of all. One is supplied by lobbyists, usually equipped with deductible expense accounts, whose concerns range from action or inaction, in the interest of pressure groups, to performance in the general public interest. Every day, in the offices and corridors of the Capitol, some member of Congress is beset with requests of the one kind or the other, and this lobbying extends into all the government departments and into the White House itself.

In one way or another all lobbyists have connections, with business, labor, popular groups, or influential constituents — these often the source of campaign funds — that gain them at the very least an attentive hearing from the objects of their pressure. And one of the commonest aspects of lobbying is the invitation, more often than not gladly accepted, to lunch or dine, attend an agreeable party or get a free ride on a private plane belonging to a company deeply interested in the outcome of legislation.

Another, but invisible, aspect of lobbying in Washington is a relationship between an important member of Congress (or of the Administration) and a lobbyist whose political philosophy is at total variance — publicly — with that of the member. There are very many instances of these under-the-table relationships in Washington, and they well serve the personal interest of each principal. Sometimes they take an extreme form. An influential member of Congress or the Executive, with no apparent means to entertain hundreds of people lavishly at a reception, début, or wedding, is host at such an affair — all but the début being an annual event. But by the employment of discreet measures the tab for the event is passed on to a lobbyist (he can be and frequently is a lawyer) for or against legislative projects that come before the host in his governmental capacity. This makes for the kind of valuable Washington friendship in which the host keeps his benefactor thoroughly and valuably posted on the course of a legislative or administrative matter in which the lobbyist has a deep personal or commercial interest. And the lobbyist-legislator relationship is crassly exploited by the party campaign committees which solicit lobbyists to buy seats at fund-raising dinners, the more (it is made clear) the wiser for the interest the lobbyist represents.

But no lobbyist can be as effective as the members of Congress themselves. In the national legislature there are bankers, market speculators, real estate operators, lawyers who still get cuts from the earnings of their firms, etc., that vote directly on legislation affecting their own private interests. Those whose consciences impel them to abstain from voting on legislation by which they may profit or lose are a rare breed. And though various reform proposals have been made, such as excluding members from committees which have jurisdiction in areas where their substantial personal interests are involved, none as yet has been adopted. And when Congress as a whole votes lavish increases in its salaries and perquisites, as happened in 1970 in the midst of floor outcries for action to stem inflation, Congress becomes the most powerful lobbyist in its own behalf.

The Communications Act of 1934, as amended, is another shining illustration of congressional self-promotion. By the lenient terms of the statute the licensed electronic stations — many gathered into the network structures — are given without compensation one of the richest public properties existing: the air. This free use is compounded by the fact that television and radio enter intimately into the homes of the tens of millions who have bought transmittal devices, and depend on electronic media for spot-news bulletins of events as the programmers choose to select and present them. This product now includes expressions of editorial comment more or less colored by commercial and personal political attitudes and doctrines — most of these "liberal."

This handout by Congress of priceless public property to a commercial interest worth billions to its owners and vital to advertisers was made by public servants, many of whom profited by it. Some profits are financial and direct — those of Senators and Representatives with a financial stake in TV and/or radio stations. Some profits are indirect, a favorable attitude by the networks and local stations in deciding whether what a politician does or says is newsworthy. And it is no stretch of the imagination to suspect that routine actions or speeches of a congressional leader or committeeman who was helpful in arranging for the giveaway that is the Communications Act would be favorably evaluated as newsworthy by the network moguls, and by the station owners in his constituency. This motivated human factor will not be eliminated by new legislation restricting the amounts a candidate may spend for television advertising.

Thus the electronic lobby is among the most powerful ever to operate at the Capitol because in a sense it includes Congress itself. It is not necessary for news broadcasters, for example, to do more than exchange a warm handshake with a legislator when any aspect of the commercial interest of the electronic media is before Congress for consideration. No lobbying by the industry is required. The TV lobby is unique because it is a non-lobby. When a Washington politician encounters a Brinkley, Cronkite, or Severeid at a party the effusiveness is all on one side.

But the representatives of the printed press are far from neglected by the political community in Washington in the hope of favorable mention, or any mention at all. The correspondents of newspapers and magazines which circulate principally in certain areas are sedulously courted by the politicians in Washington indigenous to these areas. And the reporters and commentators of nationally circulated press media, including the syndicated writers, receive even more intensive social treatment of this nature on a wider scale.

Presidents F. D. Roosevelt and John F. Kennedy, as this writer has often detailed in print, were especially assiduous in administering this flattering unction — and, it must in fairness be added, not without considerable success. But it should also be added, as a matter of balance, that compared with electronic journalism, favoritism and discrimination in the printed press do not and cannot match the power of the screen to sway an entire population for or against a figure in the news.

Conflict of interest in both the public and private sectors, and between pressure groups and the American people as a whole, necessarily has free play in any form of government that can be classified as democratic. It can be waged in behalf of the general, unorganized mass of citizens, or of self-interest groups, the difference being between what is the faithful discharge of the oath of office and what is not. But the fact that conflict of interest does and must exist in the circumstances of the American system is not in itself reprehensible.

Edmund Burke, who was perhaps the most intelligent and informed observer of the ways of parliaments, stated the case for honest trading among their members as follows: ". . . Every prudent act is founded on compromise and barter. We give and take. We remit some rights that we may enjoy others, and we choose rather to be happy than subtle disputants." But he was not speaking of the abuses of "compromise and barter." And it is these abuses by which the chosen representatives of the people betray their trust.

The betrayals which are most damaging to the general welfare no longer are self-evident and performed in the open, as in the Administrations of Presidents Grant and Harding. They are sufficiently proved by inference, but inference too often is not enough to bring that persuasion of guilt on which a roused constituency ejects a candidate for office. Consequently, corporations large and small, national and local, brazenly go to a Representative's country town or district to hire lawyers, not for their competence but for their materialistic ties to the Representative — often members of the very law firm in which the legislator was a partner or retains an oblique but lucrative interest.

This is a widespread practice by banks, utilities, airlines, railroads, oil and insurance companies, and nationwide corporations. And when the Representative is engaged with legislation affecting these companies the shrewdness of their tactic is more than likely to appear in the final form of the legislation.

That is especially so when the Representative (or Senator) is a member of the House-Senate conference committee from which this final form emerges. For the report of a conference committee takes precedence for swift action, demonstrated by the fact that a motion to adopt the report is more privileged than even a motion to adjourn. Hence, this rule can deny a House or Senate majority the debate by which the report would be rejected, or returned to conference with specific instructions to delete sections that have been slipped in against the will of a majority of the House or Senate.

Congressional trading can, however, be innocent of public betrayal and merely an example of the strategy, often amusing, that goes with the trade of politics. In his autobiography, *All in One Lifetime,* James F. Byrnes describes a classic instance of this kind of strategy:

He was a minority member of the House Appropriations Committee whose chairman was Martin Madden, a Chicago Republican from a constituency in which Negro voters numbered 50 percent. Madden privately advised Byrnes that an amendment to an appropriation bill would be offered on the floor to provide certain funds for Howard University, a private, predominantly Negro institution. At that time, in the absence of law permitting such assistance to private educational institutions, it was the duty of Chairman Madden to make a point of order against the amendment that the presiding officer of the House would certainly sustain. But for obvious political reasons Madden was not willing to make the point of order and "thought it right to advise me [Byrnes] . . . so that I could make it. He said he would then request me to withhold the point of order temporarily so that he could make a speech that would please the colored voters [of his district]." The maneuver was carried out and Byrnes's point of order was upheld.

But "when the bill reached the Senate," relates Byrnes, "where there are few rules, but much Senatorial courtesy, the appropriation was restored," agreed to in conference and remained in the bill. "The result was," wrote Byrnes, "that I sustained the House rules, Madden made his political speech and was re-elected [and] Howard University got its money."

Another instance of the play of professional politics was Lyndon Johnson's long and patient trafficking with both the Senate opponents and advocates of meaningful equal-rights legislation whereby the majority leader managed in 1957 to have legislated the first real reform of the kind since Reconstruction. Up to that time, though Johnson could not effectively be classified as a segregationist, his votes in Congress had consistently reflected this public impression of his attitude. But when President Eisenhower submitted to Congress in 1957 an equal-rights bill with provisions which Johnson knew would be successfully filibustered out of the measure by the Southern Senators, Johnson had his chance to set aside these provisions and still dispel the general impression that he was a last-ditch segregationist by steering through the Senate the very strong substance of Eisenhower's bill that ended the organized denial of voting rights to Southern blacks.

The provisions he knew the South could defeat, and with them kill the great reforms of the bill itself, authorized the Department of Justice (1) to intervene on the side of any citizen, with or without his authority, whose equal rights in any particular it considered to have been denied or menaced; (2) to call for injunctions against violations, charged or anticipated; and (3) to establish an equal-rights unit in the department, and a Federal commission with the power of subpoena.

Taking full advantage of a close personal friendship with Senator Richard Russell of Georgia, master of the Southern bloc, and in the course of innumerable conferences, Johnson for months labored to effect a modus operandi by which the bill without the extreme provisions could escape death by filibuster and be put on the statute books. He called up a thick file of legislative and other favors which were owed him by Southern and Northern Democratic Senators alike. He persuaded Russell, and through him the potential filibusters, that eventually they would get an equal-rights bill more distasteful to them if they killed the entire measure. And he persuaded non-Southern Democrats that the definition of "eventually" was many years of barren struggle.

The result was that he obtained Senate assent to what he had successfully sold as a "reasonable" equal-rights bill which would strike down the main point of discrimination against Negroes — the denial of qualified suffrage in the South.

Regrettably, there are numerous instances of intra-congressional trading that are moved by various degrees of mercenary considerations. And these blots on Congress have not and will not be expunged by the feeble "codes of ethics" that Congress has adopted under the pressure of revelations of corruption that momentarily have aroused the apathetic voting public to demand a housecleaning. The Augean stable broom may yet appear in the Capitol, wielded by a Hercules whose strength and determination will be required for effective and enduring cleansing. But neither Hercules nor his broom is yet in sight.

Meanwhile, Senators and Representatives also sit on directorates of companies which have a direct interest in the legislation they shape as members of the committees to which the legislation is assigned. Abstention in these circumstances is as rare as sainthood. And when Congress in 1969 skyrocketed its per annum salaries, together with those of hordes of government employees, to keep their favored selves ahead of inflation, the deplorably low percentage of citizens who exercise their suffrage renominated all but a handful of the Congressmen who had voted for the unconscionable raises.

A great deal of influence at the Capitol rides on the President's coattails and is an important part of his power and prestige. In an election like the landslide for President Johnson in 1964 a number of candidates come to office in its wake, and to such persons even an indicated presidential expectation of support becomes a command. On the other hand, as in the general election of 1948, the President sometimes rides in on the coattails of state candidates of his party; for example, it was Adlai E. Stevenson's overwhelming majority when he ran for Governor of Illinois that saved the state and the presidency for Harry S. Truman.

A national landslide usually assures that the President it sweeps into office will, for a couple of years at least, be the master of the Congress. When, however, a President is elected by a narrow squeak, and runs far behind the state and local candidates on his ticket, political power shifts to the Capitol, the Governors' mansions, and the headquarters of the local bosses.

But, whether or not his coattails give safe journey into office for minor candidates, a President has a vast store at his command of rewards and punishments for members of Congress, Governors and local bosses. They reach from patronage (the filling of offices), instant television time if and when he wants it, and the front pages of the press for almost every act and word, to access to income-tax returns, command of the armed forces, and moral leadership of the people.

There has been a change over the years in the concept of the relations between the congressional leadership and a

President of the same party. Before the broadening definition by the Presidents of their inherent powers, the leaders of the majority in the House and in the Senate considered their primary assignment to be spokesmen of their particular branch at the White House — to inform the President what the House or Senate would accept or reject in the legislation the Executive had proposed. And that functional concept of the primary obligation of congressional leadership endured until it was supplanted, with few exceptions, by the view that primarily the leaderships should convey the views and wishes of the President to their own bodies, and do what they could to promote legislation in the form he wanted it.

Now, with the party lines broken down by the frightening menaces of the external and internal problems of the United States, and the violence of the differences of opinion within each major party, the original concept of congressional-leadership relations with the Executive has been restored. It is again a familiar event, as in the Roosevelt, Truman, and Johnson Administrations, when a party leader in the House or Senate takes the floor or resorts to the printed press and television to announce that he cannot support the President of his party and stands with the opposition. And, because the Republican is a minority party, in Congress and in the urban areas, its leadership desertions of President Nixon have been more damaging than those of the Democrats were to that party.

Several historical examples of how the two concepts were alternately followed and rejected provide sufficient illustration.

Speaker Nicholas Longworth was extremely independent of President Taft. He advised Taft that the House would or would not accept an Executive proposal. But Oscar W. Underwood, the Senate majority leader of a few years later, though he favored U.S. membership in the League of Nations, and knew the Covenant, with certain reservations, would be approved by the Senate, refused to support any reservations because President Wilson had informed Underwood he would never accept any. The result was that United States membership in the League and Underwood's Senate leadership both were casualties.

John N. Garner's two years as Speaker were served in the Administration of a President of the opposite party, Herbert Hoover, and this automatically made him the spokesman of his branch at the White House. But when a fellow Democrat, Roosevelt, was President, Garner, as Vice-President, accepted the role of White House channel to the Capitol and used his leadership to promote the First New Deal.

With the projection of the Second New Deal, however, Garner began to stand aloof. He accepted renomination in the hope he could check the rapid administrative and congressional steps toward what he considered state socialism, and, when asked to appraise the mood of Congress, channeled the views of the Democratic dissidents into the White House. For example, during a meeting there on Roosevelt's Supreme Court packing plan, Garner was asked for his judgment on the chances of its approval by Congress. "It's a very simple matter, Cap'n [Roosevelt]," he said. "You haven't got the votes." And it turned out that the "Cap'n," his name for his chief, hadn't.

At the conclusion of his second term as Vice-President, Garner went home to Uvalde, Texas, as Speaker Sam Rayburn described him, a disillusioned, disappointed old man. (Rayburn used these words to Representative Hale Boggs and Edward H. Foley, former Under Secretary of the Treasury, when, at the Democratic national convention of 1960, they urged him to withdraw his opposition to Lyndon B. Johnson's acceptance of the vice-presidential nomination.)

Henry T. Rainey and Joseph W. Byrns, who followed Garner as Speaker, were reliably the President's men except, in Rainey's case, on certain tariff matters. But Speaker William B. Bankhead was often critical of the Administration. He reverted to the old concept that a primary obligation of the Speaker was to inform the President of what the House would or would not accept.

The next Speakers, Sam Rayburn, a Democrat, and Joseph Martin, Jr., a Republican, were uniformly faithful to the Presidents of their parties in their time, no matter what their private feelings in specific instances may have been. Speaker John W. McCormack also was faithful to Democratic Administrations; and Senate leader Mike Mansfield was until he broke with President Johnson's policy on Southeast Asia. In fact, Mansfield became the focus of the Senate disenchantment with its constitutional relations with the Executive that was initiated by Senator J. W. Fulbright of Arkansas. So the Senate in the Sixties reverted to the ancient concept of being the voice of its branch at the White House, after a lapse in which Speakers and majority leaders did pretty much what the President of their party wanted them to do, and kept their private feelings largely to themselves. And President Nixon has been confronted since his incumbency with Republican defection, including the Senate party leaders, on issues he pressed as tests of loyalty to him.

In the days of weak Presidents such as Harding and Taft, the Senate and House leaders dominated national legislative policy. Joseph T. Robinson, leader of the Senate at the time of FDR's Court packing attempt, though he had his doubts about the approach to the problem, strongly favored some effective curb on the Court majority, and Roosevelt's bill was the only proposal before Congress. Consequently, Robinson led the Senate fight for the packing bill to the hour of his sudden death in the heat of the controversy.

It was generally understood that Robinson had been encouraged by Roosevelt to expect that if the Court were enlarged he would be the recipient of one of the new places. But on the eve of his death, and however much this contributed to it, he learned he was not on the list.

Robinson was one of the most attractive men in politics. He had a hot temper and was a demanding Senate leader, but in private intercourse with friends and the press he was uniformly courteous, candid, receptive, and responsive.

Alben W. Barkley succeeded Robinson. The "Dear Alben" letter, which signified the breach between Barkley and FDR after the President had used his influence in behalf of Barkley as Robinson's successor as Senate leader, concerned their differences over a tax bill Barkley had supported. Barkley had arranged a compromise which Roosevelt denounced as taxing the poor and protecting the wealthy, whereupon Barkley instantly resigned as majority leader and was instantly re-elected. It was then Roosevelt wrote the ex post facto letter, urging him to reconsider and resume his position.

To have declined to resume his leadership post after reelection to it would have been an example of snatching defeat from the jaws of victory. For Barkley had humiliated Roosevelt; and the President had eaten a large helping of humble pie. Moreover, Barkley not only was a loyal Democrat and organization man: he generally favored the President's legislative programs, and his refusal of Roosevelt's plea would have endangered them because no new leader could have matched Barkley's strength and Senate influence.

Robert A. Taft, the Republican Senate leader, respected the great parliamentary abilities of his opposite number, Lyndon

B. Johnson. Until death terminated Taft's Senate leadership during the Eisenhower Administration Johnson made a great point of being deferential to and affectionate with Taft who responded unsuspiciously to the tactic. But Taft also was fully aware that, because of the prospect that Eisenhower's vetoes would be sustained, Johnson and Rayburn of necessity would compromise on presidential programs. This had the effect of putting on the statute books legislation acceptable to Eisenhower. And in that awareness Taft pressed the President's interest effectively.

Between Taft and Senator William Knowland of California, the deputy Republican leader, there appeared to be mutual trust and personal liking. Taft virtually anointed Knowland as his successor at a time when, a victim of terminal cancer, he knew he must soon be replaced.

But whether or not Taft realized that Knowland tended to be a bumbler, Johnson, a shrewd appraiser of his fellow Senators, certainly did. He exploited Knowland's weakness to the limit when opportunity offered, which was often. Like Lee, Jackson, and Stuart, who, because of West Point association, knew in advance what moves General Pope, the Union commander at the second battle of Manassas, would make in response to a move of theirs, Johnson was clairvoyant where Knowland was concerned.

An amusing instance of how Johnson took advantage of a blunder by Knowland occurred late in the afternoon of February 24, 1954. The Senate was in a complicated parliamentary tangle over adding a section to a proposed amendment to the Constitution by Senator John W. Bricker of Ohio that in effect required Senate approval of Executive Agreements made by the President dealing with foreign policy. Knowland, the majority leader, without observing the strict protocol of consulting Johnson, the minority leader, had suddenly announced the Senate would hold a night session.

Johnson, informed of this, rushed to the chamber to make a motion that the Senate adjourn for the day — a motion reserved by sacred custom to the majority leader. He had just said "I now move . . . " when Knowland, realizing the humiliation to which he was about to be exposed, interrupted with a plea to the Senate that it reject the "attempt of the minority to take control, and yet still charge the majority leader with the responsibility of advancing the very heavy [presidential] program that has been submitted to us." He described his position, "in which no man hitherto has been asked to serve" as being the "majority leader in this body without a majority."

Johnson, commenting on that, replied with a grin that "if anyone has more problems than a majority leader without a majority, it is a minority leader with a majority." Whereupon he moved that the Senate adjourn — an undebatable motion. It carried, forty-eight to forty-five, and Knowland was left red-faced and sputtering in the discomfiture he had brought on himself by breaking protocol with a tiger.

The vanishing of the frontier, a computerized society, the urbanization in which the native gift of humor seems to have been submerged, the hazardous exposure of television, the blurring of party lines — these are among the factors which have erased so much of the color that in past generations filled the political forum with a brightly costumed cast of entertaining characters. Congressional debates have become drab affairs. Presidents pick their way carefully along the path of act and policy where historically the foundation for bold venture was the firmest stretch of all. And the Federal judiciary emits some of the most tedious prose since Chief Justice Fuller laid down his pen.

But what is left of the constituencies of Congress that contain a significant percentage of rural and small-town voters still supplies what color there remains under the Dome. And I have chosen a few of recent vintage for illustration.

Senator Huey Long and I were on excellent personal terms. I enjoyed his brazen affrontery, and he knew it. Though his private life was luxurious — in a way he was an ancestor of the current "limousine liberals" — he managed to create a public image as the ascetic protector of the poor. But the principal reason for our agreeable association was that he knew I agreed with his belief that Roosevelt was frightened of him politically.

As his sole guest at Louisiana-style meals he cooked himself, I was an attentive listener. His comments covered all current topics and were rich in color. When he and Father Coughlin were attacking Roosevelt almost every night on the radio and Hugh Johnson was defending the President, Long decided he could entrust me with copies of his speeches without risk of having them "leak" before delivery. He brought them to my office himself, usually remarking, "I know you're not going to let Roosevelt see this." This gave the *Times* the advantage of alone having the script in type in advance of its delivery so that it was available for instant publication. Long never understood, however, the obligation to print the news that caused the *Times* to publish those speeches in full while simultaneously criticizing them on the editorial page.

As Long grew in public notice, so did his interest in meeting people of consequence outside his normal sphere of activity, an interest they shared. He was not a social climber, but he wanted to become acquainted with celebrities in other than political circles — beautiful women especially, bankers, and industrial tycoons. He would inquire whether I knew so-

and-so and if I did, ask me to arrange a meeting when he or she came to Washington. He wanted to impress such people that he was not one of your ordinary demagogues, but a champion, which he was, of fiscal, monetary, and social reforms that indeed were overdue.

Long's breach with Roosevelt was the consequence of natural causes. He had done a great deal to help FDR get the nomination in 1932 in Chicago, working closely with Louis Howe and James A. Farley. When he came to Washington for the inauguration in 1933 and called on Roosevelt at the Mayflower the night before, he felt that Roosevelt's reception was not cordial, and even had conveyed the implication that FDR wanted to keep him at something more than arm's length. This strengthened his suspicion that Roosevelt feared him as the potential rival for party power he duly became. Had Long not been assassinated, I believe he would have caused great political damage to FDR in the politics of 1936.

The Senator knew that his rough tactics made him a likely target for assassination. This is why he moved about with bodyguards, armed with sawed-off shotguns, in his automobile, at public assemblages, and adjoining his private quarters. But I saw no evidence that the possibility obsessed him, although FDR in a private group, as I have related in my book *Memoirs*, once stigmatized Long as a physical coward. (Incidentally, Long once told me that *he* considered *Roosevelt* a coward, both physically and politically, so the score of denigration is about even between them.)

Senator Robert A. Taft had a compulsive trait to which his wife, Martha, referred as "Bob's bleak honesty." He was virtually incapable of camouflaging or concealing his convictions. It was Taft alone among major American politicians

[187]

who denounced the ex post facto legal concept of the Nuremberg trials, though this involved a great risk to his prospects of reelection, with the Ohio polls drawing near. Nevertheless, he courageously asserted a sound legal principle that was most unpopular, particularly among ethnic groups he normally could have relied on to support him.

It was Taft, too, after the House precipitously voted in favor of Truman's proposal to seize the strike-bound railroads and swear the strikers into the Army, who initiated the resistance that caused the Senate to block this attempt to transform a union strike into a strike against the government. (In those law-abiding times neither the government nor the people treated a strike of government employees as conceivable or tolerable.) When the House bill reached the Senate, Taft interposed, saying in effect, "Just a minute. This is an unconstitutional use of Executive power." And, on this call for second thought, the Senate agreed, and the President's proposal was rejected.

A minor instance of Taft's "bleak honesty" occurred in 1940 during the Republican national convention in Philadelphia when he was an unsuccessful presidential candidate, the prize going to Wendell L. Willkie. A group that included my wife and me lunched every day at a table in the Bellevue-Stratford dining room: among them Alice Roosevelt Longworth, Martha Taft, Representative John Hollister, and Mr. and Mrs. John W. Hanes — except for the Haneses, my wife and I, all active in the movement to nominate Taft.

Just prior to joining this group one day I was in the lobby of the hotel. A personable man came up to me and, pointing to a gathering in another part of the lobby, asked, "Isn't that Senator Taft with those people?" I said it was. "Well, I was at New Haven with him," said the man, "and I knew him a bit but probably he doesn't recall me. Would you mind introducing me?" We walked over to Taft. "Senator," I began, "this is Mr. Jones [let's call him that]. He knew you at New Haven; he was a member of your class of 1910." Taft grasped the gentleman's hand warmly, looked him in the face and said, "I don't remember that I ever saw you before in my life." His Yale classmate backed away, horribly embarrassed. But Taft could have done no other. He didn't recall the man, and he wasn't going to pretend he did.

His convention managers were responsible for the blunders in the controversy over the Texas and Georgia delegations in 1952 that assured the defeat of Taft's presidential candidacy. Like most contenders for the highest office, Taft had been carefully excluded from knowledge of the many deals and promises his managers made. So, when they suggested that the only way to win the nomination was to propose a split in the Texas delegation Taft agreed to make the offer; also to identify himself with his leaders' motion to permit the contested delegates from Georgia and Texas to vote on the issue raised against their legitimacy. These positions provided the opening for the Eisenhower forces successfully to raise the cry of "immorality." Even so, Taft failed of the nomination by only a hundred votes plus on the first and only ballot.

Taft was a man of great moral character, of the fortitude that enabled him, bravely and uncomplainingly, to face the immediate prospect of his death from incurable cancer. Knowing this, he continued upon his Senate duties to the last, communicating his plight only to his family and a few close friends, rejecting pity, playing out his hand as he always had played it — with the stoicism and manliness that was typical of his entire public and private career.

Speaker Sam Rayburn once spoke to me privately about the Supreme Court. When I mentioned decisions in which often four dissenters accused the five-man majority of usurping legislative and/or Executive powers and in effect of amending the Constitution, Rayburn guardedly observed that there were certain areas in which one branch of the government from time to time had assumed powers and jurisdictions without constitutional warrant. I took this also to imply that he thought Roosevelt had made a mistake by getting into the bramblebush of the Supreme Court packing bill. Not that Rayburn disapproved of FDR's ultimately successful objective — to crack the anti-New Deal majority of the Court; he thought the device employed was too slick to be good political procedure.

Rayburn was a man of great charm. Though there was no one in Washington whose face was more familiar, when he joined a mixed company he would identify himself with "I'm Sam Rayburn." Once, at Clark Clifford's house, at one of the annual New Year parties where Clifford and his daughters put on talented performances of songs and skits, I came into the oyster bar where Rayburn and Senate Majority Leader Lyndon B. Johnson were standing. When Rayburn, as always, ducking his head and extending his hand, said "I'm Sam Rayburn," Johnson jokingly added "And I'm Lyndon Johnson." "I can believe that you are Mr. Rayburn," I replied to the Speaker, "because I've seen you often enough, but I'm not quite sure who this tall hombre is."

Rayburn was respected and admired by the press. He was outgiving to all, but on confidential terms with only a few. He had favorites among the reporters and kept them well informed. But, though he had a broad construction of what information was legitimate to impart, he kept high-level confidences with strict adherence to the code of the responsible politician. The press accepted Rayburn's information as gospel, but this was not always so when Johnson was the source.

The latter's "credibility gap" did not begin when he entered the White House.

Rayburn, like Garner before him, met convivially with a small group in his hideaway, known jestingly as the Board of Education, after the House adjourned, where the company, in Garner's phrase, "struck a blow for liberty" in the form of a drink or two of bourbon. Those were very pleasant occasions but sometimes they were interrupted by momentous events — once in particular.

Among those regularly invited by Rayburn to "strike a blow for liberty" was a member of my staff when I was the Washington correspondent of the *New York Times*, William S. White. On the occasion referred to above, when the gathering was interrupted by "momentous news," the company included the current Vice-President of the United States, Harry S. Truman. It was in the midst of the jollity that Truman was summoned to "come to the White House" by Stephen T. Early, FDR's press secretary. Arriving there, totally unprepared for such a shock, he learned from Mrs. Roosevelt that the President was dead.

A moving description of what followed in the "Board of Education" appears in White's book *Majesty and Mischief*. He recalls that he had "wandered over" from the Senate to the hideaway and saw hurrying away, a compact, brisk and not very impressive man whom he recognized as Truman. Then, stepping out from "a pool of darkness near an elevator shaft . . . an old friend [Lyndon B. Johnson] reached out both hands, exclaiming, 'He's dead. He's dead. . . . He was always like a daddy to me.'"

Entering the room "where Rayburn sat, so unmoving and so alone," White relates in his book that he found the Speaker in tears, "accepting the fact that the 32d President of the United States had just died in Warm Springs, Georgia," but thinking of "what was going to happen now to the American Republic. 'Now,' he said softly, as though only to himself, 'the sons of bitches will start trying to dance all over his grave. Well, by God, let them try!' "

At my request for further comment on an experience the like of which has come to few if any Washington reporters, White gave me the following:

On the first anniversary of FDR's death I was again in the Senate press gallery when Rayburn — in person — called me to come over to the Board of Education. He explained when I got there that a few other friends who had been in that room — or on the way to it or just quit of it — when Truman left it to become President of the United States had also been called in to take a drink in memory of FDR. This became an annual custom, running precisely how long I do not recall; at any rate, at the first reunion there was Rayburn, sitting, as always and in every sense, at the head of the table, meaning at his desk. There were these others: Chief Justice Fred Vinson, President Harry Truman, Lyndon Johnson (I believe) and perhaps Scott Lucas [Senate majority leader]. I can remember no others. Truman sat on a sofa, taking his turn in the conversation but in no way asserting himself and in no way suggesting that he was, after all, President of the U.S. of A. Vinson, to my vast disappointment, was solely interested in reminiscing with Rayburn et al about old races down in his Kentucky Congressional district. It was all entirely personal, on everybody's part, and if a single profundity dealing with public issues was ever mentioned I have not the slightest recollection of it. It was always a matter of in memoriam — *but* in memoriam *only allusively dealt with.*

One of Lyndon Johnson's assets, though it backfired now and then, was the gift of mimicry which he sometimes ventured to employ on the Senate floor. He was intrigued by his possession of this talent, even perfectly imitating the heavy oratory and gestures of his opposite number in the leadership, William F. Knowland.

But generally Johnson's relations with his colleagues were mutually respectful. And toward one of his fellow Democrats, Senator Earl Clements of Kentucky, the deputy Democratic floor leader, Johnson felt a very special trust and affection, an attitude unusual between men in their particular positions.

Often the congressional party leader and his deputy reflect a compromise between party factions. The faction that failed to capture the No. 1 spot is compensated, in the interest of unity, by being given the No. 2. In most of these instances the party leader and his deputy spend considerable time keeping a close eye on each other for indications of something less than full cooperation. But the Johnson-Clements relationship was of complete and mutual loyalty and respect for the following reasons:

Both were pragmatic politicians, impatient with rhetoric that delayed Senate action for which they believed the time had come. Both were born of the same American stock — some of Johnson's forebears came from Kentucky which had sent Clements to the House and Senate and made him Governor in between — and both shared the same general political philosophy.

A year after Clements was elected to the Senate he was chosen as a member of the Democratic Policy Committee where he and Johnson developed the close association that led Johnson, after he became minority leader, to select Clements as his No. 2 — an arrangement which continued after Johnson moved up to majority leader. And, on the personal side, these two pragmatists and activists and their families saw a great deal of one another and liked what they saw.

But an underlying reason was the high estimate each man had acquired for the leadership abilities and loyalties of the other.

Johnson's concern that his positions be correctly under- stood was demonstrated in my case by a flow of memoranda after most of my talks with him. These memos had the other useful quality of clarifying his own thinking. They were usually undated and unsigned, but he never marked them confidential, implying the complimentary assumption that I had sufficient discretion to know when and when not to attribute them directly. The value to me, of course, was that whenever a Johnson position was in dispute, I was in a position to check his version of it.

6

The Supreme Court

T HE SUPREME COURT was not envisaged by the writers of
the Constitution as empowered to exercise judicial supremacy over the functions, actions, or inactions of the legis-
lative and Executive branches of the Federal government. Nor
did they, as witness the Tenth Amendment, authorize the
Court to impose its current concepts of the obligations of the
Federal and/or state governments in the field of moral issues.
Jefferson, who had initiated an unsuccessful effort to remove
Associate Justice Samuel Chase from the bench, set down suc-
cinctly the Founding Fathers' concept of the limitations of the
Court's power in a letter written to William C. Jarvis in 1820:
"It is a very dangerous doctrine to consider the judges as the
ultimate arbiters of all constitutional questions. It is one which
would place us under the despotism of an oligarchy. . . . The
Constitution has erected no such single tribunal, knowing that
to whatever hands confided, with the corruptions of time and
party, its members would become despots. It has more wisely
made all the departments coequal and cosovereign within
themselves."

Thus, the Federal judiciary was not designed to proclaim
new national policy, especially on moral or sociological
grounds, or to act as a super-Congress, or otherwise to amend
the Constitution by the fiat of a group of public officials, none

of whom had been elected to their posts and in whose appointment by the President, the House, the popular branch of Congress, had no voice whatsoever.

The anticipated function of the Court was to rule on "the law of the case" before it, as prescribed in the Constitution and the statutes. Even Chief Justice Marshall, when he began, in *Marbury* v. *Madison,* the move to assert the judicial supremacy that came to its peak in the Court of which Earl Warren was Chief Justice, backed into the claim by holding that Congress, in the Judiciary Act of 1789, had given the Court unconstitutional powers — powers beyond those assigned to it by the Constitution. And by this crafty device he founded the assumption by the Court of the power to outlaw Acts of Congress.

For more than a half century thereafter only one other Act was declared invalid. Chief Justice Taney's notable ruling in the Dred Scott case (that the Fugitive Slave Act, which asserted that the right of private property extended to slaves who had fled to the free states was firmly within the letter of the Constitution) was, however, an extreme example of "strict construction" of the separation of powers among the three Federal branches that is the heart of the Charter of 1789. Yet until the sectional North-South division over the institution of slavery plunged the nation into the War Between the States, the Dred Scott decision remained the law of the land, an instance in support of the argument that "strict construction," like its opposite, can go too far.

Even Lincoln, in the Emancipation Proclamation, as previously noted, freed only the slaves in the Secessionist states — in Delaware, for example, slaves they remained. And as late as 1954, *Plessy* v. *Ferguson,* in which the Court upheld in 1895 the right of states to enforce compulsory segregation by race in public schools, was still constitutional. In 1954, however, though without benefit of intervening statute, the Court accepted Justice John M. Harlan's dissent in *Plessy*, expanding Justice Marshall's definition of the Court's authority to hold Acts of Congress invalid by claiming the power to ameliorate by judicial fiat a social condition which Congress had failed to correct by legislation the Court felt to be essential to national morality and otherwise to the national interest.

This ruling was wholly assumptive, a process invoked again when the Court ordered the reapportionment of election districts, Federal, state, and local on the basis of equal population ("one man, one vote").

But the lawyers and historians who contend that "strict construction" of the Constitution by the Supreme Court is both obsolete and unwise have one impressively strong point in their favor. The Convention of 1787 envisaged a very different United States from the nation that changing times and internal divisions have created. The Founders did not conceive of a people among whom disrespect for, and violation of, existing law would be abetted by educators, legislators, and courts as an accepted means by which groups would seek to redress their asserted grievances. They did not foresee the disappearance of civility in expressing dissent, students and professional agitators investing the streets with marching, looting mobs waving enemy flags, burning our own, and closing down the universities. They did not foresee the distortion by courts and politicians of the Bill of Rights to make it an instrument, not of *protection of* the minority but of *tyranny by* the minority.

Moreover, their otherwise valid point is greatly weakened by the fact that judicial restraint in supervening the Constitution has disappeared in the process, as when Earl Warren was Chief Justice. And it is further weakened by the fact that this lack of restraint has contributed to the arrival of a lawless national condition that, unfortunately, only such proposals as preventive detention of likely criminal repeaters and the "no knock" license for police can begin to correct. Because, what confronts and endangers the American society again, as President Cleveland said, is a "condition, not a theory," a situation in which "theory" temporarily must take second place.

Congress, of course, can refuse to appropriate the money that might be required to enforce a Supreme Court ruling; also the President can refuse to enforce it. But, through their dominance of the channels of public communication and the college faculties, the "liberals" would mount a protest which members of Congress and the Executive would not yet venture to confront because, supported as it would be by labor and combined minority groups, the protest could be politically disastrous. Apparently the American people have come to approve of judicial supremacy — except where excessive protection of criminals at the expense of society is concerned. For, though the Warren Court majority has made the Fourteenth Amendment into a bed of Procrustes stretching its occupant, the law, to fit any new doctrinal dimension fixed by five Justices — Congress has defeated all attempts to curb such grabs by the Court of jurisdiction not visible in the text of the Amendment.

Jackson, when the Supreme Court held that the Cherokees of Georgia were a separate nation, and therefore not subject to the laws of the state, refused to implement the ruling, saying in effect — though maybe not in those words — "John Marshall has made his law, now let him enforce it." And, in the expectation that the Supreme Court would invalidate President F. D. Roosevelt's revocation of the gold repayment clause in private and government contracts, the President prepared a speech in which he was to announce that for practical fiscal reasons he would, on grounds of economic necessity, regretfully refuse to honor the gold payment clause.

This speech went into the archives when John Burns, general counsel of the SEC (whom Chairman Joseph P. Kennedy had dispatched to the Court to apprise the President of the verdict), reported that the Court had refused to consider "whether or not gold certificates were an express contract with the United States, since the plaintiff had suffered only nominal damages and hence had no right to sue the government in the Court of Claims." (A. H. Kelly and W. A. Harbison, *The American Constitution,* 3rd ed. [New York: W. W. Norton & Co.], p. 737.)

The reversal of *Plessy* in 1954, since it was based on the judgment of sociologists and moralistic reformers that "separate" could not in essence be "equal" education in the public schools, was a landmark also in that the finding was unanimous.

How this unanimity was attained will probably never be known for certain until at least one of the participating Justices improbably decides to write or leave memoirs that will lift the curtain behind which the discussions of the Court, prior to decision, are conducted. But I have some authority for the belief that the following, taken from *The American Constitution* (pp. 934–935) is the explanation:

The Court, in deciding the case, significantly had issued no enforcement order; instead it asked counsel to re-argue once more the means of implementing the decision. Thus very astutely it separated its enunciation of the constitutional ban on segregation from the far more perplexing question of how Southern society was to adjust itself to the new standard. Quite conceivably, this careful separation of principle from enforcement had enabled the justices to unite in a unanimous decision. . . .

In a certain sense, the Court's resort to equity principles to enforce the Brown decision was both self-contradictory and precedent-breaking. On the one hand, the Court had found that the plaintiff school-children had a categorical right under the Fourteenth Amendment to attendance at racially non-segregated schools. At the same time, the Court had done what it had never done before — by implication denied these same children a full and instant implementation of this constitutional right. In a legal sense this was unprecedented and almost absurd; in a pragmatic sense it was vitally necessary to provide the flexibility and necessary delays which the imposition of something like a social revolution on the South now entailed. This was the meaning of the curiously contradictory phrase, "with all deliberate speed."

This explanation squares with one given me at the time by a person who was close to the Court. The rationale, he said, was devised by Chief Justice Warren in an "exercise of judicial statesmanship," based on the absence of an enforcement order that probably would have evoked widespread violence in the South and split the Court. But this formula, according to my informant, would have proved insufficient to prevent dissent if Justice Frankfurter had not contributed to the opinion the phrase "with all deliberate speed."

Eisenhower was President at that time and his concept of the presidential office with respect to the Supreme Court was that the President should neither attempt to influence the trend of opinion of the Court before a decision was reached or comment on it one way or the other after it was made. His view of his function as President was to enforce Court decisions whether he approved of them or not, on whatever ground — in this instance he felt that the 1954 decision was at least "premature."

Many Justices have maintained close personal relations with Presidents after they ascended the high bench. But the weight of the public record is that its members have sedulously refrained from discussing with anyone, even with the President, cases pending in the Court. This not only is a proper deference to the principle of the separation of powers; also it is in conformity with the Court's refusal to give advisory opinions in any circumstances.

Often appointees to the Court adopt positions on constitutional issues contrary to what the President expected of them. A notable example was furnished by Justice Oliver Wendell Holmes. In a number of instances Holmes disappointed and angered Theodore Roosevelt by opinions to the exact opposite of what the President expected them to be.

Eisenhower experienced a similar disappointment in the judicial attitudes taken by Chief Justice Warren and Justice William J. Brennan, whom he had been led to believe were moderate conservatives in the interpretation of the laws, especially those affecting the social problems of the American society. In private conversations he expressed regret that he had been persuaded to appoint them.

The Senate's rejections of Fortas's promotion to Chief Justice by Johnson, and of Appellate Court Judges Clement Haynesworth and G. Harrold Carswell to be Associate Justices, were primarily moves in the political war between the bipartisan groups of the so-called liberals and conservatives in Congress. Before Fortas's elevation was proposed Congress had made a great show of adopting codes of ethics and the Senate had censured Senator Thomas Dodd of Connecticut for using campaign contributions as personal funds.

The demand in the country for ethical reforms was mounting. Also, with Johnson's personality and his broad concept of the latitude of inherent presidential power growing unpopular in Congress, the feeling spread that confirmation of Johnson's close friend and adviser to head the Court would further increase the grip of the President on the whole governmental system.

But these considerations, standing by themselves, would not have caused Fortas's rejection as Chief Justice (he had been readily confirmed as an Associate Justice) were it not for the issue of his "ethics" that was raised by certain of his private activities after he joined the Court. These at least were imprudent and had a mercenary cast: the large sum collected for his series of lectures at American University, and his advisory role to a foundation after its creator had become involved in litigation eventually subject to reviews by the Court.

As for Haynsworth, though he profited not at all by the negligible financial dealing he had engaged in — mostly by proxy — liberal Senators who, pressured by minority and labor groups, opposed his constitutional philosophy, were able to reject him for what they *thought* he thought, since what he *did* was merely careless, not fairly vulnerable, and the ethical issue was trumped up. Haynsworth's actual "crime" was that he believed in limiting the judicial range to "the law of the case" and against rulings based on ideologies, liberal or conservative.

This was the stick to whip the dog with. Yet the charge of being lacking in "ethics" was pressed by some Senators who, in exchange for large contributions to their campaigns from labor unions, had voted the way labor wanted them to all the time they had been in the Senate.

The Republicans who supported the Democrats in opposing Haynsworth came from industrial states and big cities where there are large Negro minorities and labor unions to reckon with at the polls. These groups also account in part — for Haynsworth was the far better qualified — for the opposition to President Nixon's replacement nominee, Judge Carswell. For, though his opinions on the lower court do not rank with those of a Holmes or a Brandeis, the Senate has confirmed many others against whom this point could have been made. Haynsworth and Carswell were rejected simply because they were vulnerable on "ethical" grounds to the liberals and certain minorities who want no Justice who might move toward balancing the doctrinal radicalism of the Warren Court. And since a "strict constructionist" from the South is likely to help effect this balance, the fact that Haynsworth and Carswell are Southerners weighed the more heavily against them among the non-Southern Senators.

An amusing example of the original concept of how a Supreme Court Justice should conduct himself, and how sacredly he should view his obligation to confine all mention of the Court's business to his brethren, was provided by the experience of a reporter with the elder Justice John Marshall Harlan. (The reporter, George Rockwell Brown, was new to the journalistic and judicial protocol of Washington.) It was well known that Justice Harlan was a regular attendant, including Sunday night services, at the Central Presbyterian Church in New York Avenue Northwest. He was a large man who chewed tobacco, used earthy language, and had been a soldier in some of the toughest of the Union Army's battalions. But at church he was always attired in a frock coat and silk hat.

Neither Brown nor his editors on the *Boston Herald* knew any better, one Sunday, before a decision day of the Supreme Court, than to arrange for Brown to accost Justice Harlan when leaving the services at the New York Avenue Church, and ask him how the Court was going to decide a particular case affecting the city of Boston. Brown, full of youthful enthusiasm for his assignment, waited at the church. Out came Justice Harlan to be approached by an individual he did not know. "Sir, I'm a reporter for the *Boston Herald*," began Brown. "How are you, son?" benignly replied the Justice. "Sir," the reporter continued, "can you tell me what the decision of the Court is going to be tomorrow in the Boston case?" Slowly and steadily Harlan's visage froze, and in its terrifying chill Brown fled precipitately from the scene.

An infraction of the code but with a less menacing consequence was made by Heywood Broun at one of the regular Sunday night conversaziones convoked by the late Mrs. J. Borden Harriman. "Daisy," as she was known, had an unquenchable thirst for discussions of public affairs by persons involved in them, and her prestige assured they would accept her invitation to join the company she assembled once a week. This was in the days of a graceful Washington where the social scene was dominated by hostesses who were gentlewomen, and the "swinging" ambassadors from poverty-ridden nations and social climbers who now vie with one another to get reports of their parties in the newspaper "society columns," had not yet vulgarized the assiduous entertainment of VIP's that is a major Washington industry.

I was commissioned one Sunday night at Daisy's to produce Broun, who had been my colleague on *The World,* and Broun brought along the engaging sprite who was his second wife. Among the guests was Supreme Court Justice Owen J. Roberts. After dinner when the guests gathered in groups, as was the custom, Broun and his wife were seated opposite to Justice and Mrs. Roberts, whereupon Broun brought up the case of an Associated Press reporter named Watson, then awaiting a ruling by the Court, and began to express his views on the issue, which involved the labor relations of newspapers and press associations. Despite the indignant frowns of the Justice, Broun finished what he had to say.

While driving the Brouns to their hotel I said, "Heywood, you were way out of bounds." In the mild tones that were in such complete contrast to his bellicose writings in the press, Broun replied, "But *he* didn't seem to mind." "Well," said his wife, "you ought to have seen the dirty look *she* gave *me*."

Within the purlieus of the Court itself, and on the bench, lighter episodes often have relieved, and acerbic public comments from the bench have dramatized, the solemnity, gravity, and disputes with which both the secret conferences and open sessions of the Justices are invested. The source of the episodes that follow is Charles Henry Butler's *A Century at the Bar of the Supreme Court of the United States*. The author had long occupied the official position of Reporter Of Decisions Of The Court. Except for its longtime Marshal, John Montgomery Wright, Butler was more familiar than anyone with the Supreme Court of his day, behind the bench and upon it.

While outside activities of certain Justices, and acid personalities exchanged on the bench, have combined with some assertions of jurisdiction sanctioned neither by the Constitution nor the statutes to threaten its dignified public status, an exchange Butler relates between Chief Justice M. W. Fuller (1888–1910) and former President Grover Cleveland demonstrates how jealously the Court guards its title of "Supreme." During the interval of private citizenship between his two elections (1888–92) Cleveland, arguing his only case before the Court, announced within two minutes of the fixed closing time that he would speak only a few minutes longer. "Thereupon," according to Butler, "the Chief Justice, bowing with great courtesy, replied: 'Mr. Cleveland, we will hear you tomorrow morning.'"

The Chief Justice was President Cleveland's own appointee.

The rules and customs Butler described have since been modified on the side of informality. For example, for many years Justice Horace Gray (1882–1902) was the Court's "sartorial dictator." He permitted no relaxation by the Justices or the bar of formal attire in the courtroom, a regulation that once prompted as recent a Chief Justice as William Howard Taft (1921–30) to send word by the Clerk to a vestless lawyer either to acquire the garment during the luncheon recess or button up his coat to conceal its absence. A notable deviation was the Court's acceptance — on the ground that the costume was indigenous — of a farm-belt lawyer who appeared for argument waistcoatless and innocently clad in an olive yellow tweed suit, pink shirt, and tan shoes. Now the kind of apparel a city lawyer would wear to his office is acceptable. And their robes conceal whatever informality of garb the Justices may indulge in.

While sometimes the oral presentation of a case outweighs the quality of a brief in bringing the Court to decision — Justice Holmes (1902–32) once said that John W. Davis's ability to "skim over thin ice" in his oral arguments required the Court to stay awake — the briefs still provide the groundwork of court rulings. Moreover, unless oral arguments are noteworthy, the Justices have often shown signs of impatience with the makers. Once a Justice interrupted a pleader by saying that he would "rather give you the damn case than hear you talk." But on another occasion a lawyer turned the scales. When a Justice interrupted an oral argument with "That is not the law," he replied with a ceremonial show of respect, "It was until your Honor spoke." For, as Charles

Evans Hughes once acknowledged, with celebrated candor, the Constitution is what the judges "say it is."

Again according to Butler, for many years there was a locked cabinet in the Robing Room, containing cups of cheer, that was not to be opened unless it was raining. A Justice who ordered the lifting of the order on one sunny day explained "it is probably raining somewhere in the jurisdiction." And when Butler asked Justice David J. Brewer (1890–1910) years afterward if the cabinet was still there and available only on the same condition, Brewer impassively observed that, after all, the Court had given constitutional warrant for the acquisition by the United States of the Philippines "to be sure of having plenty of rainy seasons."

On another occasion, Butler relates, an open window on a cool day was the source of a contretemps between Justices Gray and Joseph P. Bradley (1870–92). Gray weighed in at more than 250 pounds, Bradley, much less, and consequently they had different ideas concerning ideal room temperature. "What damned fool opened that window?" demanded Bradley of an attendant. Told the culprit was Gray, he remarked, "I thought so. Shut it up and keep it shut."

It is at the Friday conferences (until recently held on Saturdays) that the base of final decision is laid and its product submitted to the Justices. In the first stage, after his colleagues have discussed the issue in the cases, the Chief Justice selects the Justice who will write the opinion to which eventually a majority will or will not subscribe and to which any dissents will be addressed. Though even the most secret sessions of the National Security Council frequently spring leaks into the channels of the press, the secrecy of what happens at these conferences of the Court has been strictly maintained. Except for the above report of how the Court came to vote unanimously on the Brown public-school decision, the only incident I ever heard about, in more than half a century of Washington reporting, was as follows:

After Justice William O. Douglas (1939–   ) had given his opinion of the law in a certain case under discussion, Chief Justice Harlan F. Stone (1941–46) inquired with raised eyebrows where Douglas had found such a law. "I learned about it from you," replied Douglas, who, when Stone was Dean of the Columbia University Law School, had been one of his shining students. "Not from *me* you didn't," said Stone indignantly.

This may serve to explain the acerbity and vigor of dissents which, notably in the Warren Court, divide the Justices five to four. Commenting on these legal conflicts, Mr. Dooley as usual went to the heart of the matter: "Mr. Justice Brown delivered the opinion of the Court and only eight Justices dissented."

7

Regulatory Agencies

T HE PIONEER among the regulatory agencies was the Interstate Commerce Commission. It was set up by the Hepburn Act when the railroads were actually bribing legislators and using other corrupt means to control all aspects of transportation in disregard of the rights of patrons. It was a very one-sided situation until a commission was established to look out for the public interest, as well as the interest of the railroads; to achieve a balance among the consumer, the shipper, the railroads, and the workers.

Hampered by a tangle of conflicting Federal and local statutes, often by cosy deals between railroad management and labor, the ICC has taken its job seriously with the result that its processes are very slow. Congress has left the Commission open to Ralph Nader's charge of swallowing whatever statistics the railroads offer for rises in rates, reduction in passenger service, and so on. However, in the first agencies that followed — the Federal Trade Commission, the Federal Power Commission, the Federal Communications Commission, the National Labor Relations Board, the Securities and Exchange Commission and the General Accounting Office — there is such a mixture of functions, quasi-judicial, quasi-legislative, and so much interlocking jurisdiction, that only a complete redefinition of their functions and the elimination of several thus made superfluous, can resolve the attendant conflicts and confusions. This process has finally been undertaken by President Nixon.

The agencies are called independent because in theory, though very frequently not in practice, they are independent of everything but the faithful fulfillment of their assignment by Congress to keep an eye on the areas under their intended jurisdictions and fairly to report to Congress what is going on. Presidents naturally have made use of the appointive power to name members of these commissions who are sympathetic with Administration aims and policies. Congress has sought to minimize this Executive control by providing for a division between the major political parties among the board members. Nevertheless, if a Republican or Democratic President is required by statute to appoint a registrant in the other major party to fill a certain vacancy in a commission, he can, and usually has, chosen a merely nominal member of the political opposition, with the hope the commissioner will not forget to whom he owes his job.

The best illustration of the partisanship this casts over the findings of a commission is the trend of rulings by the National Labor Relations Board that only now shows indications of a back-swing to impartiality. After its creation by the Wagner Act in FDR's presidency it was a packed pro-labor group because five of the seven succeeding presidential elections had been won by pro-labor Democrats. Union labor had preferential treatment, and, since for years the Supreme Court has been of the same mind, the Commission has been fairly sure of having its rulings sustained. An example is the NLRB ruling that permits unions to influence representation elections by passing around pledge cards that, being on the open record, impair freedom of choice by their workers to whom they are handed. Implicit in this method of assuring pro-union elections are threats of reprisal against employees who refuse to sign over their voting rights to the union leadership.

Thus the NLRB provided a conspicuous example of the deterioration of an independent agency into one responsive to the prevailing judicial and political philosophy. There are now moves to restore the balance but they will not fully succeed until the Executive and the Federal courts put aside political considerations to enforce on the agencies and commissions neutrality in the performance of the function they were created to exercise — riding herd on the groups that fatten at the expense of the public interest.

Among others, the Federal Communications Commission has laid itself open to the charge of favoring the applicant for, or holder of, franchises who has the better political connections. This charge has been made in the case of the award of the electronic facilities in Austin, Texas. The fact that Mrs. Lyndon B. Johnson was able to get franchises for use of the publicly owned air waves despite qualified competition was broadly viewed as supporting the allegation. Conversely, from the time the Securities Exchange Commission was created, with Joseph P. Kennedy, Sr., as chairman, the SEC, as previously noted, has been largely free of accusations that it has failed to abide by the set of honorable and objective standards he set for it. But in the spring of 1970, for the first time, complaints mounted that the agency seemed to be losing its former vigor in a web of indecision and Congress was urged to initiate a review.

The Food and Drug Administration and the Federal Trade and Power Commissions are agencies under constant and often effective pressure from industry. On the other hand the advocates of public ownership of utilities have prevailed in large sections of the country since the establishment of the

Tennessee Valley Authority and the Rural Electrification Authority by President Franklin Roosevelt. There was a great contest for the Southern field between the Commonwealth and Southern private power complex, headed by Wendell L. Willkie, and President F. D. Roosevelt. But this was finally settled by Executive acts enlarging the domain of the TVA, and giving it productive facilities not authorized in the creating statute. The general effect has been to put the TVA advantageously in competition with private business.

It is unfair competition because a public body with statutory and extrastatutory power, and tax advantages, can nearly always overcome the private industry involved, regardless of how often it is proclaimed that the intent is to protect the consumer from arbitrary policies pursued by the industry.

That was Willkie's argument and I think Willkie was right. Congress very clearly withheld from the TVA the sanction to build steam plants in direct competition with private utilities, but it built them just the same. The result was that the TVA went into business at the expense of the competitive free enterprise system.

Lyndon B. Johnson, in a pioneer effort to develop water resources in his state, addressed himself to the pressing problem of flood control. In those days there were no reservoirs of water to control the recurring flash floods. The water overran the land regularly, or in drought the streams would be too low to afford relief. A favored few had auxiliary electric plants on their farms. Johnson's district being a model example of the need for big storage dams, he was a natural exponent of this system of water conservation. Prior to that, of course, as the building of the Hoover Dam illustrates, there had been a great deal of conservation activity, but it centered on certain parts of the country and neglected others, including the state of Texas as a whole.

On the other hand, the great Shenandoah Dam project, which was nullified by the clever generalship of Thomas Byrd, the youngest brother of Senator Harry F. Byrd, Sr., is an example of the resistance to reservoirs that has exposed many areas to constant floods and droughts. The Army engineers proposed to build the Shenandoah Dam in the Valley of Virginia. It necessarily would have inundated some of the most successful soil-enrichments in the history of United States agriculture, achieved by the Pennsylvania Dutch who came to Virginia early in the eighteenth century. They had made a garden spot of Augusta County which until that time had been subject to primitive methods of farming and water distribution.

The Mennonites and the Amish, Pennsylvania Dutch who migrated to Virginia, realized that much of the land they had cultivated would be covered by a lake and the hard work of two centuries of progress in crop production would be swept away. The fact that the dam would assure a regular flow of water to the drought and flood areas did not reconcile them to the inundation of their farms. Nor did the explanation of the backers of the dam, that the lake could be stocked with fish and yield a new source of food to many more Virginians than would be deprived of their lands by the inundation.

Tom Byrd arranged a public confrontation between the Augusta County farmers and the Army engineers, designers of the proposed dam. At this hearing Byrd described the toil and the agricultural genius of the Amish and the Mennonites, and proposed a standing vote on the Army's plan. On the call of those who opposed the lake and dam there arose a group as impressive as I have ever seen. The men's long beards, deep-set eyes, square hats and plain black clothing, the women's traditional sober attire, made a spectacle that suggested a convocation of the prophets of Israel and of the Biblical Ruths and Naomis. This show of opposition was so dramatic and overwhelming that the Army engineers abandoned the project of the Shenandoah Dam.

Tom Byrd was an ardent — if, in this instance, somewhat inconsistent — conservationist, a protector of the natural beauties of the Valley, a fighter against the pollution of the Shenandoah River by the waste ejected from the Viscose plant in Front Royal. But at this hearing he demonstrated he also was a talented showman. He had craftily stage-managed what was truly a people's lobby.

Most such demonstrations of resistance to public power projects have proved abortive, once the policy was set. But some have narrowly missed adding the element needed to enforce protests against other types of governmental action. For example, the Mothers for Peace lobby in 1941 almost beat the draft. It was approved by only one vote in the House of Representatives.

The Army Corps of Engineers has been very influential because of the benefits it has brought to several communities by dredging harbors, building bridges, and by other activities paramount in one area or another. It has opened up streams for navigation that were not navigable before. But when it sought to build the Shenandoah Dam and lake that would have flooded some of the finest agricultural land in the nation, created from a wasteland by the sweat and muscle of its developers, this was more basic conservation than the Corps was able to induce the creators to accept.

8

The Power of the Press

THE SENSE OF NEARNESS the American people used to feel toward men in public life was expressed in the earlier days of what was established, and then disestablished, as a "Federal Union" by the sobriquets with which Presidents and national heroes and other celebrities were identified. Jackson was "Old Hickory"; Webster was the "Divine Dan'l"; Lincoln the "Railsplitter," and so on.

The appellations evolved not from surnames or first names, but from physical, spiritual, or mental impressions. I don't know how much modern journalism, which sharply restricts the number of letters in a headline, shares with television the responsibility for the disappearance of nicknames in political reporting, or whether this reflects the cosmopolitan fusion of races that constitutes the American people and has bred out its original folkways.

But we have been inclined, since Theodore Roosevelt's election, to refer in headlines and common parlance to Presidents by their initials: T.R., FDR, HST, JFK and LBJ, or, as in the case of Eisenhower, by his school nickname, Ike.

Nixon has not yet reached the stage of being known by his initials, but his last name is short and fits easily into a normal headline. At any rate, the change is very apparent from the use of such sobriquets as "Father of His Country" for Washington, the "Sage of Monticello" for Jefferson, "Old Rough and Ready" for Zachary Taylor, "Old Fuss and Feathers" for Winfield Scott, and "Cactus Jack" for John Nance Garner of Texas. "Five O'Clock Shadow" for ex-Senator Wayne Morse is one of the few survivors. This eponym, born of safety-razor advertising, grew out of the circumstance that, when the Senate was about to adjourn, Morse habitually chose this as the time to make a long speech.

In Kentucky, when I was reporting politics there, the custom of reference by sobriquet was widespread among the descendants of the Anglo-Saxon-Celtic pioneers who made up the overwhelming Southern majority. For example, there was a legislator, a tall, burly, expansive man with a loud voice, from Owen County, known for its pastoral beauty and quietude. He was referred to generally as the "Big Bay Horse of Sweet Owen." Ben Johnson was the "Sly Fox of Nelson [County]." In my own county there was a politician who was called the "Bullfrog of Barren," a good description of the decibels registered in his oratory. Senator Bradley, who was given to inventing nicknames, had an assistant so pure in thought and human relations that Bradley dubbed him the "He-Virgin."

Almost the last of these appellations in familiar use was given to Secretary of State Henry L. Stimson. He had backed a couple of losers in Latin America, hence he was nicknamed "Wrong Horse Harry," a witty variant of "Light Horse Harry" for Richard Henry Lee, the father of Robert E. Lee.

In the Revolutionary War, General Francis Marion was the "Swamp Fox," and in the final eponymic phase in this country General John J. Pershing was "Black Jack." "Sockless Jerry," for a Midwest Congressman named Simpson, reflected the belief that he drew on his shoes barefoot. And "Sunset" Cox, another member of the House, was called so because he, like

Morse, was inclined to take the floor in the dying minutes of the legislative day. Senator Borah of Idaho was "Big Bill," though he was not big. However, he had a loud voice and a swelling chest, and the sobriquet derived from the impression he gave of orating with an air of authority on all subjects.

The effect of the passing of nicknames has taken much of the color out of American political dialogue. Sometimes the sobriquets changed with the passage of years as American politicians developed new personalities related to new activities. Clay, who first was known as the "Mill Boy of the Slashes," a reference to his humble youth in Virginia when he worked in a grist mill, became the "Great Commoner," then the "Great Compromiser" — a reference to his leadership in breaking impasses on issues — and eventually "Prince Harry of the West," because of a bearing the people thought of as royal. But despite all these attainments he failed to realize his ambition to become President.

Some sobriquets became a sort of heritage: thus William Jennings Bryan took over one of Clay's, the "Great Commoner"; and "Swamp Fox" passed on from General Francis Marion to Representative Carl Vinson of Georgia, successively chairman of the Naval Affairs and the Armed Services Committees in his long span of service in Congress. The inheritance derived from a House cloakroom jest that Vinson could only have acquired his deft footwork by a youth spent in the great Okefenokee Swamp.

Nicknames for politicians were in common usage until the media of public communication shoved into the wings the politician who entertains more than he enlightens. Prior to this, abetted by the county fairs, Fourth of July picnics, and Mr. Dooley, only the professional stage competed with the extrovert as the source of public entertainment. But now the printed press abounds with satires and other humorous articles about politics and politicians — too many, however, diluted and dulled by their authors' conviction that projection of their own doctrines of political philosophy, their own personal loves and hates, is a patriotic obligation imposed by their command of space.

The entertaining politician, who flourished so long without competition in this field has been eclipsed, principally by television. The tube so constantly has thrust impersonators of the political animals into the living rooms that some of these impersonators are better known than the originals. And this has stifled the spontaneity from which the apt imagery of nicknames derived. Hardly a "talk" program, except for those which consist of panel interviews, fails to include an actor whose performance consists of "sounding like" a well-known public figure and who has the gift of twisting his features into a physical resemblance of the subject.

With this supervention by the media of the entertaining quality that long was principally supplied by the political orators, and the excitement of seeing and hearing candidates in the flesh confronting one another lost in cold print and electronic relay, a distance now stretches between politicians and their audiences in which apt nicknames do not flourish. For example, "the Rock," for Nelson A. Rockefeller, smells of laborious contrivance.

With few exceptions, I have encountered only honorable, conscientious, hardworking newspapermen during my career in Washington. My long experience on which this conclusion is firmly founded began with three Washington correspondents who were the leaders of the group when I joined it, not only in their coverage of the general news, but in producing news of special depth and authority due to the fact that they had quick access to Presidents, Cabinet members, and the leaders of Congress. Most of the others probably were basically as good newspapermen, but they lacked the direct entrée to important news sources that derives from representation of widely circulated newspapers.

These three leaders were Frank R. Kent of the *Baltimore Sun,* Richard V. Oulahan who was my immediate predecessor as the Washington correspondent of the *New York Times,* and John Callan O'Laughlin of the *Chicago Tribune.*

Dick Oulahan had the presence of a born leader. He was witty, handsome, charming, and a great gentleman. One day, when he was working on a big story, Oulahan came back to the *Times's* Washington bureau to write it. His custom was to report most of the front-page news himself. As he sat down to his typewriter he explained why he was later than usual in filing his copy. "I had," he said, "to see the President, the Secretary of State, the Secretary of War and the Speaker of the House." He had indeed interviewed all four, with the result that he was able to produce a balanced and completely authoritative account of a momentous affair of government, not matched in these vital elements by any report which came out of Washington that day.

O'Laughlin rose to the reportorial peak by favorably impressing President Theodore Roosevelt. T.R. did not give interviews as such, but he made himself accessible to a few reporters, among whom O'Laughlin was outstanding. In due course President Roosevelt appointed him Assistant Secretary of State and put him in charge of the Far East in connection with our difficulties with Japan over the Asiatic Exclusion Act in California, and O'Laughlin came back to his *Tribune* post in Washington with this prestige.

As a reporter, he was an avid seeker of official texts. In those days texts of legislative drafts, Executive orders and the like, were not readily available. They were officially summarized, but the sensitive documents were withheld. O'Laughlin concentrated on backing his news stories with the related texts as a special distinction of the Washington bureau of the *Tribune*. This was before the *New York Times* appropriated that field as the "newspaper of record."

He flattered me by soliciting my help in this effort, which, because of my connections with important Southern legislators as the correspondent of the *Courier-Journal,* was sometimes productive. For example, during the Taft Administration we obtained and shared exclusively the text of the Aldrich-Vreeland monetary bill, a most secret document.

O'Laughlin left the *Tribune* and, in association with James Keeley, its great managing editor, founded another Chicago paper. It failed. He then bought the *Army & Navy Journal,* which property he bequeathed to the famous Gridiron Club of which he had been president and one of its most loyal members.

Another exceptionally able and well-informed correspondent in my early Washington days was Archibald Fowler of the *New York Sun*. He had a reputation for getting exclusive news that was surpassed only by Oulahan's and O'Laughlin's. Fowler died after a rather brief period as the *Sun's* chief capital correspondent, but in the short time he was in that post he collected an impressive number of exclusive stories.

Until Frank Kent became managing editor of the *Baltimore Sun* he was the Washington correspondent for that paper and as its national political reporter acquired a countrywide readership. Kent went abroad during World War I and when he returned he wrote an article which for the first time exposed the open distrust among the Allies at the top civilian and military levels. Censorship and concealment had made this a well-kept secret. Kent's report swept the country, since his was one of the first nationally syndicated columns.

He was highly respected in and out of the press for his independence, accuracy, and integrity, though now and then his hates and loves were reflected in his column. As a reporter and news analyst he feared no one; but in his private relationships he was warm and affectionate. While Kent's political philosophy was conservative, his column, above all, was informative and revealed an intimate familiarity with political situations in all the states of the Union.

Certain basic qualities make some reporters and commentators outstanding and others just run-of-the-mill types or pompous doctrinaires. A nose for news, the industriousness to pursue it, a prepossessing personality and a zeal for fairness make the difference. Many newspapermen slide unwittingly into slanting their reports favorably toward likable politicians who clap them on the shoulder and call them by their first names. Kent was insensible to these studied beguilements, as all premier reporters and news analysts are.

After Kent left his posts as Washington bureau chief and then managing editor to concentrate on his column, J. Frederick Essary, his successor in Washington, became a leader in procuring exclusive and authoritative information, due in part to perhaps the most intense reportorial legwork I have ever observed in any colleague. He worked incessantly. He was never satisfied with the prima facie of any aspect of the news.

Between 1910 and 1915, when I was serving my first term in the Washington press corps, a famous member was Angus MacSween of the *Philadelphia North American,* a paper that no longer exists. MacSween was a crusading reporter in the tradition of Lincoln Steffens. Like Clark R. Mollenhoff, of the Cowles newspapers, who appeared decades later on the Washington reportorial scene, MacSween looked deep below the surface to expose what government tried to cover up or conceal. He also wrote in a fine satirical vein.

Another notable Washington reporter of this era, a dour, withdrawn man who at the same time put a bite in his dispatches was Sumner Curtis of the *Chicago Record-Herald*. Still another was George E. Miller of the *Detroit News*, a favorite of President Theodore Roosevelt and later editor of that paper. Fortunately for me, he was one of my patrons among the senior correspondents. Miller's dispatches acquired a national audience because of their quality, independent flavor, and penetration into the whys and wherefores of the events he dealt with.

As in the cases of O'Laughlin and Oulahan, when Miller reported that a presidential project was impending, the action could be confidently expected. Theodore Roosevelt sent up trial balloons, many marked for oblivion if they failed to rise, but Miller refused to inflate them. In 1912, when T.R. went to Chicago to oppose the renomination of President Taft, and in the hope of being nominated himself, he had a reception for the press. When George Miller came along the line Roosevelt clapped him on the shoulder and said, "I never was able to fool this old fellow."

T.R. was not the first President to make what use he could of the press to launch trial balloons, making them official only if and after they rose to the atmospheric level of public approval. The presidential successor that also bore the name of Roosevelt was equally active in this endeavor. But as the press has grown more wary of being thus exploited — usually by pro-Administration leaders in Congress or members of the Executive Department whose price for this "information" was nonidentification — the practice has been supplanted by a "feeding" system for favored reporters.

Under this system such reporters, in private converse with

Presidents and second-level officials, are fed theretofore unrevealed solid news with permission for exclusive use, in the hope of later compassionate handling of embarrassing events of public record. This hope does not always go unfulfilled. But by comparison with Washington reporting and commentary of the past, the damage done nowadays to the standards of responsible and honest journalism is minimal. It is largely in the executive offices of the printed press and the networks that slanting the news and its editorial evaluation is to be found. Important in the process are: the placement of the news by which it can be minimized or magnified; and holding back news stories called "keepers" for publication on a date when they will have the stronger impact in forming public opinion aligned with the editorial policy of the newspaper concerned.

There is considerable fire beneath the smoke of slanted journalism that impelled Vice-President Spiro T. Agnew in 1970 to roll out his engine and his hook and ladder.

Among other outstanding newspapermen in my youth was Samuel G. Blythe, formerly of *The World,* but then the political observer for the *Saturday Evening Post.* His celebrated, exclusive interview with Woodrow Wilson in 1917 ended with an unforgettable description of Wilson standing (like John F. Kennedy years afterward) with his back to Blythe, gazing out of a White House window, confronted at last with the bodeful necessity of deciding immediately whether the United States would enter World War I.

The World was a pioneer in initiating the subjective type of Washington column that has now become prevalent. This was written by the correspondent of the London *Morning Post,* Sir A. Maurice Low, and titled "A Bystander in Washington." Not distinguished for news revelations, it was a searing analysis of what was going on in official Washington. A major competitive column in the daily press at that time was on foreign affairs by Frank L. Simonds of the *New York Tribune,* the expert on that subject in the corps. (Mark Sullivan's comment on governmental affairs then still appeared in a periodical, *Collier's.*) Foreign affairs were not a very lively subject in those days, but Simonds made it so. He accomplished this by cultivating authorities in Washington and abroad, an activity that brought him important exclusive information which he analyzed as well as disclosed, and brilliantly.

But these articles were not of the highly subjective nature that has since come to characterize so many Washington commentaries on the news. Pejorative language was the exception, not the rule, and the contents were concerned with presenting and analyzing events and the forces that set them in motion. On rereading, as I have done, a few typical examples of the output of that period of signed press commentary (as distinguished from the editorial "we") my impression was confirmed that they were generally absent of the wholly subjective quality that induces contemporaries to describe, for instance, how they sat pondering over their typewriters before determining their approaches to the matter in view.

The product of these earlier commentators was absent, too, of easy persuasions that low motivations account for most of the acts and policies of public men with which the columnists do not agree. And where so many of their successors concentrate on personalized sermons and polemics, Low, Sullivan, David Lawrence, Simonds, and company devoted themselves to illuminating *situations* and their backgrounds, human and historical.

The new syndicated breed, often under the camouflage of

the label "news analysis," is wont to make such assertions as "the feeling in Washington is," although it is obvious that in the short time between researching and writing daily pieces, the commentator could not possibly make so sweeping a calculation.

There are several reasons why newspaper publishers and editors have allowed these signed contributors the liberty that verges so readily into license and was formerly reserved to editorial writers who commented in the name, and on the responsibility, of the newspaper itself.

First, they leave the newspaper in a position to disavow the views of the signed commentator to whom it has given space — a protective shield against publications which, if made by the newspaper itself, would alienate readers and advertisers. Second, small newspapers get the product at very low prices. Third, many of the syndicated columnists attract readers by their talent, so that the newspaper which publishes their articles adds to its revenues. Fourth, there are enough columnists of differing points of view that, by using both kinds, the newspaper can escape the charge of presenting only one side of a public issue. Fifth, most editors, being located outside of Washington, lack the contacts — and often the energy — of the commentators who work where the action is. And, finally, the "new American liberals" have infiltrated the press — as well as the electronic media — so deeply, and are so busy looking for material on which they can base charges of "suppression," that publishers fear the outcry sure to follow the omission or responsible editing of even rabid commentaries from a writer the liberals claim as their own.

In the bad old days when I was breaking into the business in Louisville and in Washington — prior to World War I — the kind of excessively licensed comment now signed and widely syndicated was made by editors, with the full involve-

ment of the newspaper itself. The editors have since re-
formed; this kind of "personal journalism" vanished from the
editorial columns with the passing of Greeley, Hearst,
Pulitzer, Bennett, Watterson, and their contemporaries and
equals. But under bylines and syndication it has been revived
in another newspaper compartment.

Not, it should be said in fairness, so crudely, however, as
the following examples from the past help to illustrate:

When one Louisville editor was reported to have been the
occupant of a collapsing outhouse where necessity had forced
him to pause on his way home from a convivial dinner, the
rival editor noted the event under the headline: "Fittingly
Interred."

"Scoundrel," "villain," "mountebank," and "poisoner of the
well of truth" were normal epithets exchanged between editors. And one headlined a statement by a politician to whom
he was opposed "Diseased Liar," referring to the politician's
tendency to overindulge in stimulating beverages, though the
editor fully shared it.

"Personal journalism," as practiced by newspaper editors
themselves, waned steadily from my early reportorial days.
The intervening reform was a prudent response to mounting
public distaste for superheated and/or slanderous comment;
therefore it was in recognition of the commercial need of
regaining credibility and displaying reasonable fairness. But,
though newspaper editorials in general still reflect this reform, a number of editorial columnists have reverted to the
name-calling and emotionalism which editors formerly indulged in.

I left Washington in 1915 and did not return until 1932, to
find the community much more wide open as a news source.

Mark Sullivan had moved his column into the field of daily journalism, and David Lawrence also was writing one, notable even then for its objectivity, information, and absence of personalities. Lawrence not only was and is a diligent reporter, but one with the courage to invade territory the bureaucracy sought to exclude from the press and to delineate unpopular causes — often risking reprisals from sources with the power and disposition to inflict financial damage on his property. For, in addition to his column, he had become the founder and proprietor of a gazette of official activities, the *United States News,* since expanded into the *U.S. News and World Report.*

Lawrence began his distinguished career with the Associated Press, for which he covered the invasion of New Mexico by Pancho Villa and the civil war in Mexico itself. He left the AP to become Washington correspondent of the *New York Evening Post,* and it was in this newspaper that his dispatches took their place among the best in quality ever to come out of Washington. From that day to this he has barely missed meeting a five-day-per-week writing schedule and a weekly editorial for his magazine. While he no longer actively runs the *U.S. News and World Report* and allows full scope to its editors, they draw heavily on his wisdom, experience, and judgment.

When I came back in January 1932 my principal rival was the head of the *New York Herald Tribune* bureau, Theodore Wallen. His dispatches often brought midnight call-backs from the New York office asking for their verification. He died in August 1932 and was succeeded by Bert Andrews who also soon made his mark as a competitor to be reckoned with.

Frequently, as in the case of Andrews's predecessor, I was called on the telephone by the *Times* bureau and told that the *Herald Tribune* had what was, or appeared to be, an exclusive story. This required us to check for verification at a time of night when informed sources were difficult to reach. These *Tribune* exclusives did not always stand up — far from it. But the call-backs alerted us to the useful realization that we had real competition in covering the news of Washington. It is to the widespread lack of competition in so many communities that I attribute some of the abuses of power that occur in the press.

The *Herald Tribune* was the established national Republican newspaper, and so it was natural for a young and ambitious new Republican Congressman from California, Richard M. Nixon, to cultivate Andrews. It was this Congressman who as a member of the Un-American Activities Committee, initiated the inquiry into the charge of disloyalty against Alger Hiss. That inquiry led to the inconclusive confrontation of Hiss by Whittaker Chambers. Hiss denied even knowing Chambers, aspersed his entire testimony and demanded documentation which was not then forthcoming.

One day the young Congressman was informed that Chambers had the documentation on his farm in Maryland and would produce it if Nixon would examine the papers there. Nixon complied, took Andrews with him, and enabled the latter to disclose exclusively the documentation, plus the fascinating detail that Chambers had buried it inside a pumpkin. This beat by Andrews ranks high in the history of competitive journalism, and, though Andrews died prematurely, the fame of his "pumpkin papers" beat will long survive him.

The *Herald Tribune*'s Washington bureau staff was never as large as that of the *New York Times,* but it has been crowded with professional talent which included such stars as Joseph Alsop, Albert Warner, Rowland Evans, Robert Kintner, and David Wise. All but Warner (who was suddenly immobilized by illness) became syndicated columnists with devoted, nationwide following.

It may be true that I have known, in varying degrees of intimacy, more Presidents than any other reporter in this century. If so, the distinction arises from the facts that I have lived longer than most of my contemporaries and have represented newspapers of great influence in Washington.

I have never, as the cliché goes, broken a confidence, but that can be said by most members of the Washington press. The virtue of the claim is dubious because to breach a confidence is self-defeating. The authors of gossip and other "inside" columns specialize in publishing information given in confidence, but usually the original sources are not these columnists but those who have passed on to them for various considerations — some wholly vengeful — what they themselves have been told "under the roses."

I have been accused of fabricating news, such as my report, published in the *New York Times*, November 7, 1951, that Truman had sounded out Eisenhower to determine whether the General would be receptive to the Democratic nomination for President in 1952, and had been rebuffed. This dispatch was widely denounced as a fake and some of my colleagues joined cordially in the accusation. But the incident has since been amply verified in Eisenhower's memoirs and by others who were present when it happened.

When I reported in the *Times* that Roosevelt was seriously considering the action that took form in the National Recovery Act, a distinguished contemporary and personal friend, Mark Sullivan, expressed disbelief and, at a news conference, put the question to the President, who repudiated the story. A couple of weeks later he recommended to Congress the legislation in the form I had described it.

In the campaign of 1936 I reported that Roosevelt was toying with the idea of assembling in conference the heads of states — such as the British monarch, Stalin, Mussolini, etc. — to try to avert World War II. Roosevelt, who told me of his idea one night at Hyde Park, and authorized me to circulate it, promised he would not deny the story, and technically he kept his word during the storm the publication evoked. But he encouraged Henry Wallace, after a very conspicuous visit to him by Wallace on a campaign train, to answer reporters' questions about the story that he did not believe there was any truth in it. When I acquainted Wallace with the facts he apologized and expressed regret for his unwitting part in the matter.

The higher earnings of workers in all forms of journalism (aside from inflation-bred pay increases) that the rise of unions with the capacity, the will, and the legal immunity to terminate publication has effected, have removed a principal cause of the few lapses from personal integrity in the times when newsmen were grossly underpaid. These lapses consisted of taking money and its equivalents from corporations and individuals by journalists who dealt with news in which these corporations and individuals had a special interest.

But though it was customary, in the first two decades of this century, for reporters to travel and dine free on the railroads if they chose to do so, the acceptance was rare, except in the sports departments, of financial "honorariums" from promoters and such, in the hope of favorable publicity. In the investigation by the House Rules Committee (1917) of the famous "leak" of President Wilson's note to the World War I belligerents, asking what their terms for peace would be, it developed that at least two Washington correspondents had tipped off New York brokerage houses, some hours before the note was released, that it was coming, and had speculated on what its contents would be. But no financial quid pro quo was proved for what was at least excessive friendship for the brokers on the part of one newspaperman. And the other's compensation was a pittance of $25 per month from each of two firms.

The world was guessing what President Wilson's move would be after the Germans had offered to discuss peace with the Allies in December 1916, and Prime Minister Lloyd George had replied with the condition that first the Germans must pay for their "crimes."

The reporters advised the brokers, but *not* their own newspapers, that the President had sent a note of probably "great moment" to the belligerents and the neutrals. But, according to their testimony before the House Committee, neither had thought about the possible effects of this advance information on the war-nourished market.

On December 21 the morning newspapers announced that Wilson had indeed sent a note. But, though the war-expectant market broke heavily on the afternoon of the 20th and the forenoon of the 21st, the note did not advance the peace prospect in the slightest degree. However, the bears made a killing while this interpretation endured.

The congressional committee summoned the reporters to detail just how and from whom they got the advance information on which they based their messages to the brokers. Each swore he had been given no "leak," from either official or other sources, and the statement was not disproved. The only thing proved was that neither of the reporters had been present in the forenoon of December 20 when Secretary of

State Lansing told several of their colleagues in confidence that a note would be released at 5:00 P.M. and that it dealt with the German peace proposal and its cool reception by the Allies.

My professional virtue, such as it is, was put to the test only twice in my long newspaper career, and in neither instance did the party of the second part consider that ethics, as he understood ethics, was at all involved:

The faction of the Democratic party in Louisville which was opposed by the proprietors of the *Courier-Journal* and the *Times* had got the upper hand in the coming primary contest for the party's mayoralty nomination. One morning I received, in my capacity as editorial manager of the papers, from General W. B. Haldeman, editor of the *Times* and part owner of both our publications, the text of an editorial denouncing the candidate of the other faction — Sheriff Charles Cronin, a Roman Catholic — and declaring that, if Cronin were nominated, the *Times* would not support him in the election. Assessing this as a damaging position for the paper to assume because of the anti-Catholic factor involved, I laid aside the General's editorial. The storm I was expecting duly broke over my head but subsided when General Haldeman generously accepted my explanation of the reason I gave for jettisoning his editorial — that it would be taken as religious prejudice. (Cronin was nominated and lost the election).

A week or two later, Colonel James P. Whalen, the leader of the Democratic faction which had prevailed in nominating Cronin, called on me at my office. He was dressed in full fig — fawn bowler, fawn frock coat, and a ruffled shirt adorned with diamond studs. "I know what you did for Charlie Cronin," said the Colonel, "and I want you to know how much I appreciated it." Whereupon he drew from his coat pocket a large manila envelope, obviously well stuffed, and laid it on my desk.

I thanked him and, without opening the envelope, returned it, adding that my action was taken in what I considered the interest of Democratic party unity and of the *Times* itself. "Don't you want to open it?" he asked incredulously. (I have sometimes miserably wondered how much money was in that envelope.) We parted on a friendly basis, since I understood fully that the Colonel saw no ethical involvement in his tender.

The other occasion concerned the selection by the War Department, after the end of World War I, among a number of companies that were bidding for the contract to dismantle Camp Zachary Taylor in the vicinity of Louisville and develop the tract for private and business housing. I was approached by a close personal friend, a banker, who had a large financial interest in the project, and asked if I would recommend his company to Secretary Newton D. Baker, advising me that it had reserved a substantial bloc of stock for me. The reason for this generosity soon was clarified by the banker's response to my inquiry of "how come." He answered that Secretary Baker said he would rely on me for counsel as to which bidder was most likely to execute the contract faithfully and well.

I politely explained that, if this were so, I would be betraying Baker's trust by recommending a company in which I had a financial or any other personal interest. On that note the conversation ended. But I recommended this same bidder to the Secretary when later he asked me for a judgment.

This banker was a pillar of the community and the most prominent layman in the church he unfailingly attended every Sunday. Yet he seemed to have no idea he was offering me a bribe.

I was a member of the National Press Club for nearly fifty years. Its luncheons are often of great benefit to appraisal of the news, since nearly all important people in government or the heads of foreign nations accept invitations to speak there. Rarely, of course, do these mighty folk impart any facts or define positions and policies not already known. But their presence supplies the valuable opportunity for those who attend the luncheons to appraise the personalities of the men who constantly command the headlines in the press and on the television screen. So to hear and see these dignitaries is an educational process, particularly for those members of the club who are news gatherers and news analysts.

The club's personnel is by no means confined to the press — the quota of lobbyists is considerable. Occasionally, however, the speakers make hard news. It was at one of the Press Club luncheons that Secretary of State Dean Acheson, drawing what he defined as the geographical perimeter of national security, omitted Korea and Formosa. In his recent book *Present at the Creation* he contended that he had neither stated nor implied that this line of demarcation applied to all or unforeseen circumstances and hence had no responsibility for the fact that the North Koreans took it as a sign they were free to invade South Korea. Yet the event followed the speech with a celerity that lends strong support to the belief that they acted on that interpretation of Acheson's speech.

When President Johnson made his last appearance before the Press Club he was deeply involved in the consequences of statements that had produced what became known as "the credibility gap." But he sparred so deftly with that situation, and with such good humor and wit, that he was enthusiastically applauded when he concluded. For there is something about seeing the President of the United States in the flesh,

watching him apparently baring his breast to the truth, that
cajoles newspapermen in particular. Few of them, except at
news conferences, see the President at close range and have
no means of judging him as a man. Of the thousand or more
who write or broadcast the news in Washington, only a handful have that privilege.

The White House news conference is a well-rehearsed
performance on both sides of the podium. The President's
aides have tried to anticipate what questions will be put to
him and briefed him on the replies. Sometimes it is evident he
is not prepared. But it depends on his alertness or cleverness
at evasion whether he deals effectively with the problem. Of
recent Presidents, Kennedy and Nixon have come out ahead
in such instances.

But with the dangerous exposure of instant television
coverage of a presidential news conference, the delicate conditions of world war and peace, and of domestic social-
economic woes, attest that changes in the format are vitally
required. Though reversion to the former news repressive
practice by which reporters submitted questions in writing
and in advance would probably not be ventured by any
President, he should be supported in prescribing that release
of the televised transcripts of the conferences should await his
editing of the questions and answers, for the sole purpose,
however, of assuring that an obvious slip of the tongue would
not misrepresent his real meaning.

And for their part the members of the media should insist
on being given the opportunity by the President to follow up
an important question when the President has evaded really
answering while professing to do so.

Until the 1960's the exclusive presidential interview for
publication was such a rarity that the number of times it had

been granted to the press could be counted on the fingers of one hand. Except for Samuel G. Blythe's famous interview with Woodrow Wilson on the verge of our decision to enter World War I, I don't recall any other until my interview with Franklin Roosevelt in 1937.

The press conference that followed was an angry one. Roosevelt was accused of favoritism. He was told that the White House correspondents were *working* reporters, whereas I was a bureau chief — a disparaging distinction without merit since a bureau chief who does his job is as much a working newspaperman as any "legman" on his staff. J. Fred Essary of the *Baltimore Sun,* one of my oldest friends, asked Roosevelt if they were to expect repetitions of this favoritism, ignoring the obvious fact that Roosevelt chose me primarily because the interview would appear in the *New York Times* and the *Times* was the most desirable medium for his purpose.

To the protestors Roosevelt said: "My head is on the block. Steve's head is on the block [the reference was to Stephen Early, his press secretary]. I promise never to do it again." And he didn't.

The origin of my published interview with President Truman was an offer by the President himself. He made it at a party at the 1925 F Street Club given by the late Senator Brian McMahon of Connecticut and his wife. My wife and I were present as were President and Mrs. Truman.

I was standing in a corner of the smoking room after dinner, talking with Chief Justice Fred M. Vinson, a fellow Kentuckian; and, looking at the President standing nearby, remarked that I had some questions I would like to ask him. The Chief Justice called over to the President, repeated my remark, and Mr. Truman joined us saying, "What questions? I'll answer them right now."

I was a little alarmed by that open exchange and asked for an opportunity to see the President alone. "All right," Mr. Truman said. "You arrange it with Charlie Ross [his press secretary]. I'll give you the answers and you can print them."

A couple of days thereafter Ross called me with the word that the President wanted to see me at a certain time. I appeared when and as directed, asked him the questions I had in mind, and he answered them. As in Roosevelt's case, the quantity of direct quotation was limited, but I was able to say that the rest of it was authorized by the President for direct attribution.

The press resented this interview, too, but Truman, unlike Roosevelt, did not apologize when the matter was raised at a news conference. "I'll give interviews to anybody I damn please," he said, and changed the subject.

One Sunday sometime later, when I came back from walking my dog, my wife told me the President had left a call. I telephoned Blair House, where he was living temporarily, and when he came on the line he asked me what I was doing. I said, "Nothing. I just walked the dog." Remarking "That's good for you and the pup," he added, "Come and see me but don't tell Joe Short anything about it." Short was his press secretary at that time.

We had a long conversation. I reported it in the form of the third person, though the President did not suggest this. But I felt he should have, in view of the tumult of the past occasion, and wrote two successive columns which I headlined "The President's Thinking at This Time."

The press did not protest this interview because I had not attributed it specifically and directly to the President. The average newspaper reader might not have realized that this was another interview, but the trade knew it. My colleagues saw the marks of authenticity, recognizing the now commonly employed and transparent device of quoting "a high" source or even "the highest" authority on how the President's thoughts on the issues were trending. But Joe Short was in a position truthfully to say he didn't know a thing about the genesis of the article.

9

Society

DURING MY FIRST TOUR OF DUTY in the capital city, married members of Congress rarely brought their families to Washington. The reason was simple. The pay of Congressmen was $5000 per year, and while that was a good deal of money then, their constituencies expected a Congressman to maintain his dwelling among them. Most Congressmen had children and so, unless they were rich, it was a financial necessity to keep their families at home and their children in the local schools. They lived as quasi-bachelors in hotels like the Driscoll on Capitol Hill, the Cochran, and the Riggs House.

Cordell Hull, then a Representative from Tennessee and a certified bachelor, lodged in the staid precincts of the Cochran. Many of his livelier colleagues resided at the Riggs House where the Riggs Building now stands at Fifteenth and G Streets, Northwest.

It was a tolerant hostel. There were many stories about the relaxing lives enjoyed at the Riggs House, including Boccaccian tales in which the principals were among those who have made serious contributions to political history in this century. But by and large, only the wives and families of Presidents, Cabinet members, rich members of Congress, the bureaucracy, and of course, the diplomats and the press, accompanied their spouses to Washington. (Only the Representatives from Virginia and Maryland, and those from New York City — moonlighting then as now — traveled to and from their homes every weekend.)

The sessions were shorter and the mileage allowance was much more restricted. So were the perquisites — the franked mail quota, the office personnel — usually a secretary, a clerk, and maybe an office messenger — and the stationery allowance.

The nation in this era was far less urbanized, hence the politicians who came to Washington were used to physical exercise. They were hearty, vigorous men, among whom were many who walked from their homes to and from the Capitol or the Executive offices every day. It was also customary for several members of Congress and the press to stop on their way home at Shumaker's, a famous and wonderful saloon in E Street, Northwest, where the National Theater now stands.

At Shumaker's, the floor was covered with sawdust, the liquor was stored in barrels around the walls, the bar was wholly utilitarian, and the bartenders served in shirt-sleeves. Just as in later years one would see Felix Frankfurter and Dean Acheson walking from Georgetown as far as Acheson's office every morning (Frankfurter used a cab or his own car to ride the rest of the way to the Court), in those days Reps. Ollie James of Kentucky and Tom Heflin of Alabama regularly walked down from Capitol Hill to Shumaker's, sometimes with Rep. Albert Burleson of Texas, who was to become President Wilson's Postmaster General.

It was in effect an open and pleasant club. Next door was another, patronized more by the press than by the politicians. A reporter christened it the "University of Gerstenberg," after the name of the owner of the tavern. It had a big, round table imprinted deeply over the years with the bottoms of the beer steins banged on it during drinking songs.

The Willard, though no longer a hotel, still stands at its corner, but the rest of the neighborhood has been completely changed. Also the gastronomic excellence of Washington's past has sharply deteriorated. Those were the days when the capital could justly claim to have several of the finest dining places in the United States — Chamberlain's, Harvey's, the Arlington Hotel, the Metropolitan Club and Madé's, on Four-and-a-half Street. Harvey's at Tenth and the Avenue, specialized in seafood. The Metropolitan Club was a gourmet's delight (difficult as it may be for its current members to believe). Chamberlain's had an authentic French cuisine. The Ebbett House, where the National Press Club Building now stands, ran a good restaurant, too. Also the Occidental. And the proprietors were present in person and otherwise attentive in the continental way.

In those years public transportation was limited to streetcars and hacks known as herdics and referred to as "seagoing." The herdic was a Victorian carriage, seating four, and usually drawn by a single horse. A popular evening recreation in those days was to hire a cruising herdic and drive slowly around the Ellipse. To reach the Northwest or Capitol Hill areas involved a very slow ride uphill: hence most people bound for those heights used the streetcar.*

Even electric automobiles, which were rare but less so than the gasoline driven kind, needed full-strength batteries to make the ascents. I remember vividly the time my wife developed labor pains suddenly. I managed to get a taxi for

---

* If I had used the streetcar on one particular evening I would not have found myself racing a trained bear up Capitol Hill. The bear, his trainer, and I had imbibed sufficiently at Shumaker's to induce me to accept the trainer's proposal that I accompany them home where the bear would perform some remarkable tricks. We hailed a herdic, the bear and I sitting in the back seat. But as the ascent began the bottom of the herdic fell out and there was nothing else for me to do than run uphill, *within* the vehicle, alongside the intoxicated bear. Somehow we made it, but the incident ended my association with the bear, equally amiable though he was in his cups or cold sober.

the downhill journey to Columbia Hospital in Georgetown and there I was met by our family physician, Dr. Sterling Ruffin (later President Wilson's physician during the President's incapacity). After he had safely delivered my only child, a son, he offered to take me home but the battery of his electric vehicle failed at the intersection of Connecticut and Florida Avenues. I lived on the hill above; therefore was obliged, in my excited state, to walk the rest of the way.

Washington in those days was a small, Southern city, with no traffic lights that I can recall; with policemen only at the few busy intersections. One of my permanent recollections is of old ladies, sitting straight up in electrics, and driving them without regard for pedestrians or other vehicles.

People had begun to move out to Massachusetts Avenue and Cleveland Park and Chevy Chase, but those areas did not become populous until the advent of the Model T Ford. Now the streetcar tracks are obliterated in Washington; then they ran in all directions. One route from downtown ended at Chevy Chase Circle, a considerable distance from the Chevy Chase and Columbia Country Clubs. Some bachelor members owned two-seater automobiles, and were wont to park at the Circle. When a friend with a girl in tow alighted from the streetcar, they offered to drive the lady the rest of the way — a stratagem that did not endear the poachers to her escort.

The trolley ride was often a social journey in those days because those aboard usually knew one another. It was customary to ride a trolley in full fig to any dinner, however grand. Thus, before the all-male Gridiron Dinner, for instance, you would see silk-hatted, white-tied members of the club standing with their wives or guests, or both, on street corners waiting for the trolley — the wives bound for the attendant hen parties.

Top-level diplomats and high officials had cars, but it was

on the streetcars that one encountered members of Congress and the press. In the summer the passengers were mostly male, for press wives with young children like my own usually had gone to cooler regions, and such congressional wives as came to Washington had returned to the "district." The summer streets in Washington were as unbearably hot as they are now and inside there was no air-conditioning. But citizens managed to endure the heat, especially those who owned electric fans.

In the three seasons when entertaining is a major Washington industry, the hostesses of wealth and position were not excelled at that time for taste in other capitals of the world. In Washington society few Representatives made the grade, and not many Senators. It was dominated by the cave dwellers of Washington — most of them the descendants of men of simple origins who had served in the armed forces or been appointed or elected from the "sticks" — and shared only by those officials whose "background" met the test of the eligibility the cave dwellers had acquired in a generation or two.

Such an official was W. Marshall Bullitt of Louisville, President Taft's Solicitor General. The Bullitts have long been a most distinguished family, Virginian in origin and spreading to Louisville and Philadelphia. But it was not the office held by Marshall Bullitt that provided the card of admission to Washington society — it was his ancestral background, including the Virginia explorer of the "West," Alexander Scott Bullitt, who, with Christopher Gist, discovered the Falls of the Ohio where afterward arose the city of Louisville.

Entertaining was, and still is, done largely in private houses. There was, for example, no F Street Club, now the most desirable intown locus of small mixed dinners. This was founded much later by Mrs. James Curtis, the daughter of Governor Merriam of Minnesota, who removed to Washington when appointed a Governor of the Federal Reserve Board. Beautiful, gay and highly intelligent, Laura Merriam made her debut here and, after her marriage to James Curtis of Boston, Assistant Secretary of the Treasury, lived at 1711 F Street. The Curtises also acquired the house which is now the 1925 F Street Club.

When Laura Curtis divorced her husband she started the club in the house at 1925 which had been rented or owned as living quarters by prominent officials with the essential "social" background. But until her second marriage, to John Gross, a Bethlehem Steel Company official, she continued to maintain her own residence at 1711 until after World War II (in which both her sons, James and Fielding Curtis, were killed).

The club's standards of admission rated the classification of "exclusive," a word much favored — and grown meaningless — in current obsequious journalism, and in the second half of this century in Washington only really applicable to the Alibi — an all-male group devoted to close companionship, good food, and refreshed by the constant addition to its small membership of the top-brass of the period, for example, General George C. Marshall. Members of the F Street Club were the cave dwellers, and those politicians, diplomats, bureaucrats, and journalists who were found acceptable by Mrs. Gross.

Embassy dinners were and have remained a great factor in the inner social circles of Washington. But with the proliferation of Ambassadors, some from countries composed of a patch of desert sand or a partly cleared jungle, few have the tone of the first three decades of the 1900's when a diplomat's invitation forecast an evening in distinguished company. This was particularly true of the Peruvian Embassy dinners — Ambassador Freyre was the dean of the Diplomatic Corps and a gentleman of high birth; of evenings at the Rumanian legation when Charles Davila was the Minister. He had the best chef in town, except for the French. And from the time Washington arose from its primeval mudhole, the same could be said of the companies usually assembled by the Ambassadors of Britain and France. In the pre-Bolshevik and pre-Nazi days the Russian and German Embassies were also targets of social climbers. In these diplomatic houses "everybody who was anybody" was encountered in the course of the year.

Few Representatives except the leaders of the House were invited to diplomatic dinners, and only those Senators who were party leaders or chairmen of committees were among the favored guests. Lady Lindsay, the wife of the (in my observation) ablest British Ambassador who served in my time, Sir Ronald Lindsay, got into trouble with women reporters, Congressmen and lower-echelon bureaucrats because she made no effort to know them. Hence at an especially notable royal birthday garden party Lady Lindsay gave, the House and the distaff press were almost unrepresented. This brought damaging publicity upon her that, read in the Foreign Office, blighted to a degree her husband's eminent career, though this culminated in the success of his mission to Washington — to influence the repeal of the Neutrality Act.

The married and unmarried lower-level diplomats were — and are — much sought by the hostesses without much inquiry into their origins or official activities. For example, Dr. Herbert Scholz, a handsome gangster, had been a member of the Hitler Brown Shirts in the Bierhalle Putsch in Munich, and was a Hitler spy in the United States and within the Embassy. Yet in the Thirties he was socially in evidence everywhere with his highborn and beautiful wife (selected for him from the Bavarian nobility by Hitler himself, it was said).

One night, shortly before the United States entered World

War II, Scholz figured in a dramatic incident. In N Street, Georgetown, in the prewar and "phony war" period, there lived some of the most prominent government people and their families: Representative Richard Wigglesworth of Massachusetts; F. Trubee Davison, who had served as Assistant Secretary of the Army for Air; Malcolm Baldrige, a member of the House from Omaha and an all-American Yale football player; Lewis W. Douglas, later Director of the Budget, a rapidly rising member of the House from Arizona. One night, at the Wigglesworths', the Scholzes were guests. Among others present were Joseph Alsop, then unmarried, ascending in stature among Washington newspapermen, and noted as now for his outspokenness, but not yet for his distinction as host to the most interesting and important dinner guests in the capital.

A discussion was initiated by Scholz about the war. Defending the Nazi regime he said to Alsop, "Well, suppose your country goes to war with Germany. What's the first thing you would do?" Alsop said, "The first thing I would do would be to arrest you and put you in a concentration camp." Uneasy laughter on the part of Scholz. A sensation among the other guests. The tactful host changed the subject.

Another member of the German Embassy of that time was the Counselor, Hans Thomsen, of Scandinavian extraction. He too was handsome, but, unlike Scholz, he was a gentleman. His wife was known throughout the city as "Baby." Her critical comments on Hitler were taken as indiscretions that imperiled her husband's position. At dinner parties she openly deplored the actions of the Führer, to the apparent alarm of her husband.

At a dinner given by Count George Potocki, the Polish Ambassador, among those present were the Thomsens and Signor Rossi-Longhi, the Counselor of the Italian Embassy.

He was popular for his witty cynicism, which extended to sardonic comments that audaciously infringed protocol.

The Polish Ambassador had furnished his finest dinner service; each serving-plate bore the crest of a Polish province. Baby Thomsen said to the Italian, who was sitting at her right (I at her left), "How I wish I could have these plates." "Don't worry," he replied, "you soon will." She jumped up from the table weeping, swept me into the hall, and told me she had been insulted. With what I thought was masterly pacification, I induced her to return to her seat.

Eventually it was learned that she was an active Nazi, a spy for Hitler in the Embassy and in the political community of the capital. But I thought she at least was sincere in her protection of a black squirrel that was being racially ostracized by the red and gray squirrels in a small wood adjoining her residence. I wish I had saved the letters she wrote me on this subject, soliciting my aid in getting the zoo to accept her protégé. But now I believe this was part of the cover-up of her real activity.

The Soviet Ambassadors have cultivated some Washington reporters, but only twice was I invited to their parties. The first occasion was a housewarming in the former Pullman House in Sixteenth Street. The United States had just recognized the Communist regime and the Ambassador was celebrating. The other invitation was from a press attaché, whose name I have forgotten, to see a propaganda film and feast on caviar. I don't think he was a spy, but he mysteriously disappeared after recall to Moscow. Perhaps his error was his failure to induce me to relay assurances to people high in our government that the Kremlin had no plans inimical to the United States. I think he believed that. But I never passed those messages on.

Another Soviet pressman, Vladimir Romm, often came to

my house in Kalorama Road during the cold war. When he was arrested during a visit to Moscow and put on trial, some other newspapermen and I drew up an appeal to Stalin which we forwarded through Ambassador Joseph E. Davies, asking for a fair trial, assuring the Kremlin there was nothing Romm had said or done — and we knew him quite well — that gave the slightest indication of disloyalty to his government. In time we heard that Romm had been "liquidated."

At any rate, I never heard of him again and we never got even an acknowledgment of our demarche, except from Davies, who said he had delivered it.

Most of the private clubs which have social éclat provide in their bylaws that no "business" may be transacted on the premises. But in practice this becomes a euphuism. Members in Washington who entertain government officials there, and clients (prospective and in hand), do so with the purpose of extracting information that will be of value in their business (this definitely applies to the press) and the guest hopes in turn to advance his own objectives.

A notable exception at the Metropolitan Club was provided for years by a group, important in their own spheres of life, that met regularly at a table at the south end of the long dining room on the fourth floor. None had any purpose in the association other than the good talk that was always to be heard, enriched by accounts of rare personal experiences. (The table was jocularly known to the uninvited as "The Last Supper.") For topical and historical discussion I have never been privileged to belong to a gathering where conversation covered so many areas of unique human experience in historical events. And I doubt this would have been true at this stage in history of any casually assembled group of clubmen outside Washington.

The table expanded gradually, to about a dozen regulars from the three or four who used to lunch daily with Representative Swagar Sherley of Louisville, Kentucky, after he was defeated for reelection to Congress in 1918. It was he who introduced me to the group in 1933. Among those it then included was, then and now, the dean of the Supreme Court bar, who at ninety-six is an eminent and still active American. This is John Lord O'Brian, the *a* in whose surname was the source of endless banter with another distinguished habitué of the table who came in a little later. The banterer was Robert Lincoln O'Brien, former editor of the *Boston Transcript* and the *Boston Herald,* later chairman of the United States Tariff Commission. He was one of the most gifted of those rare raconteurs who have mastered the art, and make their anecdotes more delightful by ridiculing their own part in the experiences they relate.

The regular members in my time, in addition to Sherley, O'Brian, and O'Brien, included Eugene Meyer, the financier turned publisher by his purchase of the *Washington Post;* Dr. Harry Kerr, Judge J. Harry Covington, and Edward Burling, who founded the law firm that is now one of the largest and most important in Washington; Vice Admiral Emery S. Land (now almost as old as Mr. O'Brian), who was wartime chairman of the Maritime Commission after serving as vice-chairman to Joseph P. Kennedy; Charles Warren, the standard historian of the Constitution and the Supreme Court; Major General Frank McCoy, of vast experience as a soldier and diplomat in all parts of the world, a member of the Commission that demoted General Billy Mitchell; Colonel Stephen Bonsal, whose experiences as a pioneer American foreign correspondent are delightfully recorded in his book *Heyday in a Vanished World;* my Princeton classmate Ambassador Joseph Coy Green; and the explorer Hiram Bingham, Connecticut ex-Senator and ex-Governor, who discovered the ruins of Machu Piccha, and of Vitios, the ancient capital of the Incas in Peru.

The so-called inscrutable Oriental mind often entered the conversation at the table for several reasons. The menace of Japanese militarism had already become manifest; the United States, under a token United Nations flag and token assistance from its "allies," was at war in Korea; and Colonel Bonsal and General McCoy had seen extended service in the Far East.

Mention of Korea one day led Colonel Bonsal, who had spent some years in the foreign service and had been chargé d'affaires in Seoul, to describe the easy-going government by its privileged class that made the country a sitting duck for the territory-hungry Japanese. "The Empress," said the Colonel, "had two groups of mandarins associated with her in government, the 'Help-Discuss' mandarins and the 'Help-Decide' mandarins. When a problem arose the Help-Discuss group would assemble at the capital, talk things over extensively, and then retire to the monasteries with their priests, dancing-girls and jesters and eat and drink their fill. Then the Help-Decide mandarins would take over and, after reviewing the aimless oratory of the Help-Discuss noblemen, come to conclusions that they presented to Her Imperial Majesty and were generally disregarded. This was the situation when the Japanese disposed of the Empress and the problem by the simple solution of assassination and the harshest conceivable military occupation."

This narrative produced the inevitable comment — I think by Robert Lincoln O'Brien — that often the government of the United States appeared to operate on the same two-mandarin group principle.

Bonsal knew the most unexpected people all over the world and his reminiscences shone accordingly. One was Charlie

Mitchell, the British heavyweight champion. During an interview with Mitchell on the eve of his famous match with the American Jake Kilrain, in France, Bonsal, taking umbrage at a remark by Mitchell, on impulse knocked the champion down. Bonsal weighed about 125 pounds, but, being a hot-blooded Maryland gentleman-horseman, he did what came naturally. He had been a Lieutenant Colonel in World War I (simulated rank) and at the Paris Peace Conference of 1918–19 he served as President Wilson's interpreter, an experience he related in the book *Unfinished Business*.

As aforesaid, he had known nearly every celebrity of his time. One day someone mentioned Bismarck. "When I went to Heidelberg," the Colonel recalled, "I had a letter of introduction to the Prince, and he asked me to call. Brashly I remarked that he showed none of the traditional fencing [Schlagerbund] scars that marked the faces of all the Heidelberg men I had ever seen. 'You will find them,' replied the Iron Chancellor, 'on the faces of my adversaries.'" (It is a fact that Bismarck was the only unscarred fencer up to that time in the long history of this university.)

The celebrities Bonsal hadn't known General McCoy had. To listen to them was to be introduced to the intimate biographies of the modern makers of history.

Among the other regulars at the table was Seth Richardson, a large, muscular lawyer from North Dakota. In his youth he had been the boxing mentor of Billy Petrolle, onetime middleweight champion of the world. In other respects Richardson was a true product of his rugged early environment. His role at the table was to knock down myths and pretensions with devastating comments.

Charles Warren was an outstanding contributor of personal distinction, charm, knowledge, humor, wit and wisdom. I shall not forget the ruddy face above the high wing collar; the ready smile; the quick irascibility, and the reflection, in his discourses on relationship with the great men of the law and of government, of an association covering the larger part of a century.

Mr. Warren had great dignity. And his work as the standard historian of the Supreme Court made him a famous person as well. But there was nothing stuffy about him: he enjoyed nothing more than a joke directed toward himself (the staple entertainment at the table). The principal contributor to this exercise was Mr. Warren's friend from Harvard days — Robert Lincoln O'Brien.

Mr. O'Brien knew that I was in the habit of consulting Mr. Warren on the meaning of some of the more legalistic major Supreme Court decisions so that I could make them clear in my writings for the *New York Times*. Therefore, every time such an analysis appeared in my column, Mr. O'Brien would alternately congratulate or criticize Mr. Warren for it, on the ground that it was "well-known" he was writing *Times* articles in this field "under the pseudonym of Arthur Krock." This jest never seemed to wear out for either of them, the same being true of comments on the cutaway and especially high collar Mr. Warren wore on Mondays (when the Supreme Court issued its opinion), and the inevitable neo-Crimson tie he wore as a most loyal son of Harvard.

Once, when his wing collars were again the objects of a discussion, initiated as usual by Mr. O'Brien, I ventured to draw up a "brief" arguing that this haberdashery was "constitutional"; sent it to Chief Justice Stone, who "handed down" a solemn affirmation of my plea. I recall with gratification how delighted Mr. Warren was with this foolishness, engaged in to mark his seventy-fifth birthday.

He was a "Wilson Democratic liberal" in politics, as I held myself to be. So when the Supreme Court under Earl Warren began its foray on the Constitution and the other branches of the Federal government, and President Truman issued the blueprint for what has become the Welfare State, Mr. Warren was as disturbed as I was at the trend of the Court and the Democratic party. But rarely was it possible for any of us at the table to get from him an open admission of his disenchantment. He remained a partisan Democrat — outwardly — on the Stephen Decatur platform as transposed thus: "My party, may it always be right," etc. But privately his deviations from the Decatur principle as far as the Democrats were concerned were obvious.

Mr. Warren was, I think, a most unusual combination of the merry and the serious, according to the appropriateness of the approach and the occasion. And as a social companion who neither looked down at nor up to his contemporaries, he was as pleasant to be with as any famous person I have known.

The roster, including those whose attendance was irregular, included Joseph E. Davies, former Ambassador to Moscow and once a high official of the Wilson Administration; Rear Admiral Gilbert Rowcliffe, the last defender in the Navy of the battleship versus the air carrier; John Spalding Flannery, personal attorney for many members of the Supreme Court; Walter Lippmann; Dean Acheson; and a number of Ambassadors. Among the latter were Lord Halifax and the Marquess of Lothian, British; Van Kleffens of the Netherlands; Sir Leslie Munro of New Zealand; and Lord Casey of Australia.

When distinguished visitors were in Washington they usually came to the table as guests during their stay, for among the regulars they were certain to have an old friend.

All around us we could see newspapermen interviewing government officials, and lawyers with their most valued clients. But only when papers were spread on the luncheon cloth was there a demonstrable infraction of the bylaws that brought an admonitory note from the Board of Governors. In all the clubs with which I am familiar the ideal of keeping business wholly outdoors was similarly a theoretical one.

As I write the only survivors of the regulars at the table are John Lord O'Brian, Vice Admiral Land, Ambassador Green and myself.

When I first joined the Metropolitan Club in 1933 members of the Cabinet frequently lunched there. The private dining room for high officials that now adjoins their offices had not become an appurtenance, a fringe benefit, in those simpler times. And chauffered limousines to transport officials to and from the club were rare. The occupants of the high power structure in Washington either used their private vehicles or taxicabs. Now the government limousines crowd H Street in front of the club, and from them emerge some of the most vocal criers against Federal spending and some of the most vociferous egalitarians in town.

Their intensive lip service to Jefferson's platform of "equal rights for all, special privileges for none" is also diminished by their availability to certain favorites in the swarm of lobbyists, whose Washington population explosion is attributable in considerable part to the swollen bureaucracy of the Federal government. This apparatus of government now inhabits a constantly spreading labyrinth in which only experienced representatives of special interests can find their way to the bureaucrat who has the power to assist them.

The best reporters in the capital are those who know not only the right questions, but also the right people to ask them of. With lobbyists effective performance depends just on knowing the right people.

From this useful connection has grown a segment of Washington "society" whose diversions relax the tensions of the day for officials and lobbyists alike. These diversions include cocktail and debutante parties given by officials for whom lobbyists pay the tab and list the item in disguise on their expense accounts. In addition, there are tickets to the fund-raising dinners in behalf of the major parties and their candidates that lobbyists are made pointedly aware they are expected to buy in generous quantities, and do. While this underwriting does not guarantee the success of the lobbyist in pursuing with the bureaucracy the special interests he represents, it helps to ease the labors of the pursuit.

There is nothing reprehensible about lobbying with government officials: the honorable lawyers and corporate agents cannot otherwise find a clearing in the political and official jungle in which the operations of the system are conducted. But there are ethical and unethical methods in the process. And there are far too many in office at both ends of Pennsylvania Avenue who shut their eyes to the difference.

Since, as previously noted, most members of the bureaucracy owe their jobs to the previous Administrations, lawyers and other lobbyists who have held posts in those Administrations have a special entrée to the bureaucrat who can cut red tape and otherwise simplify their missions. For the fact is often overlooked that a basic reason why the policies of new Presidents, even of the same party as the outgoing Chief Executive, are impeded and frustrated by underlings protected by the civil service, is that the loyalty of the underlings is to a preceding President and to a doctrine rejected at the polls.

Society, as the descriptive of groups of people who entertain one another lavishly and with such elegance and taste as they may be capable of, was always of special importance in Washington. But now it concentrates more intensely on catering to the members of the current political power structure at the expense of distinguished table talk. The hope behind this design is that, like the courtiers of royalty, the higher the degree of personal association of the professional party givers with those, however dull, who wield political power, the more and better will be the publicity accorded these professionals. And Washington is a capital where publicity and reputation for influence march together.

As for the celebrities at the feasts, whose promised presence assures the acceptance of invitations by other celebrities that otherwise could not be induced to attend, going out in Washington is an easy and relaxing way to establish personal relations that any time might be put to good use by any of them.

Senators who have just denounced each other on the floor as moral lepers can laugh it off over cocktails and clap each other on the back. This is a convenient provision against the day they know they will need to exchange sub-rosa favors. Diplomats can swap useful tips with others in the Corps. And the comparatively few members of the press contingent of two thousand who are invited to the small functions which — in the peculiar Washington sense — are "exclusive" can get vital information in a brief after-dinner tête-à-tête that all their industry and professional talent could not acquire. Nor does this calculated gift of privilege go always unrewarded. For inevitably the time comes when each — Senator, diplomat, reporter, commentator — can be of legitimate usefulness to the other.

For these reasons, a sketch of the power-centered hospitality which is Washington "society" is not to be scorned in an attempt, such as this one, to examine the ways and means of government.

As political power and influence shift with ups and downs

at the polls and the advent of new Administrations, so, and solely, do the guest lists. The most fallacious and worn cliché in town is that "there is no sex in Washington" — meaning that there are remarkably few "affairs," intermarital and otherwise. But the search of the professional hostesses who vie for publicity of their doings is an intensive business in which the usual attributes of sexual attraction yield to the possession of power. A Don Juan without a connection with politics would have no chance, as against an amorous bumpkin in office, with ladies disposed to dalliance, of whom I believe Washington has an average quota.

Between the two World Wars, and for a decade or so thereafter when I was often among those present, Washington society offered a combination of fashion, brains, and wit (as Enid Bagnold describes the London upper world of her youth). An evening at an embassy was likely to include a brilliant exposition of classical and light music, expertly rendered. The quality of conversation and diversity of groups such as were gathered by Mrs. Nicholas Longworth, Mrs. Robert Woods Bliss, Mrs. Truxtun Beale, Mrs. Eleanor (Cissie) Patterson, or Mrs. Robert Low Bacon, were not excelled in any other capital with which I am familiar. And the grace, elegance, and good manners of the three-a-year balls of the social group known as the Dancing Class, conferred social distinction on those who were invited to attend on the basis of standards unconcerned with their worldly possessions or how often their names appeared in the newspapers.

High in the list of American group diversions is the noble game of poker, and Washington is not behind any other city per capita, though the stakes are generally lower than those in New York. I recall with particular pleasure two regular sessions in which I participated: one, a mixture of the sexes at the house of Mrs. Longworth; the other a stag affair in the

Carlton Hotel suite of Stewart McDonald, the right-hand man of Jesse H. Jones at the Reconstruction Finance Corporation and later chairman of the B. & O. Railroad.

Both games included the variety of dealer's choice, but the second differed in that it included table stakes and seven-card high-low divide; also wild cards were conventionally confined to deuces. Among the ingenuities devised by Mrs. Longworth were kings-with-swords and (though she disputes my recollection) a deal which required a complex calculation that baffled me at least. But she did not depend on these for a high ratio of success: there may be shrewder poker players than she outside the ranks of the professionals, but not in any where I held a hand, even those I recklessly engaged in on the North Shore of Long Island in which the losses and winnings were in the thousands of dollars.

The regulars at the Carlton, in addition to Jones and Mc-Donald, included two of the craftiest players I ever have encountered — Lt. Gen. William S. Knudsen, the great engineer drafted from the automobile industry into the nation's war preparedness program, and Stephen T. Early, press secretary to President Roosevelt. The stakes were high in proportion to my income. But without an element of risk poker is not poker. I managed to survive financially, but to come down to the finals in that game always filled me with anxiety for my creditors.

It has been some years since I enjoyed the pleasure of the good company at Mrs. Longworth's and the tenseness of the combats at the Carlton. But as a feature of Washington life, both in and out of the constantly changing circle rated as "society" on the newspaper pages devoted to such doings, poker still flourishes among the diversions which briefly heal the wounds of the endless struggle for power and publicity. And I still live in the hope that some night a television special, breaking new ground, will record the table talk and playing strategies of a game where, I am told, those stars of broadcasting and printed humor — David Brinkley and Art Buchwald — are among the contenders. For, Alexander Pope despite, the proper study of mankind is of its behavior at poker.

In the relaxations of Washington life, the annual dinners of the Gridiron and Alfalfa clubs merit the gratification of the celebrities and others who are invited to attend. At both the entertainment is supplied by nonprofessionals — at the Gridiron, brilliantly satiric skits and songs dealing with public affairs; at the Alfalfa searing burlesques of standard political oratory. But until recent years there was a third evening which was quite as enjoyable and drew the same clientele. The founder and architect was John Russell Young, a tall, portly man, for years the White House reporter of the *Evening Star* and then a Commissioner of the District of Columbia.

He named his organization the J. Russell Young School of Expression of which, at the annual dinners, he appeared in the academic garb of "Dean" and performed as Master of Ceremonies. Behind him was a canvas backdrop on which was painted the school's "campus" — the White House and its north lawn. At remarkably frequent intervals, considering the human capacity to retain liquid nourishment, an assistant would march forward and present the Dean with the largest flagon conceivable, brimming with beer which Young consumed steadily throughout the proceedings.

A daisy chain, led by Jesse Jones and consisting of postgraduates of the school, was the opening feature, after which the new graduates delivered their speeches of acceptance and the class valedictorian "planted a tree." The choice of these imaginary trees was wide and ingenious, but perhaps that planted by Breckinridge Long, Assistant Secretary of State in the F. D. Roosevelt Administration took the all-time honors. "Our class," he said, "has commissioned me to plant a tree that will last, a tree with a sole — a shoe tree."

The School of Expression and its dinners died with its founder and Dean, and left a gap in the easing of the pressures that constantly assail its shakers and movers. But it will never be forgotten by those survivors who were granted the school's "degree" of Doctor of Oratory.

And in the mutation of the years to a "swinging" Washington, a talent has been developed in which the capital's most publicized party givers excel. This is the ability to detect not only the loss of the electoral or administrative power that fills with invitations the salver of the one who had it, but that this loss is impending. I would back these females against any of their kind anywhere in sensing when nothing more is to be gained by the presence at their tables of persons who long were sought there. However faintly this scent of decaying power comes to their nostrils, they can sniff it as instantly as the predatory birds can detect their unsavory comestibles from afar.

The test of whom they invite is not the famous one in the anecdote of the late Vice-President Barkley: "What have you done for me lately?" It is, "What can you do for me still?" And when the answer is negative, as so often it must be in a community where there is a regular crop of power has-beens, the only means by which these can remain even on the fringes of Washington social climbers is cash — expended on constant and costly entertainment of such of the "ins" as can be attracted by the promise that another political celebrity has been captured for the occasion.

This characteristic of Washington life probably appears in every nonmetropolitan capital city where power and social activity are closely akin. But in the great metropolitan centers of the United States there are many distinguished, talented groups which are not in the least impressed by political position or influence, or a diplomatic connection, as a card of admission.

As an example of the cultural benefit of this diversity, I recall a certain evening when I lived in New York City. The event was a party given by Jascha Heifetz's mother at her apartment on the West Side, and it was marked by a performance of chamber music by perhaps as gifted a quintet as could be assembled anywhere at that time.

Invitations were for nine o'clock and as the guests assembled they could see in the dining room a long, wide table which eventually was to bear a heaping variety of the edibles that seem to have a special appeal to that most international of groups — musicians: salami and other cold meats, pickles, rye bread, spaghetti, cheeses, huge hot casseroles of infinite succulence, black coffee, beer, wine, champagne, whiskey, and so on.

Four members of the quintet on this occasion (I forget who played the viola) were:

First violin, Jascha Heifetz; second violin, Louis Kaufman; cello, Mme. Marie Rosanoff; piano, Josef Hofmann. A galaxy indeed. They played glorious chamber music for about an hour, and then indulged in such horseplay as this — Heifetz burlesquing, by means of sudden dissonant squeaks, what he announced was a typical violin solo by a student graduating from a conservatory.

The comedy concluded, the guests, following the members of the quintet, made a rush for the dining room that accomplished its design of consuming the offerings of the buffet. This ingurgitation of supplies went on for some time, after which the quintet returned to the music room to play the second half of its program.

Among the guests I recognized a dark, black-haired, youthful man, with a lantern jaw, whom I had met several times. A rapt listener to the chamber music, he had concentrated on watching every move of Hofmann's fingers on the keyboard until the performance was concluded. On the demand of the master musicians he sat down to play some of his light compositions that already had made him famous in the Broadway theater. The members of the quintet gathered close around him, watching his fingers as he had watched Hofmann's and greeting the product with both amusement and admiration. Nor would they allow him to stop until he played at least a dozen of his repertory. The dark, slender young man was George Gershwin.

This delicious interlude was followed by another mass resort to the now replenished buffet, amid a babble of conversation, both general and à deux, until about 3:00 A.M. The last sights I recall were of one guest sound asleep on a sofa, and of Samuel Chotzinoff, Toscanini's friend and biographer and Heifetz's brother-in-law, casting a light cover over the recumbent figure and fondly surmounting the cover with a large tube of salami.

10

Problems

THE CENTRAL ISSUE of the time is how to prevent man from falling into the pit of extinction he has dug for himself.

A primary cause is man's profligate use of the fertility which the balance of nature has restrained in the so-called lower animals. It is this profligacy, indulged in without reckoning that space, air and food have a terminal supply point, that has made noxious caves of large areas of the planet, fouling them and their surrounding atmosphere with an overpopulation which neither wars nor pestilences can shrink to fit the earth's productive facilities.

The arrival of the condition in which man is devouring the sources of his daily life can be traced in part by examining the speeches made in the United States on Earth Day, April 22, 1970. In the warnings and exhortations, made in the name of "conservation" of the life-giving and life-supporting resources of the American people, a fundamental reason for their imperilment — unbridled human rut — either went unmentioned or was dismissed with routine sentences.

For, though the rate of population increase in the United States appears to be on a declining scale, this does not diminish the general problem for this country. One of the causes of our budget deficits, with their threat to the American economy, is the allocation of billions in foreign aid to nations where the constantly rising birthrate renders the money perpetually inadequate to achieve its purposes.

The accent of the orators was on disposal — of human waste, and of the indestructible packaging which disguises the mercantile gluttony that, shamelessly whetted by venal advertising, feeds the false god variously called Progress or Gross National Product.

The politicians made most of the speeches with an eye, not on the deadly effects of super-urbanization and unchecked human reproduction, but on the votes their paeans to "conservation" of the looted earth might gather at the next popular polls. And, of course, that misuse of the free enterprise system by labor-management contracts through which the greedy appetites of humanity are protected and stimulated, was unanimously omitted from the oratory.

But this industry-labor log-rolling in the free enterprise system contributes so largely to the peril of the American environment that it must be examined in the context. For it poses a question to which two books, written in the Nineteen Forties, were impressively addressed: Can Western democracy in view of selfish exploitation of its permissiveness, meet the global challenge, backed by the atomic bomb and missile, that confronts it in the United States and throughout the so-called civilized world?

One book, written by John F. Kennedy as a senior thesis at Harvard, *Why England Slept,* inspects the nearly fatal effects of the socialized British democracy, on which our own Welfare State is based, when Hitler put it to the test in World War II. Kennedy concluded that, faced by the threat to the lenient democratic system that autocracy can rapidly initiate with overwhelming armed might, Western democracy by its nature must either suspend temporarily and in time its concept of absolute individual and pressure-group freedom, or sacrifice hundreds of thousands of lives and billions of treasure before it can attain the stage of effective armed deterrent or retaliation.

The other book, addressed specifically to the same problem in the United States, *Can Representative Government Do the Job?* was written by Thomas K. Finletter after rich and varied experience in government with the workings of our own form of democracy.

Kennedy was writing after the fact, Finletter in the growing shadow of the ultimate test. Kennedy's argument already had been established at Dunkirk. Finletter's was a speculative proposition. But with the rise in Soviet Russia's potential for nuclear destruction, the misbegotten American military action in Indo-China, the war in the Middle East, Communist China's emergence toward the status of a nuclear power, and the undermining of the American economic structure by the alliance between political and self-interest pressure groups, Finletter's speculation has been transmuted into a frightening reality.

The basic problem raised by our democracy, as he saw it, was its built-in delays in grappling with obviously oncoming emergencies in which delay was either fatal or ruinously costly in blood and treasure. There are scores of examples, but the following are sufficient to prove Finletter's thesis insofar as the United States is concerned:

Politicians, irresponsibly exploiting for votes the public indignation against the denial by employers of the basic rights of labor that characterized the advent of the industrial age, went far beyond the other extreme. In the Thirties they crowded the statutes with special privileges for organized labor, granting legal immunity for practices which, imposed by management, would have sent its members to prison and loaded them with punitive fines.

Thereby Congress gave organized labor the unrestricted power to paralyze the daily life of the community. Under the superficially fair commandment that differences between management and labor be resolved by "collective bargaining," the Wagner Act set organized workers in the driver's seat.

With the power, which management cannot legally exercise, to bring to a halt the nation's economy, the teamsters' union, for example, can suspend the transportation and distribution of necessities of life until its demands, however excessive and inflationary, are met substantially or in their entirety. And, though the Taft-Hartley Act put certain legal limits on this union power, these can be and are disregarded and actively violated by picket lines, enforced by violence against, and coercion of, those workers who venture to attempt to cross them. So, with the tolerance of Congress and the judiciary, the picket line has become the supreme law of the land.

The specifications in the laws of what are "unfair labor practices" for years were applied by the National Labor Board and the courts to employers only. As has constantly been demonstrated in the recurrent "negotiations" between newspaper proprietors and newspaper unions, the property of an employer can be destroyed while he presses before pro-labor commissions and courts the charge of such "unfair labor practices" as slow-downs, "sick" calls, and other breaches of contract.

Strikes against the government, Federal, state, or local, by its tax-supported employees also are tolerated by executive, legislative, and judicial authorities, regardless of statutory bans and of the peril to which they subject public health and safety and a responsible fiscal policy. Sanitation workers can condemn the taxpayers they subsist on to several of the plagues of Egypt. Electrical workers can return whole communities to the Dark Ages. And all this is made possible by the latitude doctrinaire judges have read into the Fourteenth Amendment while simultaneously turning the guarantees of the Bill of Rights, the capstone of the American democratic system, from protections against tyranny of the majority to tyranny of the minority. For years the Supreme Court, though often by a margin of one vote, concentrated its zeal in behalf of individual rights on the citizens who violated the criminal laws instead of on the society that is their victim.

Employer-employee contracts which require a worker to affiliate with a union in its plant or lose his job — a glaring violation of individual rights — have the sanction of the laws and the courts. And, though the Supreme Court imposed the principle of one man one vote throughout the political process, from a presidential election to a contest for membership of a local schoolboard, it struck down a heavily affirmative vote in Colorado for an electoral system which authorized the creation of state senatorial districts on a basis other than population.

Hence, despite grave threats to the national security from enemies abroad and explosive social conditions at home, the American democratic system, under the libertarian political philosophy long dominant, is demonstrating, as Finletter feared, its failure to put down anarchy, rescue the government from the insolvency that is threatened by the greed of economic groups, and at the same time keep the people secure from external aggression and inner subversion. He offered the following proposal whereby this debacle might be averted — a loan from the parliamentary government system that the makers of the Constitution rejected in the 1787 atmosphere of the autocracy of George III:

[277]

The remedy is, I believe, to amend the Constitution so as, first, to give the President the right to dissolve Congress and the Presidency, and to call a general election . . . whenever a deadlock arises between Congress and the Joint Cabinet [a body to be composed of congressional leaders and presidential appointees]; second, to make the terms of the Senate, House and Presidency of the same length, say six years from the date of each election. . . . If such a remedy had been available, many of the distressing periods of our history, which were caused by conflicts between Congress and the Executive would have been avoided. . . . Why, for example, should the country not have been given the chance to decide in 1919 whether or not it wanted to join the League of Nations instead of having the issue decided in such tragic consequences by bitter fighting between an ill President and a Senate determined to reassert its authority?

The Joint Executive-Legislative Council, wrote Finletter, could be set up by a joint Senate-House resolution and an Executive order of the President. And its members would be subject to questioning on the House and Senate floors. The presidential candidates of each major party in the special election would present to the voters a slate bearing the names of the Joint Cabinet he would choose if elected.

In the absence of a solution, Finletter's or another, factional division, campaign promises made not to be redeemed, and the blurring of clear issues between political parties and candidates have so confused the voting public that some remedy of the situation is desperately needed to produce an overwhelming popular mandate for candidates, irrespective of their party labels, who will equip an elected President with a majority in both branches of Congress that will support his nonpartisan legislative proposals and policies until they are rejected by the people.

Although British parliamentary democracy, like its raddled counterpart in France, allowed the nation to remain almost totally unprepared while Hitler, Mussolini, and the Japanese war party made ready the military machinery for World War II, party government in the United Kingdom, so absent in the United States, was ultimately restored by the devastating experience. With a House of Commons majority of only three, Prime Minister Harold Wilson in the Sixties was able to hold its ranks intact from the assaults of the Opposition. But in this country no party leader, even one who firmly wielded and held the powers of the presidency, and whatever the number of Congressmen and Governors under his party's label, has matched this record.

Republicans defecting from the party line rescued President Kennedy from defeat in the House on several occasions. Defecting Democrats, on the other hand, slowed the pace of inflationary spending for a more egalitarian society that was proposed by Presidents Truman and Kennedy. Most of President Nixon's defeats in Congress — including the overriding of vetoes and two nominations to the Supreme Court — have been inflicted by defecting Republicans. And with the exception of the Japanese sneak attack on Pearl Harbor that united the American people in support of Roosevelt's military retaliation, the Senate has intermittently obstructed presidential formulation and conduct of foreign policy.

But it is the *causes* of this disarray among the people and in the governmental structure that have produced the flaws in the workings of the constitutional system. And since there will be no reversion here to the parliamentary system, and both major parties are and are likely to remain fragmented, such changes as have been proposed by Finletter and others can only be meditations on the problems. Their roots, in addition to the prime menace of overpopulation, are, as I see them:

We are the most, if not the only, heterogeneous people living under a democracy. When the identities and power jurisdictions of the states were preserved by Congress and the courts from the intensive Federal centralization of recent years it was far more possible to attain a loose but strong national unity by taking into consideration, in the making of general laws, the local economies and ethnic preferences that vary in contiguous states or multi-state areas. But when, as now, the laws and their administration are gathered under the tent of Federal compulsion, the constitutionally based "Federal Union" is demolished, and the state boundaries become imaginary lines, the heterogeneous makeup of the American people becomes a crucible of perpetual social discontent and disorder instead of the "melting pot" which the founders of the Republic envisaged as the grand design of American democratic liberty and justice for all.

The denigration of the states by the Supreme Court, as self-governing units, established as such both by specific constitutional allocation of powers and the general allocation of Article X, may in time be repaired by a Supreme Court less disposed to transfer all authority to the Federal system, and above all to itself. But since the denigration has been so sweeping that a century might well be required to restore essential state powers, the present might be the right time to consider a fundamental revision of the components of the Federal Union.

This would consist of a re-division of the country into like-minded regions, instead of states whose parts are in incessant political conflict. And because the trend of the Supreme Court since the Nineteen Thirties has been to obliterate state boundaries and reduce state sovereignties to the vanishing point, the elimination of the states as presently constituted would amount to no more than practical recognition of what the Supreme Court has done.

By this re-division small-town and rural areas would become sections of like-minded areas in neighboring states, and no longer be dominated politically and economically by the vast urban and suburban complexes now within the same state borders. Where these complexes contain a population of two million or more each would constitute a separate Region — for example, the complexes centering in New York City, Boston, Chicago, Detroit, Los Angeles, Philadelphia, Pittsburgh, St. Louis, and San Francisco-Oakland. Each Region would have representation in the United States Senate equivalent to the sum of its former state parts. And regional membership in the House of Representatives would be determined by factors of which population would be only one, to balance each region with the others.

Common economic and sociological interest would fix the boundaries of the new Regions. In the reallocation process Congress would remove from the Supreme Court the asserted jurisdiction by which it decreed that all election districts should be substantially equal in population — the one man one vote principle — thereby nullifying this decree. As for the mandate of Article V — that no state can be deprived of a quota of two Senators without its consent — this would cease to apply because the states as such would have disappeared.

In the interchanges among these Regions as represented in Congress, each would have greater influence than now over legislation directly affecting it, and minorities less opportunity to divide and conquer. This influence would also be kept in fair balance by retaining the method of selecting as President the candidate with a sufficient number of electors, but electors allocated to each Region, instead of each state, by a computerized system of calculation.

This reallocation of United States territory, including Alaska, and Hawaii, could not, of course be constitutionally attained (by amendment) until or unless the present myth that there still are self-governing states can be dispelled sentimentally as thoroughly as the Supreme Court has shattered it by judicial fiat. But every great reform, however urgent, is confronted by high, stubborn obstacles. And, acknowledging that my proposition is vulnerable in both sentimental and practical aspects, I propose it merely in the hope it might advance a discussion of how to restrict and reverse the centralization of all government in Washington.

The official competence, courage, and conscientiousness that the nation requires as the price of preservation of a democratic system are at one of the low levels in American history. Two of the principal products of this condition are our involvement in the war in Southeast Asia, and the steadily rising price inflation in a falling industrial and financial market.

The fundamental error of engaging American ground forces on the Asian continent should have been as clearly visible to the Johnson Administration as it was to President Eisenhower and to the few who, from the time President Kennedy initiated the involvement by enlarging the American military presence in Vietnam and moving it to the combat zones, opposed the venture. (At the beginning of 1964 the United States military personnel in Vietnam numbered 23,300; after the combat troops began to arrive in 1965, the approval by Congress of the Tonkin Gulf resolution and the North Vietnamese attack on Pleiku, the number mounted through 184,300 to 485,000 and then to 543,000.)

As previously noted, the last opportunity to halt the inflation originating in the fiscal policies of President Kennedy before it got out of control was in 1966. The chance was lost when President Johnson rejected the advice of leading economists that he ask a tax rise from a heavily Democratic and pro-Johnson Congress. Vote-getting considerations, instead of the courage that was acutely required, were allowed to shape the decision. And for the same reason both the Administration and a bipartisan majority in Congress continued to increase spending programs.

The extreme character of the social ferment that has manifested itself in anarchic violence on the campuses and in the city streets of the nation is a direct responsibility of judicial and other politicians with a low quotient of courage and conscience. Closely associated with them in responsibility are the faltering college administrators and faculty members who have allowed education to be subverted by New Left colleagues, professional agitators, and their student dupes.

The rise of extremist influence with Negro citizens is the evil product of reckless, ruthless promises by white politicians that a genetically different minority race would be fully integrated overnight; and of the growing awareness among Negroes that violence, even to the point of anarchy, would largely go unpunished in the frightened and overloaded courts. As for the white students who have occupied and burned down school and adjoining properties, in one special instance destroyed the notes that a teacher had been assembling for a lifetime, and shattered the educational process by destroying its disciplines, I offer as the soundest analysis of their conduct with which I am familiar a comment by a European exchange student. The comment appeared in an article by Robert Conquest in the *New York Times* Sunday Magazine of May 10, 1970, and is as follows:

A Czechoslovak student who spent time in the United States commented last year in the journal Dissent *that Americans he had met were "pampered children of your permissive, affluent society, throwing tantrums because father gave them only education, security and freedom — but not Utopia." He found irony in the students' discontent: "They bitterly resent society because it does not treat them as the fulcrum of the universe, though from what they told me of themselves it seemed that their families did treat them that way. I can't take them seriously. They seem to have no idea of the cost or the value of the privileges they receive. . . . What surprises me most is not that they take themselves seriously — students always do, and we are no exception — but that their elders take them seriously. In the West it seems possible to grow quite old without having to grow up — you have so much slack, so much room, so much padding between yourselves and reality. . . . You simply haven't faced up to the fact that you can't build a Utopia without terror, and that before long, terror is all that's left. We've had our fill of Utopia."*

This comment bears directly on an observation, made by a columnist dealing with the violent encounters between youthful demonstrators and the police on the streets of Chicago during the Democratic national convention of 1968. Denouncing the conduct of the deliberately provoked police, he urged his readers to remember that the demonstrators were "our children." But also, as the Czechoslovak exchange student noted, these were (our) "pampered children of your permissive, affluent society, throwing tantrums because father gave them only education, security and freedom" and "not Utopia." And it is the failure of parents to enforce the disciplines and stress the values these disciplines maintain that was heavily responsible for the actions that produced the reactions.

The large crop of the male and female unwashed and malodorous hippies and yippies, drug addicts, communal VD-ridden sexualists, and anarchists — that have created another of the grave problems of the American society — is the harvest of the cult of child worship in this country. And before the problem can effectively be dealt with, the cult must be recognized and attacked as one of its fundamental causes, not only by doting parents but by those who have access to the media of public information.

This bristling array of deep national troubles — and there are others — must somehow be catalyzed if the United States is to remain the foremost world power or even the largest viable democracy. Proposed solutions flow in by the thousands from as many groups and individuals at home and abroad. But until 1972 at least the catalyst must be the current President of the United States. And the extent and quality of his accomplishment depend on the answers to these questions:

Can he overcome the obstacles which Democratic partisanship will erect in the interest of regaining office and power — a question which only the American people can resolve?

Has he the intestinal fortitude to serve the general interest as he sees it, regardless of whether this will end any prospect he may have of being reelected?

If the answer is in the affirmative, will the measures he pursues make the national problems manageable — a question which time alone can resolve?

Will the promises Nixon has made, especially with respect to military withdrawal from Southeast Asia and the curb of inflation, be sufficiently redeemed in the time he has for the purpose — a question which involves the constant issue of the credibility of an Administration and the manageability of the areas?

He has the rare advantage of having been elected without the support of any minority. To labor, ethnic minority groups, and the like he owes nothing except to govern justly. He is confident that his goals — which, in the domestic area, a traditional Republican could hardly recognize with that party label — represent the aspirations of the unorganized majority of Americans. And he is gambling he will have enough time to attain them, regardless of the percentages of members of Congress under one or the other major party label. These goals are:

School integration stopping short of the point where the quality of education and the neighborhood school are sacrificed to it.

Withdrawal from Vietnam except for a watchdog force for as few years as necessary.

A Supreme Court (he prospectively will have three or more places to fill) that will restore the proper judicial balance in applying the Constitution to "the law of the case" and not to five Justices' idea of what it *should* have meant.

An economy in which price inflation has been put under control and the value of the dollar stabilized.

The restoration of a transport system by rail that will serve to relieve the congestion which reliance on motor transport has created.

A return by the people to trust in their government, thereby enabling the democratic process to withstand the threats to its future at home and abroad.

The most intensive concentration in our history on law enforcement in the matters of the supply, distribution, and use of drugs that is a basic source of crime and violence committed by American youth on all the economic-social levels.

To progress substantially toward these goals Nixon seems fully aware he may have to pay the usual price the voting American majority has exacted from Presidents who press unpopular measures, requiring common sacrifices. This price is defeat for reelection. If he proves as resolute in these purposes as he appears to be, as patient in waiting for concrete results, and as resistant to the pressures for surrender of basic principles that will grow steadily with the approach of the election of 1972, he may win his great gamble.

There really are no *solutions* for the problems enumerated here. They won't just go away. However, I believe Nixon has at least evolved a courageous, promising, and definite program; but, only if it is supported by the unorganized majority, will it effect a congressional bipartisan coalition committed to bringing these problems under partial control.

As generally was proved again in the elections of 1970, a President's courting of trade union leaders by social amenities and trying to make them his political partners by words alone, will not induce them to abandon the inflationary pressures they have steadily applied to the wage and price economy. Presidents before Nixon have found that labor leaders instantly become the implacable foes of any public official who seeks by any means in any degree to reduce the exercise of the excessive economic and political power they possess. And the same is true if, out of respect for and obedience to the laws on which a just and orderly society depends, a President or any other politician undertakes positive measures against those who, in the name of "civil rights," justify crimes ranging from unpunished looting, arson, and murder to established anarchy.

With both groups the price of cooperation is abject surrender by the President of his responsibility to protect and serve the national interest above their own.

There are three means, it seems to me, by which the United States can yet avoid a debacle of its democratic structure and maintain the strength of the arsenal of the free world: (1) The restoration of a balanced economy in which advancement and protection of the general welfare will prevail over the special-interest pressure groups whose blind greed is a basic cause of the inflation that has greatly contributed to turning "the American dream" into a nightmare. (2) The restoration of discipline in the permissive society. (3) A presidential leadership that will forsake the drive of political ambition for a determination to "take arms against a sea of troubles, / And by opposing end them."

Without the full, dedicated employment of No. 3, I see no prospect of effective employment of Nos. 1 and 2. To do this a President must forsake politics-as-usual for statesmanship in formulating and fighting for measures by which the erosion of the American system could be halted; and regain credibility in his willingness to be a one-term President if this shall be the price of his crusade. For a professional politician like Richard M. Nixon, in a society deeply divided on the means for its salvation, and prone to the false teaching that prosperity can be preserved without individual sacrifice, no test of high resolve could be more severe.

I have sought, through inquiry of those who know him intimately, to determine whether the current Chief Executive is resolved to risk defeat in 1972 for asserting the leadership of which the country stands in dire need, and have acquired some hope that he is. But to be fully equipped for this dubious battle Mr. Nixon must first gain control of the policies and acts of his own Administration, overcoming, for example, such resistance as has been displayed in the ranks at the Department of Health, Education and Welfare.

Another vital thrust of the leadership that is required must be against the favoritism and political cowardice which has given organized labor the unilateral power to paralyze the national economy and social order until its constant pressures for wage increases unrelated to production are met. This will call for the enactment of a new labor relations law subjecting all unions, including those composed of government employees, to heavy fines, to be imposed by the judiciary and rigidly enforced by the Executive, for each day of suspension of any publicly vital service in any area.

Except for a brief period during the Eisenhower Administration the political community has steadily yielded to organized labor blackmail since 1933. And Mr. Nixon should have discovered, from the outset of his effort to gain the cooperation of the labor leaders, that the product of flattering personal attention is zero. With these leaders and their incessant demands, it is a case of all or nothing. Not even a President can create a partnership with the George Meanys that lasts longer than a friendly round on the links at Burning Tree if he seeks to curb labor's monopoly to any substantial degree.

The same is true of a presidential attempt to limit the waste of public revenues, inherent in the Welfare State, by a compromise in which its enervating social quality is maintained. And also of a presidential leadership which shrinks even from identifying the ethnic groups where crime in the streets is concentrated.

"The inventions of man," wrote Pascal, "advance from age to age, but the goodness and malignity of man remain constants." For more than thirty years legislation and administration in the United States have been founded in "liberal" government policy that shuts its eyes to the quotient of malignity, and actually protects it by judicial technocracy and political toleration.

History supplies enough instances to encourage the hope that, when a leader undertakes so great a mission as this by Mr. Nixon would be, the reward of the political risk can yet be extended tenure in which the mission can be completed.

December 1970

Index